Global Monitoring Report 2011

Improving the Odds of Achieving the MDGs

Improving the Odds of Achieving the MDGs

Heterogeneity, Gaps, and Challenges

1818 H Street NW
Washington DC 20433
Telephone: 202-473-1000
Internet: www.worldbank.org

1 2 3 4 14 13 12 11

ISBN: 978-0-8213-8700-9
eISBN: 978-0-8213-8701-6
DOI: 10.1596/978-0-8213-8700-9

The painting on the cover, "Faces of Diversity," is by Tola Wewe; the painting is from his 'Beauty is Everywhere' series and is part of a private collection.

Tola Wewe is a member of the African Artists' Foundation (AAF), which is a nonprofit organization dedicated to the promotion of African art and artists, and the promotion of relevant social issues through artistic endeavors. AAF plays a significant role in art communities in Africa through its art exhibitions, competitions, art classes, and workshops with the aim of unearthing and developing talent, creating societal awareness, and providing a platform to express creativity. Visit www.africanartists.org for more information on AAF.

Cover design by Debra Naylor of Naylor Design

Interior photographs: All photographs are from the National Geographic Society Image Collection. Lynn Johnson (page 10); James P. Blair (page 42); Lynn Johnson (page 70); W. E. Garrett (page 102); Randy Olson (page 124).

Contents

BOXES

FIGURES

MAPS

TABLES

Foreword

This year we are facing historic development challenges—from natural disasters, to food and fuel price spikes, and profound change in the Middle East. Despite high average growth in the developing world, it is crucial to provide opportunities to those that are being left behind. Wealthier economies are experiencing slower growth—but development assistance needs remain high. In our interconnected world, sustainable recovery means supporting inclusive growth.

Only four years remain until the 2015 deadline for reaching the Millennium Development Goals. The *Global Monitoring Report 2011: Improving the Odds of Achieving the MDGs—Heterogeneity, Gaps, and Challenges* underlines the urgency of helping countries that are behind on meeting key targets for extreme poverty, hunger, disease, and child and maternal mortality. The report lays out the challenges that remain; analyzes efforts to improve human development; and assesses the role of growth, policy reforms, trade, and donor policies in meeting the MDGs.

The findings from this year's report offer reason for both hope and concern.

Two-thirds of developing countries are on target or close to being on target for all the MDGs. Among developing countries that are falling short, half are close to becoming on track; with improved policies and faster growth, these countries could still achieve the targets in 2015 or soon after. Yet even those middle-income countries on track to achieve the MDGs are home to indigenous and socially excluded groups that are still very poor and often well behind in reaching the goals. Moreover, progress could stall without stronger global growth, expanded access to export markets for developing countries, and adequate assistance from donors.

We are making headway against poverty: based on our best economic projections, the world remains on track to reduce by half the number of people living in extreme poverty. We project that by 2015, 882.7 million people will be living on less than $1.25 a day, compared with 1.4 billion in 2005 and 1.8 billion in 1990. Yet a substantial portion of this progress reflects rapid growth in China and India, while many African countries are lagging behind: 17 countries are far from halving extreme poverty, even as the aggregate goals will be reached.

Developing countries as a whole will also likely achieve the MDGs for gender parity in primary and secondary education, for access to safe drinking water, and will be very close on hunger and primary education completion. But progress is too slow on meeting goals for child and maternal mortality as well as access to sanitation.

Many of the poorest countries—even some that have made substantial progress—face severe difficulties in achieving the MDGs. This is particularly true for those affected by violence and fragility. The difficulties reflect the drawbacks of their initial conditions; by contrast, many middle-income countries, which entered the 1990s with better policies, better institutions, and higher growth, are now in a better position to achieve the goals. Yet we have seen how improved policies in low-income countries did contribute to strong growth in the years before the financial crisis. Policy buffers that allowed for active countercyclical policies softened the impact of the crisis and drove a relatively rapid return to precrisis growth rates. To substantially reduce poverty and meet the MDGs, low-income and other developing countries need to grow faster and shore up their ability to guard against future shocks.

To help us better understand results on the ground, this year's report presents findings and lessons from impact evaluations in health and education. Such evaluations often show that progress in human development has not improved as much as might be expected, given substantial recent increases in resources devoted to health and education services. This is partly because, too often, scant attention has been given to improving incentives for rural doctors and health workers, for example, so as to improve the quality of services. This might explain the slower progress toward MDGs measured by outcomes (such as those for health), than those MDGs measuring access to services, (such as those for education). A key lesson is that strengthening institutions and improving incentives—by enhancing the role of performance in setting the pay of health workers, for example—are vital to better outcomes.

To regain momentum toward achieving the MDGs, we need international cooperation on three fronts:

First, low-income countries in particular require a strong and stable global economic environment to continue growing. While advanced economies are facing subdued growth and high unemployment, many fast-growing emerging markets are seeing inflation pressures build. With global growth projected at 4.4 percent this year and next, advanced market economies will need to repair and reform their financial systems and tackle their fiscal imbalances in order to strengthen the recovery. Emerging market economies must adjust their macroeconomic policies to reorient growth domestically and avoid possible overheating.

Second, low-income countries need to achieve and sustain more rapid economic growth and restore their policy buffers. One major challenge for growth is addressing the infrastructure gap through stronger public investment management systems and enhanced efforts to mobilize domestic revenue. Another is to create private sector opportunities, for local business people as well as foreign investors. Entrepreneurs' small enterprises can create jobs, opportunity, and hope. International organizations can offer policy advice and technical assistance; donors need to meet aid commitments and strengthen the overall effectiveness of aid. The world can also assist by expanding trade opportunities, particularly for the poorest countries. Key steps include completing the Doha Round, and expanding and improving Aid for Trade, connected to trade facilitation and building capacity.

Third, fragile states lag the furthest behind in reaching the MDGs. These countries require additional support in building institutions and moving toward a virtuous circle of development, peace, and security, as discussed in the Bank's recently released *World Development Report 2011: Conflict, Security, and Development.*

The MDGs were designed to provide a framework for the entire international community to work together toward a common end: making sure that human development reaches everyone, everywhere. If these goals are achieved, billions more people will have the opportunity to benefit from the global economy. We have four years left to reach the targets. International financial institutions, including regional development banks, are adapting policies, procedures, and tools to respond to the postcrisis world and to tailor support for unique country circumstances and needs—including economies and peoples hit hard by banking problems, food and fuel crises, and natural disasters. In doing so, we need to keep the MDGs firmly in our sights. Reaching these goals is central to global development.

Robert B. Zoellick
President
The World Bank Group

Dominique Strauss-Kahn
Managing Director
International Monetary Fund

Acknowledgments

This report has been prepared jointly by the staffs of the World Bank and the International Monetary Fund (IMF). The cooperation and support of staff of several institutions are also gratefully acknowledged: the African Development Bank (AfDB), the Asian Development Bank (ADB), the European Bank for Reconstruction and Development (EBRD), the Inter-American Development Bank (IDB), as well as the Netherlands Environmental Assessment Agency (PBL).

Delfin S. Go was the lead author and manager of the report. Brad McDonald led the team from the IMF. The principal authors of the chapters were: chapter 1–Delfin S. Go and Jose Alejandro Quijada; chapter 2–Brad McDonald; chapter 3–Gayle Martin and Shwetlena Sabarwal; chapter 4–Harry Anthony Patrinos; and chapter 5–Amy Heyman (aid), Mariam Malouche (trade), and Stefano Curto (international financial institutions). Jose Alejandro Quijada, Sachin Shahria, and William Shaw were key members of the core team in the overall preparation and coordination of the report.

Bruce Ross-Larson was the principal editor.

The work was carried out under the general guidance of Justin Lin and Hans Timmer at the World Bank. Supervision at the IMF was provided by Hugh Bredenkamp and Catherine Pattillo. Advisers to the report include Shantayanan Devarajan, Shahrokh Fardoust,

Deon Filmer, Ariel Fiszbein, Ann Harrison, Jeffrey Lewis, Mohammad Zia Qureshi, Martin Ravallion, and Ritva S. Reinikka. Several people also provided specific suggestions: Andrew Burns, Jeffrey Chelsky, Punam Chuhan-Pole, Rui Coutinho, Aart C. Kraay, Barbara W. Lee, Sonia Plaza, Luis Serven, Lucio Vinas de Souza, Dominique van der Mensbrugghe, and Adam Wagstaff.

Several staff members also made valuable contributions and inputs, including the following from the World Bank: Harold Alderman, Uranbileg Batjargal, Jinzhu Chen, Shaohua Chen, Stacey Tai Sie Chow, Yohana Dukhan, Yoichiro Ishihara, Lauren Murphy, Victor Hugo Orozco Olvera, Israel Osorio-Rodarte, Prem Sangraula, Jennifer Sturdy, and Edit Velenyi. Other contributors from the IMF included Sibabrata Das, Nisreen Farhan, Shaun Roache, Manrique Saenz, Mika Saito, and Joe Thornton. Contributors from other institutions included Paul Lucas, Henk Hilderink, Marcel Kok, Ben ten Brink, and Stefan van der Esch (PBL); Patrica Laverley and Agnes Soucat (AfDB); Indu Bhushan, Valerie Reppelin-Hill, Manju Senapaty, and Gina Marie Umali (ADB); and Murat Jadraliyev, Anita Taci, and James Earwicker (EBRD).

Guidance received from the Executive Directors of the World Bank and the IMF and their staffs during discussions of the draft report is gratefully acknowledged. The report also benefited from many useful comments and suggestions received from the Bank and IMF management and staff in the course of its preparation and review.

The multilingual web sites accompanying the report were produced by Vamsee Kanchi, Roula Yazigi, Rebecca Ong, and Swati Priadarshini Mishra; the main GMR Web address is www.worldbank.org/gmr2011. Rebecca Ong and Merrell Tuck-Primdahl managed the communication and dissemination activities. The translation process was coordinated by Jorge del Rosario.

The design and production of the *Global Monitoring Report 2011* was handled by the World Bank's Office of the Publisher, under the supervision of Stephen McGroarty, Susan Graham, and Denise Bergeron.

Abbreviations and Acronyms

ADB	Asian Development Bank	IDA	International Development Association
AfDB	African Development Bank		
AIDS	acquired immune deficiency syndrome	IFC	International Finance Corporation
BRICs	Brazil, Russia, India, and China	IFI	international financial institution
CAT DDO	post–natural catastrophe deferred drawdown option	IIA	independence of irrelevant alternatives
CCT	conditional cash transfer	IMF	International Monetary Fund
CFM	capital flow management	LDC	least-developed country
CPIA	Country Policy and Institutional Assessment	MDB	multilateral development bank
		MDGs	Millennium Development Goals
CRW	Crisis Response Window	NTM	nontariff measure
DAC	Development Assistance Committee	OECD	Organisation for Economic Co-operation and Development
DDO	deferred drawdown option		
DFQF	duty free, quota free		
DIME	Development Impact Evaluation	PBL	Netherlands Environmental Assessment Agency
DMC	developing member-country	PCL	Precautionary Credit Line
DPL	development policy lending	PRGT	Poverty Reduction and Growth Trust
EBRD	European Bank for Reconstruction and Development		
		PRST	Poverty Reduction Strategy Paper
FCL	Flexible Credit Line	QuODA	Quality of Official Development Assistance Assessment
FDI	foreign direct investment		
GDP	gross domestic product		
G-20	Group of Twenty	RPGs	regional public goods
HIV	human immunodeficiency virus	SDRs	special drawing rights
		SMEs	small and medium enterprises
HRF	Haiti Reconstruction Fund	TFP	Trade Finance Program
IADB	Inter-American Development Bank	WBG	World Bank Group
		WEO	World Economic Outlook
		WTO	World Trade Organization

All amounts are presented in U.S. dollars, unless otherwise indicated.

Goals and Targets from the Millennium Declaration

GOAL 1	ERADICATE EXTREME POVERTY AND HUNGER
TARGET 1.A	Halve, between 1990 and 2015, the proportion of people whose income is less than $1.25 a day
TARGET 1.B	Achieve full and productive employment and decent work for all, including women and young people
TARGET 1.C	Halve, between 1990 and 2015, the proportion of people who suffer from hunger

GOAL 2	ACHIEVE UNIVERSAL PRIMARY EDUCATION
TARGET 2.A	Ensure that by 2015, children everywhere, boys and girls alike, will be able to complete a full course of primary schooling

GOAL 3	PROMOTE GENDER EQUALITY AND EMPOWER WOMEN
TARGET 3.A	Eliminate gender disparity in primary and secondary education, preferably by 2005, and at all levels of education no later than 2015

GOAL 4	REDUCE CHILD MORTALITY
TARGET 4.A	Reduce by two-thirds, between 1990 and 2015, the under-five mortality rate

GOAL 5	IMPROVE MATERNAL HEALTH
TARGET 5.A	Reduce by three-quarters, between 1990 and 2015, the maternal mortality ratio
TARGET 5.B	Achieve by 2015 universal access to reproductive health

GOAL 6	COMBAT HIV/AIDS, MALARIA, AND OTHER DISEASES
TARGET 6.A	Have halted by 2015 and begun to reverse the spread of HIV/AIDS
TARGET 6.B	Achieve by 2010 universal access to treatment for HIV/AIDS for all those who need it
TARGET 6.C	Have halted by 2015 and begun to reverse the incidence of malaria and other major diseases

GOAL 7	ENSURE ENVIRONMENTAL SUSTAINABILITY
TARGET 7.A	Integrate the principles of sustainable development into country policies and programs and reverse the loss of environmental resources
TARGET 7.B	Reduce biodiversity loss, achieving by 2010 a significant reduction in the rate of loss
TARGET 7.C	Halve by 2015 the proportion of people without sustainable access to safe drinking water and basic sanitation
TARGET 7.D	Have achieved a significant improvement by 2020 in the lives of at least 100 million slum dwellers

GOAL 8	DEVELOP A GLOBAL PARTNERSHIP FOR DEVELOPMENT
TARGET 8.A	Develop further an open, rule-based, predictable, nondiscriminatory trading and financial system (including a commitment to good governance, development, and poverty reduction, nationally and internationally)
TARGET 8.B	Address the special needs of the least-developed countries (including tariff- and quota-free access for exports of the least-developed countries; enhanced debt relief for heavily indebted poor countries and cancellation of official bilateral debt; and more generous official development assistance for countries committed to reducing poverty)
TARGET 8.C	Address the special needs of landlocked countries and small island developing states (through the Programme of Action for the Sustainable Development of Small Island Developing States and the outcome of the 22nd special session of the General Assembly)
TARGET 8.D	Deal comprehensively with the debt problems of developing countries through national and international measures to make debt sustainable in the long term
TARGET 8.E	In cooperation with pharmaceutical companies, provide access to affordable, essential drugs in developing countries
TARGET 8.F	In cooperation with the private sector, make available the benefits of new technologies, especially information and communications

Source: United Nations. 2008. *Report of the Secretary-General on the Indicators for Monitoring the Millennium Development Goals.*
E/CN.3/2008/29. New York.
Note: The Millennium Development Goals and targets come from the Millennium Declaration, signed by 189 countries, including 147 heads of state and government, in September 2000 (http://www.un.org/millennium/declaration/ares552e.htm) and from further agreement by member states at the 2005 World Summit (Resolution adopted by the General Assembly–A/RES/60/1). The goals and targets are interrelated and should be seen as a whole. They represent a partnership between the developed countries and the developing countries "to create an environment—at the national and global levels alike—which is conducive to development and the elimination of poverty."

Overview

With less than five years remaining to achieve the Millennium Development Goals (MDGs), the international development community has to set priorities that focus on lagging countries and sectors and take onboard lessons from past interventions, reflecting the limited resources available. To inform this effort, *Global Monitoring Report 2011* analyzes the diverse record in improving human development across and within developing countries; summarizes the results of impact evaluations of health and education programs; and reviews recent developments in global growth, trade, and donor policies.

The key messages:

- Global progress toward the various targets continues to be mixed, and country performance is predictably diverse. Among developing countries that are off track, the top half are, on average, within 10 percent of the on-track trajectory. While countries close to the target may still miss the 2015 deadline, they could achieve the targets soon after, with improved policies and an acceleration of growth to precrisis levels.
- For countries that are on track, or close to it, solid economic growth and good policies and institutions have been the key factors.

Progress on both fronts has been evident since the 1990s. Indeed, policy responses in the recent global economic downturn have softened the negative impact, particularly for low-income countries (especially in Africa).

- This substantial progress is not a reason for complacency. Without a stable expansion of the global economy, continuing access to advanced and developing-country markets, and adequate assistance from donors, progress could still break down. Enhancing the resilience to adverse economic shocks, including the provision of social safety programs, will need greater attention and support.
- Reaching the MDGs is only one milestone, for there still is much work to do in fostering inclusive growth, reducing inequality and poverty, and improving health and education outcomes in even the most successful countries. Even the middle-income countries on track to reach the MDGs have trailing pockets of indigenous and socially excluded groups whose odds of reaching the goals are slim.
- Unsurprisingly, countries with slower growth and poorer institutions are farthest behind. Many countries far from the target are fragile states, reinforcing the need

for the international community to step up support to these countries.

- Impact evaluations show that the quantity of health and education services has increased, but not the quality. This might be one reason that progress has been slower for MDGs measured by outcomes (like those for health) than for those measured by access (like those for education). That is why improving the incentives for service providers and consumers—especially making service providers directly accountable to consumers—is so essential to improving outcomes.
- The growing assistance from new donors—many in the developing world—will not compensate for a significant future fall in aid from traditional donors, particularly if they pursue different development priorities and practices. The changing aid landscape could also have implications for the transparency of official flows and for the policies and programs that aid supports.

The diversity of country performance

The global numbers tell a mixed story. Progress has been substantial in achieving the MDGs for gender parity in primary and secondary education, completion of primary education, access to safe drinking water, and eradicating extreme poverty and hunger, in that order (figure 1). On current trends, and despite the recent global economic crisis, developing countries are on track to reach the global target of cutting income poverty in half by 2015, thanks in large part to rapid growth in China and India. Developing countries will also likely achieve the MDGs for gender parity in primary and secondary education and for access to safe drinking water, and will be very close on hunger and on primary education completion. Progress is too slow, however, on health-related outcomes—such as child and maternal mortality and access to sanitation—so the world will likely miss these MDGs by 2015. Most regions are lagging on these health goals, but East Asia and Pacific, Latin America and the Caribbean, and Europe and Central Asia are doing better than other regions.

Poor countries and regions tend to lag in attaining the MDGs. The low-income countries lag on all the MDGs. While poverty in Sub-Saharan Africa has fallen steeply with the acceleration of growth since 2000, the region is not on track to meet the poverty reduction goal. Middle-income countries—both lower and upper—generally exhibit the best performance. Eighty percent of the upper-middle-income countries (23 of them) have achieved

FIGURE 1 **The distance to global MDGs ranges widely**

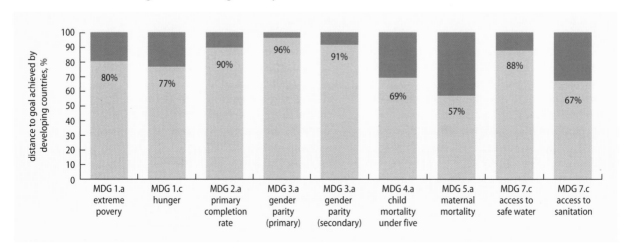

Source: World Bank staff calculations based on data from the World Development Indicators database.
Note: Distance to goal achieved in this graph is a weighted average of the latest indicators, using population weights in 2009.

or are on track to achieve the extreme poverty eradication target. And 72 percent of lower-middle-income countries (34 of them) are set to reach the target for gender parity in secondary education. Both low- and middle-income countries have made good progress on gender parity in primary education.

Even so, the targets remain within reach for many developing countries. Although more developing countries are off track than on track in achieving the targets, many off-track countries are closer to the goals, thanks to more than a decade of better policy and faster growth. A country is "close to the target" if its distance to getting on target is smaller than the average gap of all lagging countries. Others are "far from the target," if their distance to getting on target is bigger than the average gap.

Indeed, two-thirds or more of developing countries are, on average, on target or close to being on target for all the MDGs (figure 2). Many countries are on track to achieve several MDGs: gender parity in primary education (89 of them), gender parity in secondary education (82); access to safe drinking water (66); primary completion rate (55); and wiping out extreme poverty (47). For instance, about 70 percent of developing countries

have achieved or are on track to achieve the targets for gender parity in primary and secondary education. Although half the monitored countries (57) are off target for the primary education completion goal, two thirds of them (38) are very close.

Progress is still mixed or poor for access to sanitation, maternal mortality, and child mortality. For example, more than 40 percent of low- to upper-middle-income countries (58 of them) are lagging significantly on access to sanitation.

The variation among lagging countries is still large, but the average gap is not. Lagging countries are, on average, 23 percent behind being on track to achieve all the MDGs (table 1). They are close to being on track for gender parity in primary education (7 percent); gender parity in secondary education (16 percent); hunger (19 percent); primary education completion (20 percent); and, to some extent, under-five mortality (23 percent). But for each target there are countries with scant progress. For example, 17 countries are far from halving extreme poverty, even as the global goal will be reached.

More important, among countries that are off track, the top half are, on average, about

FIGURE 2   **More than two-thirds of developing countries are on track or close to being on track**

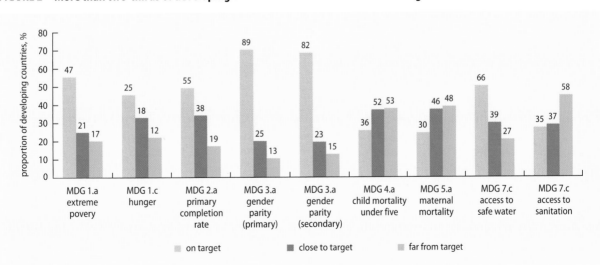

Source: World Bank staff calculations based on data from the World Development Indicators database.
Note: The figure above each bar is the number of countries.

TABLE 1   **Lagging countries are close to getting on target**

	Average distance to getting on target (gaps, %)		
	All off-target countries	Countries close to the target	Countries far from the target
MDG 1.a Extreme poverty	39 (96)	17	67
MDG 1.c Hunger	19 (60)	9	35
MDG 2.a Primary education completion	20 (96)	9	40
MDG 3.a Gender parity in primary education	7 (22)	4	14
MDG 3.a Gender parity in secondary education	16 (52)	8	29
MDG 4.a Child mortality under five	23 (59)	8	38
MDG 5.a Maternal mortality	32 (80)	11	51
MDG 7.c Access to safe drinking water	25 (76)	14	41
MDG 7.c Access to sanitation	27 (50)	16	34
Simple average	23	11	39

Source: World Bank staff calculations based on data from the World Development Indicators database.
Note: A country is "close to the target" if its distance to getting on target is smaller than the average gap of all lagging countries. It is "far from the target" if its distance is bigger than the average gap. Figures in parentheses indicate the range of variation (maximum value minus minimum value) of countries off target, by MDG. Averages and numbers of countries cover only those with data, which can vary by MDG.

10 percent off the on-track trajectory. Their mean distance is only 4–9 percent for gender parity in primary and secondary education, child mortality, primary education completion, and alleviating hunger. Indeed, these countries close to the target need to increase primary education completion by only 9.2 percent, on average, to become on track.

Reducing data gaps will improve the assessment of progress. Poor data availability may fail to convey progress or understate deterioration resulting from shocks and conflicts. Among the MDGs, the collection of data on poverty seems to lag the most. Conducting household income and expenditure surveys in both large and poor countries is difficult, often delaying global or regional poverty updates when the countries with missing data account for a large share of the total. The new household surveys employed in the analysis covered about 43 percent of the population in developing countries in 2008 and 7.6 percent in 2009. However, gaps for 2008–10 household surveys remain in several regions—particularly, South Asia (pending India's new household survey, 10.8 percent of the population is covered), Middle East and North Africa (19.1 percent), and Sub-Saharan Africa (20.1 percent). Efforts are already under way at the World Bank to close the remaining gaps before the end of 2011 to complete and update the time-series

estimate of poverty at the global and regional levels for 2008. There is also spotty information about infectious diseases, such as malaria and tuberculosis. Other data issues include reporting errors that severely hamper the accuracy of the maternal mortality ratio.

The quality, timeliness, and availability of data are gradually improving, which can be seen from the World Bank Statistical Capacity Indicator (http://bbsc.worldbank.org); but additional effort and support for statistical capacity-building activities will be required to improve data and close gaps for all MDG-related indicators.

The role of growth and policy

Starting points—inherited initial conditions—count in MDG performance, but subsequent growth and policy also matter greatly. Countries with a higher per capita GDP in 1990 generally have better MDG performance. Countries starting with good policy and institutions also tend to do better. But initial conditions do not fully determine outcomes, and economic growth and policy performance after the initial year may be more important in meeting the goals. Countries that have reached or are on track to reach the targets show, on average, the fastest per capita GDP growth over 1990–2009 (table 2). Similarly, countries close to the

TABLE 2   **Growth and CPIA scores are higher in countries on track or close to being on track**

Average values across MDGs (weighted by the number of countries in each MDG category)

	On target	Close to the target	Far from the target
Average GDP per capita growth (1990–2009)	2.4	1.8	1.2
CPIA index (2009)	3.7	3.5	3.3

Source: World Bank staff calculations based on data from the World Development Indicators database.
Note: The pairwise correlation between average GDP per capita growth and the CPIA index is 0.32 (significant at 0.01). A country is "close to the target" if its distance to getting on target is smaller than the average gap of all lagging countries. It is "far from the target" if its distance is bigger than the average gap.

target tend to have faster per capita growth than countries far from the target. A strong policy and institutional framework, as measured by the World Bank's annual country policy and institutional assessment (CPIA), appears to be associated with improved MDG performance.

Both factors—initial conditions and subsequent growth and policy—also point to why the MDGs are such big challenges for the poorest and most fragile countries. Middle-income countries, having grown earlier, often have better policies and institutions.

Growth has an all-encompassing bearing on the progress of MDGs, while policy is vital for outcome-based MDGs. Preliminary econometric results suggest that economic growth has a pervasive association with the odds of achieving the MDGs. For those countries currently far from the goals, a strong growth performance seems to catalyze progress toward the MDGs. And for those that are closer to becoming on target, growth seems to be significantly correlated with specific goals such as primary education completion and gender parity. Improved policy and institutions appear to be especially important for health-related MDGs, such as maternal mortality, under-five mortality, hunger alleviation, and access to safe drinking water; as outcome-based goals, they depend (in addition to growth and resources) on a myriad of factors that improve the quality of public expenditures and service delivery.

Overall, an increase in growth and in the quality of policies equivalent to one standard deviation would appear to put 32 more developing countries (44 percent) on track to meet the MDGs. Increasing average growth

in developing countries by one standard deviation is feasible, although the implied rate of 3.8 percent in average developing-country per capita growth is roughly double its historical 1.8 percent rate (see table 2), it is comparable both to recent periods of accelerated growth and to current forecasts of growth for 2010–15. Achieving the assumed improvement in policy and institutions may be more challenging, given the few years to 2015. Because policy reforms can take time to implement and bear fruit, it is important to begin now. Although many close-to-target countries may still miss the 2015 deadline, with higher growth and better policies they could still achieve the targets soon afterward.

Prospects and challenges for economic growth

The global economic recovery is proceeding along multiple tracks. Advanced economies are slowly recovering from the recent global economic crisis and face continued high unemployment. By contrast, emerging economies have seen a robust recovery, and some faster-growing economies are experiencing inflation pressures amid signs of overheating. Thanks in part to their countercyclical policy responses to the crisis, low-income economies are seeing a relatively rapid return to precrisis growth rates. Higher commodity prices are supporting growth in commodity-exporting countries, but are sparking concerns over the affordability of food for the poorer segments of the population in some low- and lower-middle-income countries. Global GDP is forecast to rise by about 4.5 percent in 2011 and 2012, with rates in advanced economies

TABLE 3 Global output, 2007–14

annual percentage change

Region	2007	2008	2009	2010	Projections 2011	Projections 2012–14
World output	**5.4**	**2.9**	**−0.5**	**5.0**	**4.4**	**4.6**
Advanced economies	2.7	0.2	−3.4	3.0	2.4	2.5
Emerging and Developing Economies	8.8	6.1	2.7	7.3	6.5	6.6
Central and Eastern Europe	5.5	3.2	−3.6	4.2	3.7	3.9
Commonwealth of Independent States	9.0	5.3	−6.4	4.6	5.0	4.6
Developing Asia	11.4	7.7	7.2	9.5	8.4	8.5
Middle East and North Africa	6.2	5.1	1.8	3.8	4.1	4.5
Sub–Saharan Africa	7.2	5.6	2.8	5.0	5.5	5.7
Western Hemisphere	5.7	4.3	−1.7	6.1	4.7	4.0
Emerging Economies	9.2	6.3	2.6	7.5	6.7	6.7
Other Developing Economies	7.2	6.0	5.2	6.2	6.1	6.4
Least Developed Countries (LDCs)[a]	9.0	6.9	5.2	5.3	6.1	6.4

Source: World Economic Outlook.

a. United Nations classification, a subset of developing countries.

several percentage points below those in emerging and developing economies (table 3).

Good macroeconomic policies remain crucial to the recovery. Continuing accommodative monetary policy in most advanced economies has alleviated the financial crisis and recession, and monetary conditions in most emerging and developing countries began to normalize in 2010. Fiscal policy is shifting from supporting recovery to cutting deficits, although easy credit conditions may be slowing the pace of fiscal consolidation among major emerging economies. Low-income countries have, appropriately, begun to reverse the unprecedented countercyclical fiscal response that softened the impact of the crisis. In many countries, policy makers can also take steps to improve employment opportunities, including for young adults.

Sustaining the global recovery demands greater effort. To avoid unsustainable debt burdens, the advanced economies must redress fiscal imbalances and repair and reform financial systems. Emerging economies face policy challenges of overheating and strong capital inflows. Although core inflation remains subdued in many of them, inflationary expectations are rising and policy targets have been exceeded in some cases. Inflation could threaten otherwise sound policy frameworks, but concerns about further

currency appreciation are resulting in a sluggish monetary policy response in several emerging economies. Differences in interest rates and growth prospects have spurred strong capital flows from the advanced to the emerging economies, adding to the overheating and complicating the policy response.

The challenge in low-income countries is to sustain and accelerate growth through better policies and greater investment in infrastructure. Closing the large infrastructure gap by raising productivity and encouraging private investment could substantially increase per capita income growth. Effective public investment management—better strategic planning and analyses of the feasibility of projects—is critical. The financing of additional investment also needs to be carefully managed, to ensure that debt sustainability is preserved, and should be supported by parallel reforms to strengthen tax revenue.

Rebuilding policy buffers can help protect growth in the face of future shocks. Good policies in low-income countries contributed to strong growth before the crisis. The policy buffers established then also created the space for countercyclical policies that softened the impact of the crisis and drove a fairly rapid return to precrisis growth rates. To ensure that higher growth is sustained in the face of future shocks—a prerequisite for meeting the MDGs—low-income and other developing countries need to rebuild their policy buffers as the recovery proceeds. In addition to strong, well-designed national policies, international cooperation is required to restore a global economic environment conducive to development and poverty reduction, and to support the most vulnerable countries.

Making the right policy interventions—lessons from impact evaluations in education and health

Improving the likelihood of more countries attaining the MDGs depends not just on more resources but also, and quite critically, on improving the quality of service provision through better policies and stronger institutions. But not much is known about how exactly to do this. To help inform this question, a special feature of this year's report presents the findings and lessons from impact evaluations in health and education.

Development assistance for health and education has risen to unprecedented levels in volume, but has not generated the expected improvements in outcomes. And given the current global economic environment, citizens in developed and developing countries alike are demanding more value for their money. This requires closer attention to the causal chain linking spending to outcomes and actions to isolate and strengthen the weak links in this chain. In recent years, impact evaluations have emerged as a tool to do this; and even though their evidence base is still far from complete, some interesting lessons are beginning to emerge.

Impact evaluations highlight the disconnect between increased public spending and changes in outcomes. The outcomes have been disappointing, partly because the spending focus has been narrowly trained on input provision, ignoring other parts of the causal chain that links public spending to better outcomes. Inputs continue to be important, but alone they are not sufficient for attaining the goals in many developing countries. Policies have failed to account for the incentives facing both service providers and consumers. Too much effort has been devoted to increasing inputs, and not enough to ensuring that institutions provide services efficiently and responsively—and that consumers have the ability and incentive to use services efficiently and hold service providers accountable for quality. Some of the lessons are these:

- Reducing user costs and providing cash transfers has improved the uptake of health and education services, but issues of quality remain.
- Health inputs have had to grapple with uptake and use by citizens, and school-based and community-based approaches are tackling this. But more research and impact evaluations are needed to discover when and how these approaches work.
- Increasing traditional schooling inputs has often been ineffective in improving learning outcomes—as in Bolivia, Colombia, Kenya, and Nicaragua.
- Service delivery too often fails the poor—as in Bangladesh, Brazil, Ecuador, Ghana, India, Indonesia, Morocco, Peru, Tunisia, and Uganda.
- Pay for performance improved student learning outcomes—as in India, Israel, and Kenya. The Rwanda health center pay-for-performance program increased institutional deliveries and preventive care visits by young children and improved the quality of prenatal care.
- New approaches are being designed to improve service delivery, and an evidence base on the effectiveness of these approaches is beginning to take shape.

These are just some of the compelling messages from the evaluations summarized in chapter 3.

Although designing the right approach to improving outcomes is complex and depends on context, a systematic evidence base generated through rigorous impact evaluations can provide useful guidance for policy makers. The information base on impact evaluations is far from complete, and much more work is needed before the most pressing questions can be answered. But some new approaches show promise in improving incentives and in strengthening the accountability of service provision.

Assisting the poorest of the poor—socially excluded groups

Reaching the MDGs requires addressing the plight of the world's socially excluded groups, including indigenous people, ethnic minorities, and linguistic groups. They make up a sizable proportion of the world's people and an even greater share of the world's poor. Turning the situation around will therefore require widespread and sustainable economic growth, as well as specific interventions to reach these groups.

Most MDG indicators for indigenous people and ethnic minorities are worse than population averages. This is true for under-five mortality; adult literacy; school enrollment, completion, and achievement; gender equity; water deprivation; child nutrition; and, especially, poverty reduction. Most countries in Latin America with sizable indigenous populations, for example, show almost no poverty reduction for those groups.

Programs can meet the needs of indigenous people and ethnic minorities. Bilingual education programs can promote national language acquisition, school completion, and subsequent earnings gains, contributing to multiple goals—and be cost effective. Conditional cash transfer programs can promote schooling, health, and poverty reduction; and these programs result in disproportionate gains for minority populations, particularly in countries with large vulnerable populations.

Attaining the MDGs for indigenous people and ethnic minorities requires innovative approaches. These people may be hard to reach because they live in remote locations with poor transportation. They may also suffer from social and economic discrimination and government neglect. So assisting them may require more complex interventions than those for the general population. The lack of data also complicates the design

and evaluation of programs. The more successful programs, such as those in Asia, have extended economic opportunities and provided cash or in-kind assistance, thus allowing these groups to use the targeted assistance more effectively. Other countries may need to target these groups more tightly and raise the quality of services by increasing the accountability of service providers to their clients.

In addition to assisting the indigenous peoples, more inclusive growth and equality within countries will also benefit people in the bottom quintiles and lift more people out of poverty. The case of Brazil points to two lessons: (1) reforms to social policies and programs to make them more pro-poor (if fiscally possible) can play an important role in sustaining poverty reduction, even during a period of economic stagnation; and (2) sensible macroeconomic and trade policies need not hurt the poor and, in the specific case of taming hyperinflation, are likely to make a significant contribution in the fight against poverty, even when that is not the primary objective.

Progress in the international development framework

The international development framework functioned well in coping with the crisis. Governments and international institutions cooperated well in the face of recession, thus avoiding the perils of a downward protectionist spiral, maintaining aid, and boosting emergency financial resources. Financing from the international institutions jumped sharply, leading to a general increase in their resources. Although recent research suggests that declines in aid have tended to deepen for several years after banking-related crises, aid levels from countries in 2010 have not yet been constrained by concerns over rising fiscal deficits. Some major-donor governments remained dedicated to maintaining aid levels and others announced cuts. Even so, official development assistance (ODA) from members of the Development Assistance Committee (DAC) of the Organisation for Economic Co-operation and Development (OECD) rose to its highest level, at $128.7 billion, an increase of 6.5 percent over 2009 in real terms. Developing countries are also benefiting from new donors (including disbursements of some $9–$10 billion a year from donors that are not members of DAC) and from a sharp rise in donations from the private sector in advanced countries.

The past tumultuous decade has ushered in significant changes in the assistance policies of international institutions. They have developed a results-based, country-driven assistance framework grounded in regular reviews of country strategy and independent evaluations. A more diverse and flexible range of financing instruments helped them tailor assistance to the needs of particular countries (such as those affected by conflict) and in particular situations (such as disaster relief and crisis assistance). They are also doing more in providing knowledge—through loans and technical assistance, and global programs and projects—as well as free information to the global community.

The growing assistance from emerging donors (many in the developing world) is welcome but may not compensate fully for a significant fall in aid from traditional donors, to the extent that the emerging donors pursue different development priorities and practices. This changing aid landscape could also have implications for the transparency of official flows and the policies and programs that aid supports.

Trade integration and facilitation remain essential for inclusive growth and poverty reduction. World trade, now recovering at about double the 2002–08 rate of growth, remains well below the precrisis peak and even lower than the level it would have achieved if it had continued the 1995–2008 trend. The rise in protectionist measures during the crisis, which particularly affected the exports of least-developed countries, appears to be receding. Solidifying an open, rules-based international trade regime can be accomplished best by concluding the Doha Round.

The global community can support poverty reduction through improving trade integration in low-income countries. Poor-country market access could improve significantly if rich countries extended duty-free, quota-free access to all poor-country exports and simplified rules of origin in preference agreements. Efforts also are required to ensure that poor countries can access trade finance at reasonable cost, along with improvements in data and a review of whether banking regulations impose excessive capital requirements on trade finance transactions. Regional trade agreements should support open trade through low external tariffs, while technical assistance to developing-country trade negotiators would support deeper regional integration. More financial resources and technical assistance are needed to strengthen trade facilitation and to reduce supply constraints on poor-country exports. These efforts should include increased commitments for aid for trade (which in real terms stagnated in 2009) and greater use of public-private partnerships. Further efforts are required to connect landlocked countries and lagging regions to regional and international markets. Logistical improvements at the subnational level are also critical for connecting rural and remote areas in developing countries.

1

The Diversity of MDG Progress

With less than five years left to achieve the Millennium Development Goals (MDGs), the international development community is showing renewed urgency to assess the various development efforts, especially in light of the recent global economic crisis and the still-fragile recovery. What are the prospects and challenges for reaching the goals? Answers are clearly linked to the complex tapestry of progress that lies below the global numbers.

The Global Monitoring Report [GMR] 2011 *extends the forward-looking analysis started in last year's report by examining more carefully the diversity of progress and its implications for the remaining gaps and challenges. It complements that report's analysis of the impact of the global crisis on the MDGs.*

A key observation on the progress toward the MDGs is its diversity. At the aggregate and regional levels, low-income countries, particularly fragile states and those in Sub-Saharan Africa, lag because of a combination of low starting points and difficult circumstances. Behind those aggregate numbers, however, the great diversity of performance across indicators, countries, and groups of countries requires further analysis. That is the subject of this chapter.

Several questions demand answers: How many countries are off target, and how far are they from the goals? Why are some countries behind? And what factors are key to improving the odds that off-target countries can reach the goals?

Looking under global progress

The global numbers tell a familiar, mixed story (figure 1.1). The latest information confirms that progress toward the MDGs remains substantial on gender and education, access to safe drinking water, extreme poverty, and hunger, in that order. On current trends and despite the recent global economic crisis, the world is on track to reach the global target of cutting income poverty in half by 2015. Thanks to rapid growth in China, the East Asia and Pacific region has already halved extreme poverty. Developing countries will also likely achieve the MDGs for gender parity in primary and secondary education and for access to safe drinking water, and will be very close on hunger and the primary education completion rate.

Progress continues to lag in health-related development outcomes, such as child and maternal mortality and access to sanitation. New data and methodologies indicate much

Rendille villagers in northern Kenya scoop the dregs from a water tank filled only the night before by a government truck but already drained below the level of its spigot. They must wait a week for the next delivery.

FIGURE 1.1 **Current global distance to the MDGs is wide ranging**

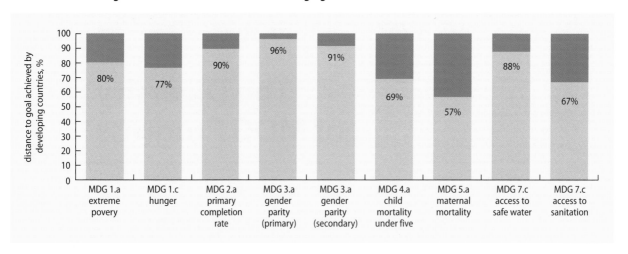

Source: World Bank staff calculations based on data from the World Development Indicators database.
Note: Distance to goal achieved in this graph is a weighted average of the latest indicators, using population weights in 2009. In this and other graphs in the chapter, the focus is on MDGs with well-defined targets and time-series data to assess progress.

more progress than previously thought in reducing maternal mortality, but that is still the MDG that lags the most. On current trends, the world will likely miss these three targets by 2015. Most regions are off track, but East Asia and the Pacific, Latin America and the Caribbean, and Europe and Central Asia are doing somewhat better than others.

Poor countries and regions tend to lag in attaining the MDGs. As a group, they lag on all the MDGs and are unlikely to reach a single target by 2015. Generally, fewer low-income than middle-income countries are on target to achieve each MDG (figure 1.2). The number of countries in each income group does not differ greatly, so this is not the result

FIGURE 1.2 **Fewer low-income countries are on track to achieve the MDGs**

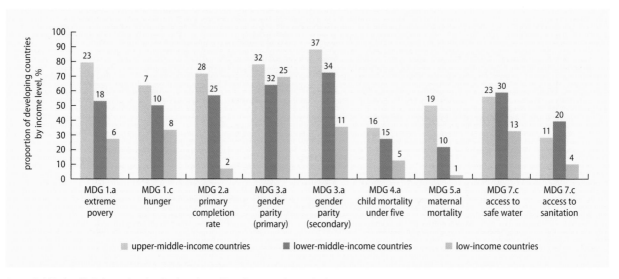

Source: World Bank staff calculations based on data from the World Development Indicators database.
Note: The number above each bar refers to the number of countries attaining that MDG.

of the distribution of countries. In fact, about 40 countries are currently classified as low income, compared with 54 lower-middle-income and 48 upper-middle-income countries (see appendix 1 for the classification). Nor do the results arise from missing data in low-income countries because the availability of data also shows little variation among income groups (see appendix table A1.1). At the global level, the latest poverty data remain at 2005, and box 1.1 explains why.

The pattern more likely stems from the starting points—especially incomes, which matter greatly in attaining the MDGs. As several studies show, recent achievements are obscured by poor past performance and by the disproportionate challenges the MDGs pose in many Sub-Saharan African and other poor countries.[1] The longer the distance to the 2015 targets, the more ambitious the goals appear and the steeper the path to achieve them. Ravallion and the World Bank and IMF discussed how higher starting poverty rates are generally associated with a lower responsiveness (elasticity) of poverty to economic growth.[2] Countries in Sub-Saharan Africa implemented reforms later than others and therefore benefited much later from accelerating economic growth. However, after showing no decline for much of

---

BOX 1.1   Poverty data and projections

New poverty projections at the World Bank are the result of several changes—new and more recent household surveys, updates of historical consumption per capita from national accounts, and a new forecast of per capita consumption growth. For this report, the poverty forecast includes 62 new household surveys out of a total of 123 countries, which reflect methodological advances in newer surveys and changes in the underlying distribution of income not measured by changes in mean income or expenditure. The forecast therefore captures changes in income inequality in the new surveys. However, it assumes inequality is unchanged in other countries. Some of the effects of food and fuel price shocks in 2008 are captured in the new surveys.

Based on the economic projections of developing countries at the International Monetary Fund and the World Bank, the world remains on track to reduce by half the number of people living in extreme poverty. The number of people living on less than $1.25 a day is projected to be 882.7 million in 2015, which is lower than the previous estimate of 918 million (see the table on the next page). The decline results mainly from data changes for India, which showed a more rapid growth of per capita consumption than previously reported in the national accounts. This estimate will be updated further when India's forthcoming household survey for 2008 is completed. That survey will provide a more accurate estimate of household consumption for different income groups. Although the poverty numbers for East Asia and the Pacific remain relatively stable, China's poverty rate and number (at the poverty level of $1.25 a day) have decreased further, based on the new 2008 household survey and a higher growth rate of its household income. Projections for Sub-Saharan Africa are slightly better than previously estimated: its extreme poverty at $1.25 a day is projected to be 35.8 percent in 2015, lower than the previous forecast of 38.0 percent, because of its higher recent growth performance and growth forecast. However, several of Africa's household surveys for 2008 still need to be completed (see the discussion of gaps below).

The new household surveys employed in the forecast cover about 43.1 percent of the population in developing countries in 2008 and 7.6 percent in 2009 (see the figure on the next page). However, gaps for 2008–10 household surveys

continued

BOX 1.1   Poverty data and projections (continued)

Estimates of poverty reduction on a poverty line of $1.25 and $2.00 a day, by region

Region	1990	2005	2015	1990	2005	2015
	Population living on less than $1.25 a day (%)			People living on less than $1.25 a day (millions)		
East Asia and Pacific	54.7	16.8	5.9	873.3	316.2	119.0
China	60.2	15.9	4.8	683.2	207.7	66.1
Europe and Central Asia	2.0	3.7	1.2	9.1	17.3	5.8
Latin America and the Caribbean	11.3	8.2	4.7	49.6	45.1	29.1
Middle East and North Africa	4.3	3.6	1.3	9.7	11.0	4.8
South Asia	51.7	40.3	22.4	579.2	595.6	379.3
India	51.3	41.6	22.4	435.5	455.8	276.8
Sub-Saharan Africa	57.6	50.9	35.8	295.7	388.4	344.7
Total	41.7	25.2	14.4	1,816.6	1,373.5	882.7
	Population living on less than $2.00 a day (%)			People living on less than $2.00 a day (millions)		
East Asia and Pacific	79.8	38.7	19.7	1,273.7	728.7	399.4
China	84.6	36.3	15.4	960.8	473.7	213.4
Europe and Central Asia	6.9	8.9	4.5	31.9	41.9	21.4
Latin America and the Caribbean	19.7	16.6	10.7	86.3	91.3	66.3
Middle East and North Africa	19.7	16.9	7.2	44.4	51.5	26.2
South Asia	82.7	73.9	57.1	926.0	1091.5	967.2
India	82.6	75.6	56.9	701.6	827.7	702.0
Sub-Saharan Africa	76.2	73.0	57.7	391.2	556.7	555.6
Total	63.2	47.0	33.1	2,753.5	2,561.5	2,036.1

Source: World Bank staff calculations from PovcalNet database.

remain at the regional level: South Asia (pending India's new household survey), 10.8 percent of population is covered; Middle East and North Africa, 19.1 percent; Sub-Saharan Africa, 20.1 percent; Latin America and the Caribbean, 84.1 percent; East Asia and the Pacific, 90.3 percent; and Europe and Central Asia, 94.4 percent. Efforts are already under way at the World Bank to close remaining gaps before the end of 2011 to complete and update the time-series estimate of poverty at the global and regional levels for 2008.

Population coverage of the latest available household surveys is increasing

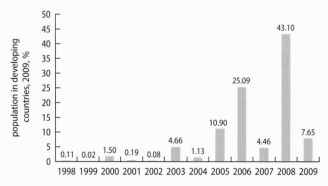

Source: World Bank staff calculations based on household data from the PovcalNet database.

the 1990s, Sub-Saharan Africa's poverty has fallen steeply since 2000.

Middle-income countries—both lower and upper—generally exhibit the best performance. For example, 80 percent of countries in the upper-middle-income bracket (23 countries) have achieved or are on track to achieve the extreme poverty target. Similarly, 72 percent of lower-middle-income countries (34 countries) are reaching the target for gender parity in secondary education. In one area, however—gender parity in primary education—progress in both low-income and middle-income countries is substantial.

Latin America and the Caribbean is showing excellent results and leading in several indicators: hunger, primary education completion, gender parity in secondary education, access to safe drinking water, and access to sanitation. Even so, it faces serious challenges on maternal mortality, with just 10 percent of countries (three countries) that have reached or are on track to reach the 2015 target (figure 1.3).

East Asia and Pacific is progressing in many areas, particularly on education, gender parity, and access to safe drinking water. Its performance is particularly good for gender parity in secondary education, where 82 percent of countries (14 countries) are on target.

South Asia is also closing the development gap. Its performance is encouraging for primary education completion, gender parity, maternal mortality, and access to safe drinking water, although performance needs to improve for extreme poverty and hunger.

Eastern Europe shows important progress on extreme poverty (the region's countries account for 32 percent of countries on target). Advances are also significant for child and maternal mortality. Challenges remain, however—particularly in Central Asia, where progress on extreme poverty, child and maternal mortality, and access to safe drinking water is relatively low. For instance, no Central Asian country is on track to achieve the child mortality goal; but the target is still within reach or close to becoming on target for five countries in the subregion (see below and appendix 1 for a discussion of the concept, close to becoming on target).

The Middle East and North Africa is performing relatively well on gender parity in secondary education and on access to sanitation. However, it needs faster progress on extreme poverty, hunger, and maternal mortality.

FIGURE 1.3   Countries on target to achieve the MDGs, by region

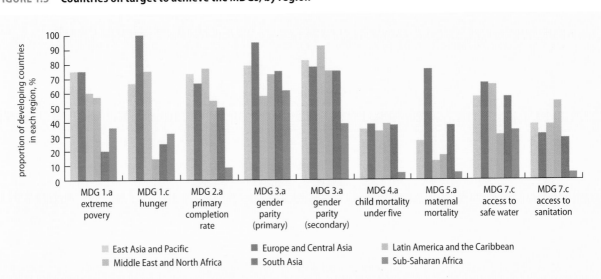

Source: World Bank staff calculations based on data from the World Development Indicators database.

Sub-Saharan Africa lags the other regions but can point to some encouraging results. Progress is quite good on extreme poverty (9 countries), hunger (8 countries), gender parity in primary education (27 countries), and access to safe drinking water (15 countries). Goals related to child and maternal mortality, access to sanitation, and primary education completion require stepped-up efforts.

Several low-income countries are doing well. A look beneath the aggregate global statistics shows not just middle-income countries doing well, but many low-income countries, too (table 1.1). A recent study by

TABLE 1.1   Several low-income countries are achieving the MDGs

Selected MDG	Low-income countries that have achieved the goal	Low-income countries that are on track to achieve the goal
Poverty	Cambodia Kenya Mauritania	Central African Republic Ethiopia Ghana
Universal primary education	Myanmar Tajikistan Tanzania	None
Gender parity in primary education	Bangladesh Gambia, The Ghana Haiti Kenya Kyrgyz Republic Madagascar Malawi Mauritania Myanmar Rwanda Tanzania Uganda Zambia Zimbabwe	Benin Burkina Faso Burundi Cambodia Comoros Ethiopia Guinea Nepal Sierra Leone Solomon Islands Togo
Gender parity in secondary education	Bangladesh Kyrgyz Republic Myanmar	Gambia, The Malawi Mauritania Nepal Rwanda
Under-five mortality	None	Bangladesh Eritrea Lao PDR Madagascar Nepal
Access to safe drinking water	Afghanistan Burkina Faso Comoros Gambia, The Ghana Korea, Dem. People's Rep. Kyrgyz Republic Malawi Nepal	Benin Cambodia Guinea Uganda
Access to sanitation	Lao PDR Myanmar Tajikistan	Rwanda

Source: World Development Indicators database (as of March 2011).
Note: List of low-income countries is based on the new World Bank classification for fiscal year 2011 (see appendix 1).

Leo and Barmeier confirmed that progress in individual African and poor countries was surprisingly strong.[3]

Variation behind the aggregates. The typical global and regional summaries amass data for countries of dissimilar development and types—fragile, low-income, and middle-income countries. For example, the Europe and Central Asia region covers such middle-income countries as Albania and Bulgaria and such low-income countries as Tajikistan and Uzbekistan. Among the developing countries in Sub-Saharan Africa, some are middle-income countries (such as Mauritius and South Africa); some lower-middle-income countries (such as Angola and the Democratic Republic of Congo) are resource rich, but their levels of development may be closer to those of low-income countries. Progress has been more heterogeneous than is shown by the aggregate figures.[4]

Country progress, not just global or regional

Although the MDGs were conceived as global targets to spur development efforts and support to poor countries, it is necessary to measure and describe progress at the country or other level to better understand advances and remaining gaps (see box 1.2). To untangle the aggregate numbers, we introduce alternative ways of analyzing MDG progress with a focus on lagging countries. Our approach characterizes MDG progress by country performance and by different typologies—such as initial income and policy-institutional conditions, subsequent growth and policy-institutional achievement, the poorest countries versus the others, level of fragility, and export sophistication and shipping connectivity (broadly following Collier and O'Connell[5]). This approach provides some empirical explanations of the links between development's drivers and different rates of MDG progress.

Where do countries stand?

Several global targets will be missed, but the following questions also matter: How many

countries are attaining the goals, and how many are behind? Are lagging countries far from the goals? And how many are already close? Answers from available information are surprisingly hopeful.

To examine them, we distinguish countries that are on target (or on track)—that is, their annual rate of progress between the reference year of MDGs in 1990 (or the closest available) to the latest year of data implies the right trajectory or trend to meet or exceed the goals—and those that are off target (or lagging). We look first at the gaps of off-target countries because they are the countries that need most attention.

First, the variation among lagging countries is large, but the average gap is not (table 1.2). Lagging countries are, on average, only 23 percent away from being on track to achieve all the MDGs. They are especially close to the targets for gender parity in primary education (average gap is 7 percent); gender parity in secondary education (16 percent gap); hunger (19 percent gap); primary education completion (20 percent gap); and, to some extent, under-five mortality (23 percent gap). But for each target there are countries where progress has been scant. For example, several countries are far from halving extreme poverty, even as the global goal will be reached.

Progress is mixed or poor on access to safe drinking water, access to sanitation, maternal mortality, and extreme poverty. Even so, the mean gaps of all lagging countries are less than 50 percent from the targets on access to safe drinking water (25 percent) and access to sanitation (27 percent), and no worse than 40 percent on maternal mortality (32 percent) and extreme poverty (39 percent).

Different starting points will imply a unique trajectory for each country to reach a specific goal. Hence, comparing the slope or growth rate of the historical path with the required one is a good way to assess progress. Leo and Barmeier define lagging countries as close to target if their trajectory is within 50 percent of the required progress to reach the goals, earning half a full score.[6] In our methodology, we do not assign numerical scores in

---

BOX 1.2   Gaps and issues in measuring development outcomes beyond 2015

Measuring broad development outcomes through specific indicators is never precise, so the diversity in MDG performance is partly the result of indicator or measurement issues. Although the purpose of this report is not to focus on these issues, they are important for future deliberations of MDGs beyond 2015. Some of the issues are the following:

- *Outcomes versus outputs.* Some MDG indicators (such as under-five mortality and maternal mortality) quantify development outcomes, whereas others (such as the primary education completion rate and ratios of girls to boys in education) are specific intermediate outputs. It is not surprising that the more outcome-based health MDGs often progress more slowly than others. But poverty reduction, a broad development outcome, is progressing rapidly. Because of the inherent and varying difficulty of demonstrating progress and results, choosing between outcomes and outputs may touch on issues of political economy. For example, a target like universal primary school enrollment is easily embraced because it is easier to show progress by getting children through school than it is to make sure they learn something, which may also be harder to measure. By contrast, learning outcomes as an objective are often resisted when the jobs and pay of

teachers are at stake, partly because the outcomes also depend on other factors beyond the control of teachers. Take Tanzania as an example. It received an MDG award at the 2010 United Nations summit for its rapid progress on the primary education completion rate, but the ultimate development goal of improving learning outcomes of Tanzanian children remains problematic.[a] The point is that some meaningful development outcomes rest outside the scope of the MDGs, and it is important to begin to develop the auxiliary indicators and information base to monitor them.

- *Missing targets.* Some specific development outcomes are not defined or are missing. Economic growth, particularly inclusive growth, is also excluded from the MDGs, as noted by many commentators. Its centrality as a means to achieve the MDGs is nonetheless monitored in the *Global Monitoring Report* framework. Missing global public goods include climate change–related goals (such as reducing carbon emissions) and market access for developing countries.

- *Targets versus trends.* Although Sub-Saharan countries as a group will find it difficult to meet the poverty goal by 2015, they are progressing far above historical trends. Therefore, deviations from the targets versus deviations from past trends also

this manner or use an arbitrary cutoff point of 50 percent. Although we use the trend deviations or differences in the two growth rates to define the gaps, the actual gaps are retained to classify countries into groups according to their progress, to measure the mean gaps of each group, and to identify countries that are within 10 (or 20) percent of becoming on target. The mean gaps of lagging countries are all less than 50 percent across the MDGs, and they provide data-specific cutoff points to split the off-target countries into two subgroups: above average and below average. Countries in the top half are "close to the target," whereas countries in the bottom half are "far from the target" (appendix 1 explains the approach in more detail).

More important, among countries that are off track, the top half are, on average, only about 11 percent away from being on target. The mean distance of this subgroup is only 4–9 percent for gender parity in primary and secondary education, child mortality, primary education completion, and hunger. Indeed, countries close to the target need to increase primary education completion only by 9.2 percent (or 1.5 percent a year), on average, to be on track to reach the 2015 target.

However, the rather uneven distribution also points to serious problems for the bottom half of the off-target countries, those far from the target among the lagging countries—they are disproportionately far from the targets, especially for poverty (67 percent)

BOX 1.2 (continued)

matter. A related, wider issue is whether the MDGs should be absolute or relative targets.[b]

- *Data gaps.* Poor data availability may fail to convey progress or understate deterioration resulting from shocks and conflicts. Among the MDGs, the collection and dissemination of poverty aggregates seem to lag the most. Conducting and completing household income and expenditure surveys in large countries is difficult, often delaying global or regional poverty updates because of the weights of these countries in the aggregates. There is also spotty information about infectious diseases, such as malaria and tuberculosis. Other data issues include reporting errors that severely compromise the accuracy of the maternal mortality ratio. And hunger is assessed only indirectly, through minimum food intake and its deprivation.

- *Metrics issues in some MDGs.* When targets are measured in proportionate amounts, such as *reducing by half the proportion of people living on less than $1.25 a day*, problems can arise at both extremes. For low-income countries with high initial poverty rates, many of which are in Africa, the greater distance to the goal makes the target harder to reach; for middle-income countries where poverty rates are less than 10 or even 5 percent, reducing the rate further is also difficult and may entail assisting

the hard-to-reach populations (chapter 4). The ratios of girls to boys in schools may be stagnant at 97–99 percent in some higher-middle-income countries because of different enrollment ratios between girls and boys. Boys may be lagging in completion rates (for example, at the primary level in Uruguay and at the secondary level in the Russian Federation). In addition, country figures can vary from international ones because of differences between national education systems and the International Standard of Education Classification (ISCED) used in multilateral development agencies—as well as differences in coverage and even population estimates.

- *Averages and weights.* Large countries such as China, India, and Nigeria dominate their respective regional averages, especially on measures, such as poverty, where population is the weight. So the pattern would likely change if the reference unit pertained to individual countries, not regional or global aggregates. For example, many poor countries, including Bangladesh, Bolivia, the Lao People's Democratic Republic, Malawi, Mozambique, Nepal, and Niger are registering major achievements on difficult MDGs such as child mortality.

a. Uwezo Tanzania 2010.
b. ODI 2010.

TABLE 1.2 **Lagging countries are close to getting on target**

	Average distance to getting on target (gaps, %)		
	All off-target countries	Countries close to the target	Countries far from the target
MDG 1.a Extreme poverty	39 (96)	17	67
MDG 1.c Hunger	19 (60)	9	35
MDG 2.a Primary education completion	20 (96)	9	40
MDG 3.a Gender parity in primary education	7 (22)	4	14
MDG 3.a Gender parity in secondary education	16 (52)	8	29
MDG 4.a Child mortality under five	23 (59)	8	38
MDG 5.a Maternal mortality	32 (80)	11	51
MDG 7.c Access to safe drinking water	25 (76)	14	41
MDG 7.c Access to sanitation	27 (50)	16	34
Simple average	23	11	39

Source: World Bank staff calculations based on data from the World Development Indicators database.
Note: A country is "close to the target" if its distance to getting on target (that is, its gap of trajectory) is smaller than the average gap of all lagging countries. Otherwise, it is "far from the target" (that is, its distance is greater than the average gap). Figures in parentheses indicate the range of variation (Maximum value—Minimum value) of countries off target, by MDG. Averages and numbers of countries cover only those with data—and that may vary by MDG. See appendix 1 for more details.

TABLE 1.3 **Many countries are within 10–20 percent of being on target**

	Distribution of lagging countries			
	Gap ≤ 10 percent		Gap ≤ 20 percent	
	Number of countries	Proportion of countries (%)	Number of countries	Proportion of countries (%)
MDG 1.a Extreme poverty	9	24	13	34
MDG 1.c Hunger	10	33	18	60
MDG 2.a Primary education completion	23	40	39	68
MDG 3.a Gender parity in primary education	28	74	36	95
MDG 3.a Gender parity in secondary education	16	42	23	61
MDG 4.a Child mortality under five	33	31	48	46
MDG 5.a Maternal mortality	20	21	37	39
MDG 7.c Access to safe drinking water	10	15	32	48
MDG 7.c Access to sanitation	6	6	25	26
Simple average	17	32	30	53

Source: World Bank staff calculations based on data from the World Development Indicators database.

and maternal mortality (51 percent). And the range of variation is considerably large among countries off target. For extreme poverty and primary education completion, the gap between the countries closest to and farthest from being on target is 96 percent, a fact that clearly illustrates the diversity of performance. This is the case for El Salvador and Uzbekistan on extreme poverty reduction and for Bhutan and Djibouti on primary completion rates.

Indeed, many lagging countries are already within striking distance. From another perspective, table 1.3 provides the proportion of countries within 10 percent

or 20 percent of getting on target. A third of off-target countries have, on average, a gap of 10 percent or less from being on target across the MDGs. Countries like Bangladesh (extreme poverty, hunger, and maternal mortality), Indonesia (hunger, child and maternal mortality, access to safe drinking water), and Mali (gender parity in primary education and access to safe drinking water) are in this category. (Table 1.4 lists these countries by MDG.) More than half have a gap of 20 percent or less. Of the countries within 20 percent of target, the best results are for gender parity in primary education, primary education completion, gender parity in secondary education,

TABLE 1.4 **Lagging countries within 10 percent of being on target to achieve the MDGs**

MDG 1.a Extreme poverty	MDG 1.c Hunger	MDG 2.a Primary education completion	MDG 3.a Gender parity in primary education	MDG 3.a Gender parity in secondary education	MDG 4.a Child mortality under five	MDG 5.a Maternal mortality	MDG 7.c Access to safe drinking water	MDG 7.c Access to sanitation
Bangladesh	Bangladesh	Bhutan	Belize	Bulgaria	Algeria	Algeria	Azerbaijan	Botswana
Burkina Faso	Bolivia	Cambodia	Cape Verde	Congo, Rep.	Antigua and Barbuda	Bangladesh	Colombia	Brazil
El Salvador	Egypt, Arab Rep.	Comoros	Chile	Georgia	Argentina	Brazil	Eritrea	Dominican Republic
Guinea	Indonesia	Cuba	Congo, Dem. Rep.	Grenada	Belarus	Cambodia	Haiti	Morocco
India	Jordan	El Salvador	Congo, Rep.	Guatemala	Bhutan	Cape Verde	Indonesia	Peru
Lao PDR	Kenya	Gambia, The	Djibouti	Macedonia, FYR	Cape Verde	Dominican Republic	Iran, Islamic Rep.	Turkey
Lesotho	Nigeria	Ghana	El Salvador	Madagascar	Colombia	Egypt, Arab Rep.	Kiribati	
Philippines	Pakistan	Guatemala	Grenada	Morocco	Dominican Republic	Ethiopia	Mali	
Uganda	Rwanda	Honduras	Guatemala	Pakistan	Ecuador	Haiti	Myanmar	

TABLE 1.4　Lagging countries within 10 percent of being on target to achieve the MDGs (continued)

MDG 1.a Extreme poverty	MDG 1.c Hunger	MDG 2.a Primary education completion	MDG 3.a Gender parity in primary education	MDG 3.a Gender parity in secondary education	MDG 4.a Child mortality under five	MDG 5.a Maternal mortality	MDG 7.c Access to safe drinking water	MDG 7.c Access to sanitation
	Zambia	Iraq	Guinea-Bissau	Russian Federation	Ethiopia	India	Venezuela, R.B. de	
		Jamaica	Jamaica	Senegal	Guatemala	Indonesia		
		Kyrgyz Republic	Lao PDR	Solomon Islands	Honduras	Lao PDR		
		Lebanon	Lebanon	Sudan	Indonesia	Mongolia		
		Lithuania	Maldives	Swaziland	Kazakhstan	Morocco		
		Macedonia, FYR	Mali	Vanuatu	Kiribati	Nepal		
		Mauritius	Mozambique	Zimbabwe	Kyrgyz Republic	Peru		
		Moldova	Nigeria		Liberia	Rwanda		
		Morocco	Paraguay		Libya	Syrian Arab Republic		
		Nepal	South Africa		Malawi	Tunisia		
		Philippines	St. Vincent and the Grenadines		Moldova	Yemen, Rep.		
		South Africa	Sudan		Montenegro			
		Tanzania	Suriname		Niger			
		Turkey	Swaziland		Paraguay			
			Tajikistan		Russian Federation			
			Tonga		Samoa			
			Uruguay		Sri Lanka			
			Vanuatu		St. Vincent and the Grenadines			
			Venezuela, R.B. de		Suriname			
					Syrian Arab Republic			
					Tajikistan			
					Turkmenistan			
					Uzbekistan			
					Yemen, Rep.			

Source: World Bank staff calculations based on data from the World Development Indicators database.
Note: See also box 1.2, which covers metrics issues concerning some MDG targets.

and hunger. The worst results are for access to sanitation, extreme poverty, and maternal mortality, with access to safe drinking water and under-five mortality in the middle.

All told, developing countries have been doing much better than thought until recently. Although many more developing countries are off track than on track to achieve the targets, two thirds or more of developing countries are actually on target or close to being on target, thanks to more

than a decade of better policy and growth (figure 1.4). Many countries are making substantial progress in several MDGs: gender parity in primary education (89 of them), gender parity in secondary education (82), access to safe drinking water (66), primary completion rate (55), and extreme poverty (47). For instance, about 70 percent of developing countries have achieved or are on track to achieve the targets for gender parity in primary and secondary education. Although

FIGURE 1.4   **More than two-thirds of developing countries are on track or close to being on track**

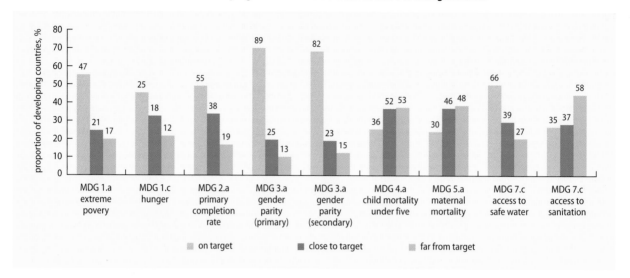

Source: World Bank staff calculations based on data from the World Development Indicators database.
Note: A country is "close to the target" if its distance to getting on target (that is, its gap of trajectory) is smaller than the average gap of all lagging countries. Otherwise, it is "far from the target" (that is, its distance is greater than the average gap). The number above each bar indicates the number of countries. See appendix 1 for more details.

half the monitored countries (57) are off target for the primary education completion goal, two-thirds of them (38) are very close to being on track.

Progress is mixed or poor on access to sanitation, maternal mortality, and child mortality (box 1.3). Unfortunately, more than 40 percent of low-income to upper-middle-income countries in the sample (58 countries) are significantly off target for access to sanitation.

Regional patterns vary. The maps in this report show global and regional patterns (see map 1.1). Because the gaps in the top half of lagging countries are small, the ratio of countries close to the target to the total number of off-target countries also provides a relative measure of progress among MDG underachievers (table A1.2 and related tables in appendix 1). Within this group, Sub-Saharan Africa shows encouraging results. For instance, 81 percent of the region's lagging countries are relatively close to the extreme poverty target. Fifty percent of the region's countries are very close to the target for gender parity in secondary education, and 53 percent are quite close for hunger. Progress is also evident in access to safe drinking

water (69 percent of countries are close to the target).

Many South Asian countries that face difficulties in reaching the 2015 targets are also performing better than average in the off-target group. For instance, all the region's countries are within reach of the extreme poverty target, and 80 percent are close to the access to sanitation goal. For 67 percent of South Asian countries, the hunger target is within range.

In the Middle East and North Africa, 67 percent of countries are close to the target for gender parity in primary education. Even more encouraging: 80 percent of countries in the region are within reach of the primary education goal.

In Latin America and the Caribbean, Europe and Central Asia, and East Asia and Pacific—the regions with better MDG performance—most off-target countries are close to several goals, such as hunger, primary education completion, and gender parity. Results are less promising for maternal mortality and access to sanitation. Interestingly, for countries that have low poverty rates (that is, less than 10 percent), reducing extreme poverty at $1.25 a day to a much greater extent may not be easy (see box 1.2).

BOX 1.3   Improving children's health through sustainable access to food, water, and energy

Sustainable access to food, safe drinking water, basic sanitation, and modern energy sources can decrease child mortality significantly.[a] Of the estimated 10.5 million child deaths annually, the vast majority are from preventable and treatable diseases and conditions, including low dietary energy consumption (underweight), unsafe drinking water and the lack of basic sanitation (diarrhea), and indoor air pollution related to solid fuel use for cooking and heating (pneumonia).

Based on socioeconomic and environmental trends, we project the population that lacks adequate access to food, water, and energy, and the resulting effect on child mortality. Except for Middle East and North Africa, progress is not enough to reach the MDG target on child mortality; and Sub-Saharan Africa does not even come close by 2030. Accelerated progress significantly improves this situation (see the figure below). This is especially the case in Sub-Saharan Africa, where approximately one-third of the child mortality gap can be achieved by achieving other MDGs.

Rising demand for food, water, and modern energy will put pressure on scarce natural resources (for example, fertile land for food and bioenergy; oil resources for clean fuels, such as kerosene for cooking). This will increase the prices of (especially) food and energy. And it will hurt poor people in importing countries in Sub-Saharan Africa and South Asia whose governments are unable to guarantee affordable prices when global prices increase.[b] Furthermore,

provision of food, water, and energy becomes more difficult when natural resources are not properly managed or degrade as a result of global environmental change.[c] For example, climate change induces changes in rainfall and temperature patterns, potentially increasing the likelihood of short-term crop failures and long-term production declines as well as deterioration in water quality. The most vulnerable are poor and food-insecure countries at lower latitudes (especially in seasonally dry and tropical regions) that largely depend on rainfed farming—again in Sub-Saharan Africa and South Asia. Many such pressures are slow moving and cannot easily be stopped because of major inertia, including the pressures of fertility transition and greenhouse gas accumulation. They become apparent only in the long term, after 2015 or even after 2030, trapping people in their poverty and reversing progress.

Therefore, to achieve the MDG target on child mortality, accelerated growth in the other MDGs is key—particularly access to food, improved drinking water, basic sanitation, and improved energy sources. Furthermore, policies addressing increased access to food, water, and energy should take global scarcities and global environmental changes into account. This could both help in achieving the MDGs and in making those achievements more sustainable.

a. PBL 2009b.
b. PBL 2011.
c. PBL 2009b.

Projected child mortality results from various causes, 2015 and 2030

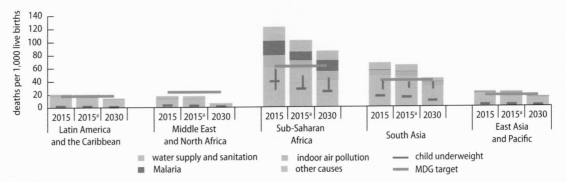

Source: PBL 2009a.
Note: Because being underweight is usually not a direct cause of a child's death (although it increases the risks of dying from pneumonia, malaria, and diarrhea), it is reported separately.
a. The accelerated progress scenario for 2015 achieves the MDG targets on food, water, malaria, and energy (GISMO model, PBL 2008).

Country diversity generally softens the gloomy global picture. All these statistics are remarkable, revealing progress that is much more diversified and much more hopeful than the recent pessimism about achieving the MDGs. That pessimism was likely colored by the gaps at the global level, the difficult circumstances of poor countries, the potential negative impact of the recent global crisis, and the lack of recent data to assess outcomes. For example, although only 27 percent of low-income countries are on track to achieve or have achieved the extreme poverty target, almost 90 percent of these countries with data are in the top half of the lagging group and, therefore, have the poverty goal within their reach. Similarly, around 40 percent of low-income countries are close to the primary education completion goal, even though only 7 percent of the countries in this income group are on target.

What the data also suggest is that the reference unit matters. Simple country averages that give equal importance to each country qualify the global story, which uses weighted averages that give more importance to countries with large populations. This can work in both directions. For example, the progress in reducing world poverty and in meeting the goal is essentially the result of rapid advances by China and India, with the absolute number of poor people falling rapidly in China. Too many countries, however, still lag on the poverty goal, and their average shortfall of 39 percent to be on target is the biggest among the MDGs. In contrast, the average distance to becoming on target for under-five mortality is only 23 percent for lagging countries, somewhat less daunting than the global distance derived from the population of all under-five children.

Country analysis generally brightens the global picture, but both global and country perspectives are necessary for the complete view. In an unprecedented manner, the MDGs as global targets have galvanized development efforts to help the world's poor; however, the country unit is relevant because these efforts are still geared to individual countries, given that country-owned strategy and capacity are important aspects of development assistance.

What important lessons therefore emerge from the complex tapestry of progress? Why are some countries on target, but others are not? Of the lagging countries, why are some close to target and others far away? The two main drivers often cited as key to attaining MDG-related development outcomes are economic growth and sound policies and institutions (fundamental to effective service delivery to the poor).[7] Although it is easy to cite these two drivers, it is hard to provide empirical substance to their impact on achieving the MDGs.

We pursue this tack in the next section by examining the country pattern against growth and policy accomplishments, continuing the forward-looking analytical work started in the 2010 *Global Monitoring Report*.[8] More specifically, we ask whether initial conditions or subsequent growth and policy improve the odds of reaching the goals. The analysis looks at these elements in two ways: using prima facie evidence from graphical associations and patterns, which point to these elements' likely association with the diverse progress of countries; and using a statistical investigation of their significance in increasing the likelihood of attaining MDG-associated outcomes.

The role of growth and policy

Initial conditions count in MDG performance, but subsequent growth and policy also matter greatly—or more. In most cases, countries that are doing better (those on or close to the target) exhibited favorable starting conditions around 1990 (the reference year). A higher per capita GDP in 1990 is generally associated with better MDG performance (figure 1.5).

Although there is no perfect indicator of the overall quality of policy and institutions in developing countries, the World Bank's annual Country Policy and Institutional Assessment (CPIA) provides a broadly consistent framework for assessing country performance on 16 items grouped in four clusters: economic management, structural policies, policies for social inclusion and equity, and public sector management and institutions.

MAP 1.1　The world is still on track to meet the poverty reduction target

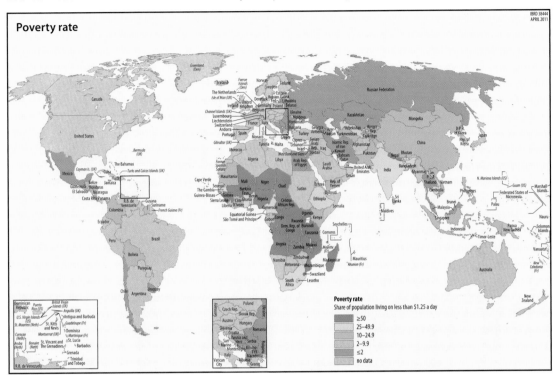

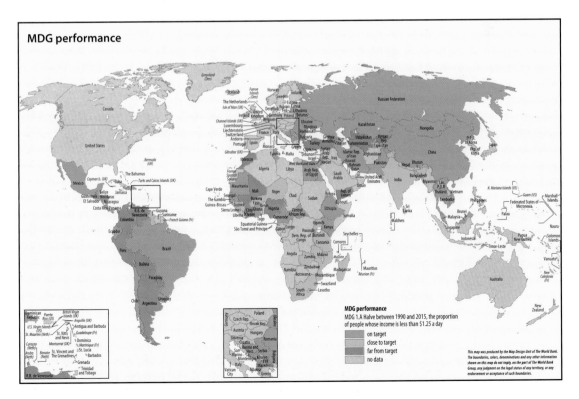

Source: World Bank staff calculations based on data from the World Development Indicators database.

FIGURE 1.5   MDG performance is stronger in countries with good initial conditions

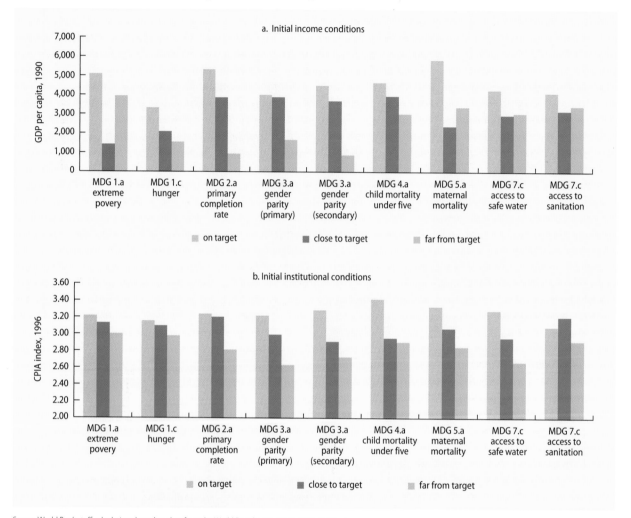

Source: World Bank staff calculations based on data from the World Development Indicators database.
Note: A country is "close to the target" if its distance to getting on target (that is, its gap of trajectory) is smaller than the average gap of all lagging countries.
Otherwise, it is "far from the target" (that is, its distance is greater than the average gap).

The score is from 1 (low) to 6 (high) for each policy that covers a wide range of issues.[9] The index focuses on policies and institutional arrangements—the key elements that are within the country's control—rather than on actual outcomes (for example, growth rates) that are influenced by elements outside the country's control. Over time, good policies and institutions are expected to lead to favorable growth and poverty reduction outcomes, notwithstanding possible yearly fluctuations caused by external factors.[10] Using the 1996 CPIA, the earliest index with comparable scale and criteria available,[11] suggests

that countries starting with good policies and institutions tend to do better in the MDGs.

Starting points—inherited initial conditions—explain why middle-income countries generally do better than low-income countries. Having grown earlier, they also tend to have implemented earlier a better set of policies and institutions. But there are variations. For extreme poverty and gender parity in primary education, countries making the fastest progress are those that experienced medium poverty and female-to-male primary enrollment ratios in the 1990s (see table A1.5 in the appendix). The latter results draw attention

FIGURE 1.6   Subsequent economic growth and policy seem to matter more

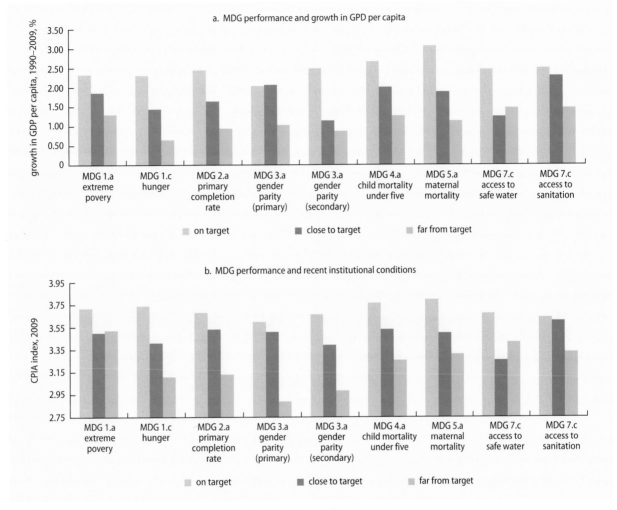

Source: World Bank staff calculations based on data from the World Development Indicators database.
Note: A country is "close to the target" if its distance to getting on target (that is, its gap of trajectory) is smaller than the average gap of all lagging countries. Otherwise, it is "far from the target" (that is, its distance is greater than the average gap).

to the challenges of poverty reduction in the proportionate way that MDGs are defined at low-income and middle-income levels— for poor countries, the distance to the goal is long; for middle-income countries, halving already low poverty rates is not easy.

So, although starting points (given their inherited nature) do not say much about what countries can or should do, they need not pre-ordain outcomes. The good news is that economic growth and policy performance after the initial year appear to count greatly, if not more than the starting points (figure 1.6). On average, countries that have reached or are on track to reach the targets (excluding gender parity in primary education) show the fastest per capita GDP growth over 1990–2009. In the same way, countries close to the target tend to have grown faster, in per capita terms, than countries far from the target. Likewise, a strong policy and institutional framework in the most recent year, 2009, tends to facilitate service delivery to the poor and to improve MDG performance (table 1.5).

Both factors—initial conditions and subsequent growth and policy—also point to why the MDGs are such big challenges for the poorest and most fragile countries. The

TABLE 1.5 **Growth and CPIA scores are higher in countries on track or close to being on track**
Average values across MDGs (weighted by the number of countries in each MDG category)

	On target	Close to the target	Far from the target
Average GDP per capita growth (1990–2009)	2.4	1.8	1.2
CPIA index (2009)	3.7	3.5	3.3

Source: World Bank staff calculations based on data from the World Development Indicators database.
Note: The pairwise correlation between average GDP per capita growth and the CPIA index is 0.32 (significant at 0.01 level).
GDP per capita, purchasing power parity constant 2005 international dollars. A country is "close to the target" if its distance to getting on target (that is, its gap of trajectory) is smaller than the average gap of all lagging countries. Otherwise, it is "far from the target" (that is, its distance is greater than the average gap).

world's 79 poorest countries serviced by the World Bank's International Development Association (IDA) have a threshold per capita gross national income of $1,165 for fiscal year 2011, with average per capita growth and recent institutional performances well below average.[12] Half the IDA countries are in Sub-Saharan Africa. With lower incomes and a late start in policy reforms and growth, IDA countries' MDG performance tends to lag that of middle-income and non-IDA countries (figure 1.7a). Despite the greater distance to the MDGs set by low starting points, the poverty target is within reach for more than 70 percent of IDA countries as a result of more recent economic growth and policy improvement. That is also true of the hunger target for 58 percent of IDA countries. Results are also good for gender parity in primary education.

Fragile conditions in conflict-affected countries are also associated with very poor MDG performance because these countries may experience growth collapses and disastrous policy and institutional environments (see box 1.4).[13] In broad terms, the proportion of on-target countries tends to rise with declining state fragility (figure 1.7b). Fragility in the graph is the index from the Center for Global Policy, which ranges from 0 (no fragility) to 25 (high fragility), divided into four categories ranging from little to extreme fragility (for more information on fragile states and the policy toolbox, see box 5.4).[14]

Export sophistication and shipping connectivity also have positive associations with MDG performance. In a period of rapid globalization and trade expansion, these two trade dimensions tend to be related to MDG performance in developing countries. Countries with a higher level of export sophistication are generally more on track to achieve the targets (figure 1.8a). Likewise, countries more integrated into global shipping networks are more likely to be on or close to the target (figure 1.8b).

We also looked at simpler dimensions of trade—commodity versus noncommodity exporters as well as landlocked versus other countries—but the associations tend to be less defined than those shown in figure 1.8. In any case, export sophistication, shipping connectivity, and state fragility are likely to be correlated with a country's level of development, growth performance, infrastructure, and with its policies and institutions for trade, private sector development, and doing business.[15]

Assessing the odds of achieving the MDGs

Is it possible to link and simulate the impact of growth and policy to the likelihood of achieving the MDGs in a manner more rigorous and statistical than with graphical associations? Although formal econometric analysis, in principle, can isolate partial effects that are not apparent from the simple correlations in the previous section, there are caveats: the direction of impact between development outcomes as measured by the MDGs and the two basic drivers (growth and policy) can go both ways; the two drivers themselves are likely to be correlated; and some factors that affect the progress of MDGs are not readily measurable and available. Data constraints are also problematic. For these reasons, the findings

FIGURE 1.7   MDG performance lags in IDA and fragile countries

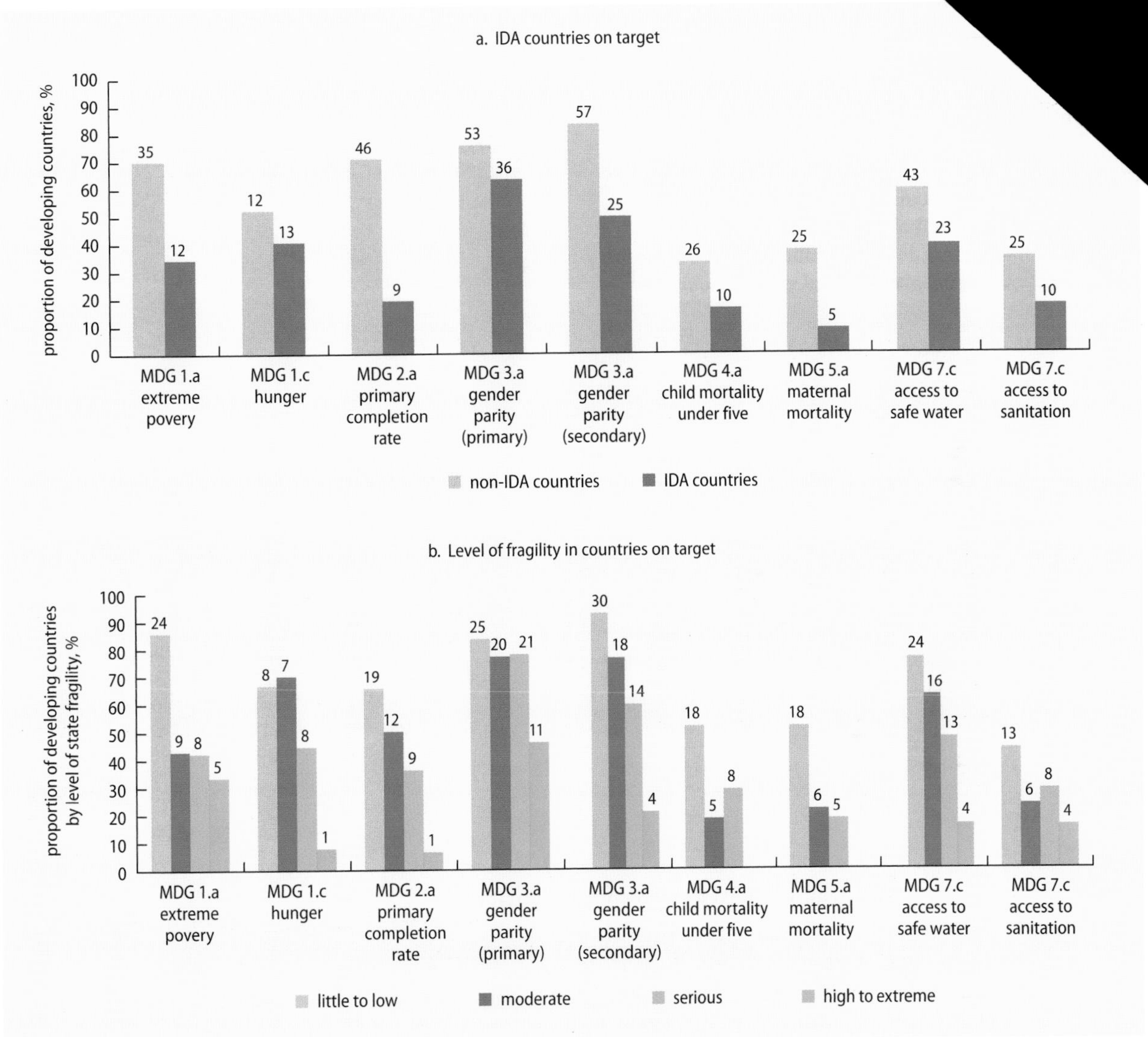

a. IDA countries on target

b. Level of fragility in countries on target

Source: World Bank staff calculations based on data from the World Development Indicators database and Marshall and Cole 2010.
Note: The number above each bar indicates the number of countries. See appendix 1 for more details.

in this section are preliminary; they are specific to the approach and presentation of data taken; and they may not apply when using other approaches or treatment of the MDG variables.

With these caveats and building on the empirical patterns, previously defined measures of MDG progress, and the basic drivers of progress in the GMR framework,[16] we introduce a simple and intuitive model that is suited to assessing the probability of a country falling into one of the three defined categories, linking performance to the two drivers. For a given development indicator associated with each MDG, the likelihood of a country being on target, close to the target, or far from the target is expressed as a function of

- economic growth (annual per capita GDP growth, 1990–2009);
- recent quality of the policy and institutional framework approximated by the current

MDGs

onflict,
d social
e. Devel-
rly every

tates are
more liable to be impoverished *ished and*

to lack access to basic health services and safe drinking water. Children born in these countries also tend to miss out on schooling; they are twice as likely to be undernourished and nearly twice as likely to die before age 5 (bottom figure below).

Violence poses a major challenge to meeting the MDGs

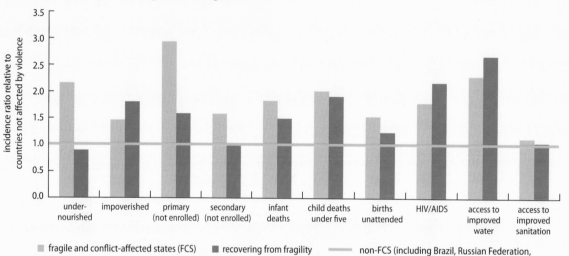

Countries affected by violence account for:

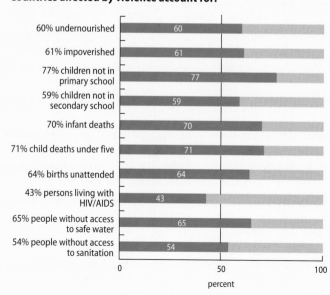

FIGURE 1.8   **MDG performance is better in countries with greater export sophistication and shipping connectivity**

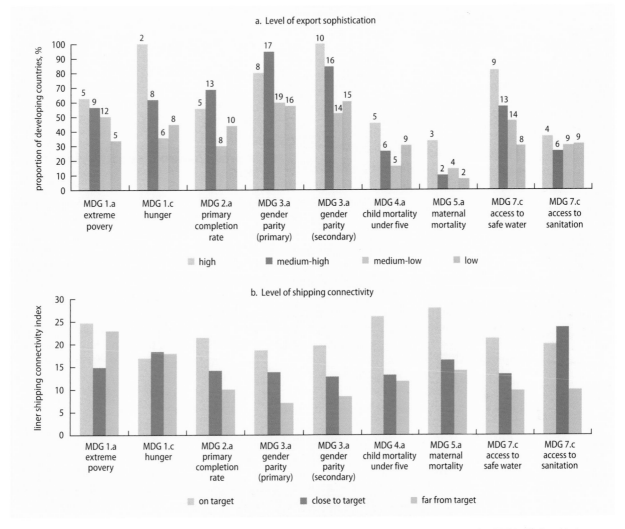

Source: World Bank staff calculations based on data from the World Development Indicators database, Lall 2000 for export sophistication, and UNCTAD 2010 for liner shipping connectivity.
Note: The index of export sophistication measures the technological content of exports from developing countries, standardized and distributed into four export groups. The shipping connectivity index has a base year of 2004. The number above each bar indicates the number of countries. A country is "close to the target" if its distance to getting on target (that is, its gap of trajectory) is smaller than the average gap of all lagging countries. Otherwise, it is "far from the target" (that is, its distance is greater than the average gap). See appendix 1 for more details.

CPIA, which assesses recent changes in policies and institutions and, by design, does not correlate with recent growth[17];
• initial conditions (per capita GDP in 1990 and CPIA index in 1996); and
• controls (specific development indicators around 1990).

The probability function across the different states of MDG performance is estimated using the multinomial logit model. Estimations are performed for each of the nine development targets under consideration using "far from the target" as the reference group or base category (see appendix 1 for a technical discussion). The statistical analysis therefore pools all country information and focuses on the probability of a country being in one of the three states of MDG performance.

Most of the literature on the determinants of MDGs, at country or regional level, focuses on demand-side factors (such as income and growth, demographic characteristics, and cultural values and preferences) and on supply-side interventions (such as public social expenditures, infrastructure, institutional quality, and civil service performance). Accordingly, empirical cross-country analyses usually relate supply and demand factors to development indicators in levels.[18] In the 2010 *Global Monitoring Report,* the scenarios of the impact of the recent crisis on the MDGs also used such an approach, and those scenarios remain generally valid. For this report, the emphasis is shedding light on the likelihood of countries attaining the development goals.

The statistical probability of achieving the MDGs is positively correlated with growth and improved policy. The correlation is significant at a 10 percent or better level of statistical significance (see figure A1.1 and marginal probabilities in the appendix). As expected, growth and policy effectiveness are positively related with the predicted probabilities of achieving or being on track for achieving the MDGs.

Both development drivers count, but growth has an all-encompassing bearing on progress toward the MDGs. A closer look at estimation results (table A1.6 in appendix 1) reveals that economic growth has a pervasively significant and positive impact on the odds of achieving all MDGs under consideration, apart from gender parity in primary education. The quality of policy and institutions also has a positive and statistically significant relation with MDGs for hunger reduction, gender parity, and child and maternal health.

Consequently, based on the average pattern thus far and at the aggregate level, growth might have a broader impact on attaining MDGs than the quality of policy and institutions. This is likely because growth has a more immediate effect and can be generated from several sources, including better policy as well as beneficial exogenous shocks and flows in the global economic environment. By

contrast, policy improvements as defined by the CPIA cover myriad areas and interventions that need a longer time to come through. In any case, given the short time left until 2015, the statistical results confirm the centrality of growth in improving countries' odds of achieving the MDGs. (In addition to growth, reducing inequality also helps decrease poverty in the case of Brazil [box 1.5]).

Improving the odds of achieving the MDGs

How much will higher growth and better policy improve these odds? We consider an increase of one standard deviation in growth and in the quality of policy institutional assessment to be equivalent to about 1.8 percentage points in added growth and to the CPIA index rising by 0.5 points.

Economic growth can jump-start countries particularly far from the goals. For countries that are far from the target (starting from a low base), the effects of a one-standard-deviation simulated increase in per capita growth on the probabilities of reaching some MDGs tend to be distinct and large (figure 1.9b). It would raise 12-fold the probability of reaching the targets for primary completion and gender parity in secondary education, more than double it for under-five child mortality and sanitation, almost double it for extreme poverty and hunger, and increase it by more than half for access to safe drinking water.

For countries close to the target, higher growth rates still appear to have a significant impact on primary education completion and gender parity, but not to the same extent as for countries far from the target (note the scale of the y-axis in figure 1.9a). This is doubtless because growth is already higher in this group (see table 1.5), which likely needs better policy to move to a higher plane.

Good policies and institutions are vital for outcome-based MDGs. For lagging countries far from the target, this seems true for several health-related MDGs—under-five mortality, maternal mortality, and hunger—as well as for gender parity in primary education. A one-standard-deviation simulated improvement in the quality of policies and institutions would increase the probability of achieving the hunger target nearly four-fold. For the remaining targets, the impact ranges from 152 percent to 67 percent.

For lagging countries close to the target, effective policies and stronger institutions also appear important to the progress on health-related MDGs. For instance, the odds of reaching targets such as maternal mortality and access to safe drinking water improve by more than 30 percent after a one-standard-deviation increase in the CPIA index.

Why do policies and institutions seem to play a greater role in the chances of reaching health-related MDGs in both groups of off-target countries? The reason is likely because the targets are outcome-based measures that depend not only on growth and resources but also on myriad factors in the system: the flow of budgets to localities where resources are needed, accountability and transparency, incentives of service providers and clients, and other institutions for service delivery. If the goals for education and gender parity were also outcome based (for example, based on learning outcomes or equal pay for workers

---

BOX 1.5   Reducing inequality and poverty in Brazil

In addition to faster growth and better policies, more inclusive growth and equality within countries will benefit people in the bottom quintiles and lift more people out of poverty. However, despite reduced inequality across countries over the last 25 years, within-country inequality has generally increased in most developing countries since 1980.[a] Brazil is a notable exception.

At the end of the 1980s, Brazil was one of the most unequal countries in Latin America and the developing world. According to the World Development Indicators database, Brazil's Gini coefficient of income inequality peaked at 63.0 in 1989—the highest among 70 countries with data, just above Sierra Leone's 62.9 and Zambia's 60.5. Since then, Brazil has experienced extraordinary progress in reducing both poverty and inequality—in fact, the country's Gini coefficient has fallen 10 points, while gross domestic product and real household consumption have grown steadily since 2003, after earlier stagnation.

Reduction of income inequality has significant effects on poverty in Brazil

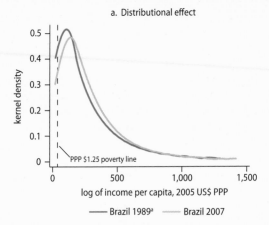

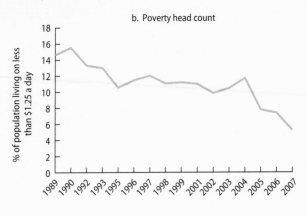

Source: World Bank staff calculations based on PovcalNet database.
a. Brazil 1989 is a projection of the structure of income distribution in 1989 with the average income in 2007.

continued

BOX 1.5   Reducing inequality and poverty in Brazil (continued)

The 1990s marked the expansion of social safety nets in Brazil. Public social expenditure, including conditional cash transfers such as the *Bolsa Família*, targeted to poor families rose from 17.6 percent of GDP in 1990 to 26 .0 percent of GDP in 2008—an increase of almost 50 percent in education, health, housing, and social security. Recent evidence suggests that this increase in social spending and better targeting contributed much to reducing poverty and inequality.[b] From 1994 to 2004, sound macroeconomic policies also lowered inflation from high levels and improved economic growth in more recent years.

Without the reduction in income equality from 1989 to 2007, the $1.25-a-day poverty rate would have been 14.5 percent, instead of the 5.2 percent attained. An additional 17.5 million Brazilians would have remained in extreme poverty. Using regression decomposition methods, Ferreira, Leite, and Ravallion calculate that without the social transfer policies and programs, the poverty head count index in Brazil would have been about 5 percentage points higher in 2004.[c]

Brazil's encouraging results illustrate the importance of inclusive economic growth and reduction of inequality in the fight against poverty and social exclusion. Ravallion identifies two main lessons from the Brazilian experience: "First, reforms to social policies to make them more pro-poor [if fiscally possible] can play an important role in sustaining poverty reduction, even during a period of economic stagnation. Second, sensible macroeconomic and trade policies need not hurt the poor and, in the specific case of taming hyperinflation, are likely to make a significant contribution in the fight against poverty, even when that is not the primary objective."[d]

Brazil is also taking steps to reach its indigenous peoples. Between 2002 and 2007, the number of indigenous schools rose by about 45 percent, and school enrollment among indigenous populations increased by 50.7 percent. The "Indigenous Portfolio" (*Carteira Indígena*) Initiative implemented in 2004 has approved over 250 projects to support economically and environmentally sustainable productive activities for the benefit of 12,000 indigenous families and 60 ethnic groups across 18 Brazilian states; the participation rate by indigenous organizations and communities is more than 80 percent.[e] Within-country variation and inequality being important, chapter 4 of this report examines one segment of the population—indigenous and socially excluded groups of people—that is lagging behind even in countries that are already on track to achieve the poverty goal.

a. See World Bank (2007, ch. 3) for a more detailed discussion of the trends and issues of global and within-country inequality.

b. Ferreira, Leite, and Litchfield 2008.

c. Ferreira, Leite, and Ravallion 2010.

d. Ravallion 2011, p. 17.

e. Government of Brazil 2009.

of similar characteristics), the results could be similar. The lack of data and defined goals in these areas makes it hard to test this more systematically. (See appendix 1 for more discussion.)

The simulation results generally show that economic growth and policy effectiveness can contribute significantly to achieving the MDGs. Although per capita GDP growth tends to have a broader impact on development targets, sound policies and institutions—basic dimensions of effective service delivery to the poor—appear crucial for achieving health-related MDGs.

Many more developing countries can get on track. A one-standard-deviation rise in both growth and the CPIA would mean that as many as 32 more developing countries can get on track for the MDGs—an average increase of 44 percent in the number of on-track countries (figure 1.10). This forecast is based on a greater than 50 percent probability of each country getting on track. Statistically, the probability of lagging countries can only

FIGURE 1.9   The odds of getting on target rise substantially with faster growth and better policy

Effects of a one-standard-deviation increase in selected development drivers from the multinomial logit estimates

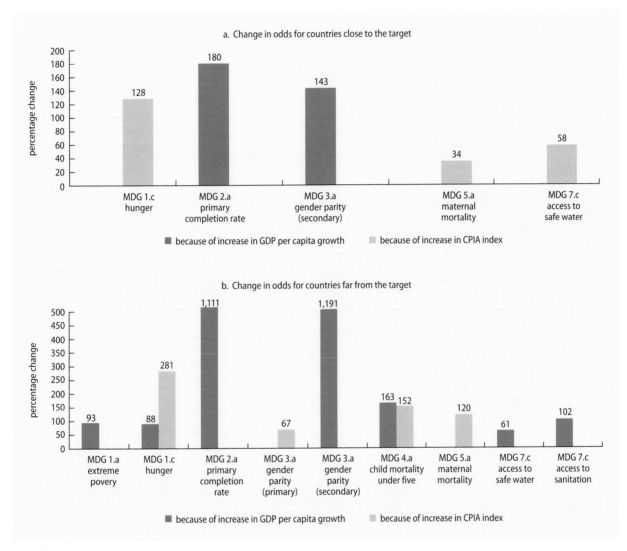

Source: World Bank staff calculations. See appendix 1 for details.
Note: For simplicity of presentation, only those countries with significant percentage changes at the 0.10 level or better are shown. Marginal probabilities and odds ratios are presented in appendix 1. Percentage variations are not comparable across indicators. Average standard deviation increase in GDP per capita growth ≈ 1.8. Average standard deviation increase in CPIA index ≈ 0.5. GDP per capita, purchasing power parity constant 2005 international dollars.

reach 100 percent as an upper (asymptotic) limit, but a 95 percent confidence interval of a 50 percent increase will generally cover that upper limit. The percentage increase in the number of countries getting on track generally rises most for the targets farthest behind—targets such as under-five mortality (89 percent), hunger (64 percent), access to sanitation (54 percent), maternal mortality (37 percent), and access to safe drinking water (36 percent). For the other MDGs (such as poverty, primary education completion, and gender equality in primary and secondary education), the increase in the number of countries is about 30 percent, still substantial. Individual countries that are good candidates to get on track

FIGURE 1.10   Growth and policy reforms will put many countries on track

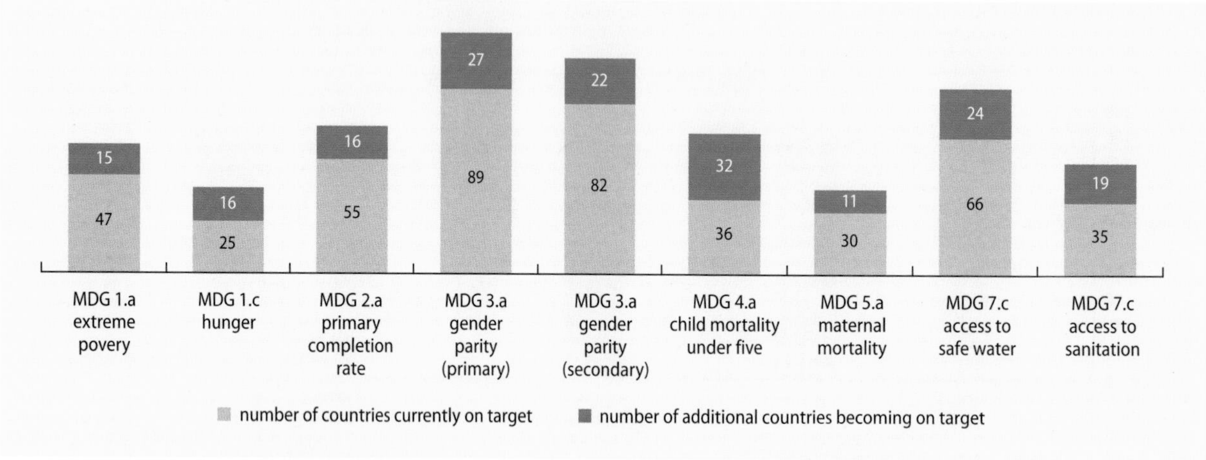

| MDG 1.a extreme poverty | MDG 1.c hunger | MDG 2.a primary completion rate | MDG 3.a gender parity (primary) | MDG 3.a gender parity (secondary) | MDG 4.a child mortality under five | MDG 5.a maternal mortality | MDG 7.c access to safe water | MDG 7.c access to sanitation |

■ number of countries currently on target   ■ number of additional countries becoming on target

Source: World Bank staff calculations based on a one-standard-deviation increase or improvement in growth and policy. See appendix 1 for details.

are those currently very close—that is, within 10 percent of getting on track (table 1.4).

How achievable are these gains? Recent history suggests they may be. Achieving the growth assumption for developing countries appears possible. To put the one-standard-deviation growth increase in context, per capita GDP growth will need to double from its historical rate of 1.9 percent a year. Even so, the historical rate is an average covering all types of developing countries and the uneven subperiods during 1990–2009, including

the recent global crisis years (2008–09). The increase, in fact, is very much within the realm of actual performance for Sub-Saharan African countries during periods of growth acceleration (3.9 percent), including the high-growth period 2000–07.[19]

For the two off-target groups, growth during the recent global crisis did not fall below the rates in the reference period (1990–2009), corroborating other economic assessments that low-income countries did relatively well (table 1.6). Three factors explain why the

TABLE 1.6   A one-standard-deviation increase in growth is definitely achievable

Growth period	Years covered	Developing countries (GDP per capita growth rate)		
		on target	close to the target	far from the target
I. Reference period	1990–2009	2.42	1.77	1.22
II. Recent growth accelerations				
Modern trend-break	1995–2007	3.46	2.61	2.01
New millennium	2000–07	3.97	2.90	2.25
Boom years	2003–07	4.82	3.65	3.07
III. Recent global economic crisis				
Crisis years	2008–09	1.48	1.79	1.48
Peak crisis	2009	−1.09	0.28	0.65
IV. Growth prospects	2010–15	3.58	3.33	3.22
V. Growth assumption	n.a.	n.a.	3.57	3.02

Sources: World Development Indicators database. Growth prospects are from the IMF's *World Economic Outlook.World Economic Outlook.*
Note: The growth assumption is growth during reference period plus one standard deviation, or 1.8. Growth rates are all simple averages, giving equal weight to each country GDP per capita, purchasing power parity constant 2005 international dollars.
n.a. = not applicable.

MAP 1.2   Sub-Saharan Africa and Southern Asia are home to the vast majority of children out of school

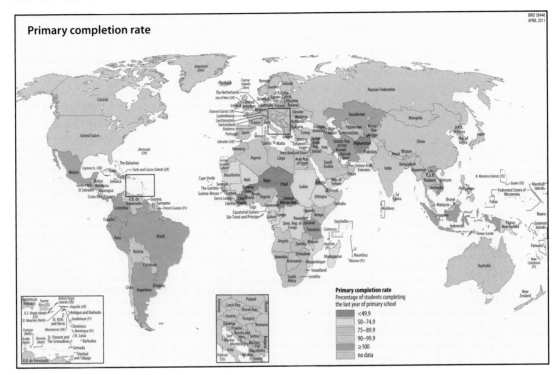

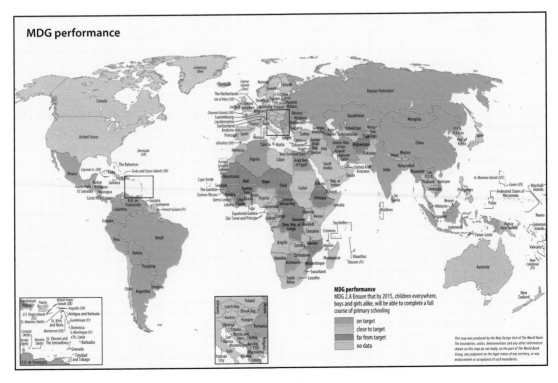

Source: World Bank staff calculations based on data from the World Development Indicators database.

recent crisis was different for low-income countries. First, policies and institutions improved before the crisis, and economic growth accelerated after the mid-1990s—particularly after 2000. Second, unlike previous crises, the recent one was not caused by domestic policy failure, which would have severe impacts on human development outcomes—particularly on child and maternal mortality. Third, spending on social safety nets was protected by governments with the assistance of international financial institutions and the donor community.[20] Even during the peak in 2009, their average growth stayed in positive territory. Their recovery is now expected to be strong, with growth prospects for 2010–15 similar to the growth assumption (which is higher than in the reference period, but as good as the recent growth accelerations, variously defined).

The global crisis struck the on-track developing countries much harder. At its peak, growth in this group was negative. However, many of the countries are higher-middle-income ones—particularly in Eastern Europe, where the MDGs were less of a challenge. The growth forecast for 2010–15 is still higher than the record in the reference period or the recent trend-break (1995–2007).

Where a problem may surface is in improving policy and institutions, given the few years left until 2015. A one-standard-deviation improvement in the CPIA is equivalent to a 0.5-point increase, or about the difference between the CPIA for on-target countries and for countries far from the target (see table 1.5). A 0.5-point increase in a CPIA rating is the normal award for an improvement in any policy area in a country. But to do this consistently for all the 16 questions in the CPIA is much harder. In any given year, a 0.1-point increase in the overall score represents a significant policy improvement for a country; a 0.2- or 0.3-point increase represents a substantial policy shift or regime change—rare for any country.

But it is certainly conceivable over time. The World Bank's CPIA has undergone changes to improve its assessment and is only broadly consistent over time. For instance, from 1998 to 2003, 32 countries (24 percent of developing countries for which scores are available) experienced an improvement of 0.5 points or better, especially countries in Eastern Europe. More recently, during the period 2004–09 when the new system has been stable, countries that have achieved an improvement of 0.5 include Georgia, Nigeria, and Seychelles. As one of the few broad measures available for policy and institutions, it is a proxy for the point that significant policy reforms are needed, especially for outcome-based or system-oriented MDGs. Because policy reforms can take time to implement and bear fruit, it is also important to undertake significant reforms sooner than later.

What is in the rest of this report

Developing countries are doing better when looking at country-level figures than at global figures. Lagging countries, on average, are very close to the targets, and their odds of getting on track can improve dramatically with stronger growth and sounder policy. Economic growth has a pervasive effect on all the MDGs and can jump-start countries far from the target. The implications are clear. With 2015 only a few years away, growth in developing countries needs to be taken quickly to a higher plane, the fastest way to lift more countries to the MDGs. Chapter 2 examines the prospects and challenges for economic growth in developing countries, how they are recovering from the recent global economic crisis, and what they need to do to boost growth further.

The quality of policies and institutions is more crucial for MDGs that are health related or are lagging the most, as well as for countries close to the target. What constitutes good policies and institutions in developing countries is complex, however, covering a wide range of areas.

Interventions can be broad and wide ranging or specific to local circumstances and problems. Much has been written about the broad issues, but less about microeconomic interventions, precisely because of specificity and local context. But thanks to the World Bank's Development Impact Evaluation Initiative and similar efforts, more documentation has emerged in recent years. To help untangle the difficult challenge of improving policies and institutions in developing countries, chapter 3 presents findings and lessons from impact evaluations in health and education, where several of the studies have already been completed.

Chapter 4 examines what countries can do to help the bottom 10 percent of society, usually indigenous and socially excluded groups.

Because a beneficial global environment (Goal 8) also helps support MDG progress in developing countries, chapter 5 reviews global trade, aid, and the actions of international financial institutions for developing countries. Goal 7 on environmental sustainability and biodiversity has no well-defined targets but it affects other MDGs, such as child health and human development more generally. Appendix 2 describes some aspects based on contributions from the Netherlands Environmental Assessment Agency.

Notes

1. World Bank 2010; Easterly 2009; Clemens, Kenny, and Moss 2007.
2. Ravallion 2009; World Bank 2010.
3. Leo and Barmeier 2010.
4. See, for example, Bourguignon et al. (2008), Leo and Barmeier (2010), and ODI (2010).
5. Collier and O'Connell 2006.
6. Leo and Barmeier 2010.
7. See, for example, the first *Global Monitoring Report* (World Bank 2004).
8. World Bank 2010.
9. Issues include macroeconomic and fiscal policy, debt policy, trade, human development policy in education and health, gender equality, social protection, budgetary and financial management, and corruption in the public sector.
10. See World Bank (2009) and footnote 17.
11. An earlier version of the CPIA goes back to 1970s but uses a different scale and criteria.

For example, the assessment of governance issues was not included in the earlier CPIA.

12. Average GDP per capita growth in IDA countries (1990–2009) is 1.36, a point below average growth in non-IDA countries (2.38). The CPIA index in 2009 is, on average, 3.26 in IDA countries versus 3.69 in non-IDA countries. Fragile or conflict-affected countries (one or more years, 2006–09) exhibit average per capita GDP growth (1990–2009) close to 1.03 percent and a CPIA index of 3.00 in 2009. However, nonfragile states have grown, in per capita terms, at an average rate of 2.27 percent since 1990. The CPIA index for these countries is 3.68 in 2009.
13. World Bank 2010. Harttgen and Klasen (2010) show that fragile countries perform worse on MDG *levels*, but that their MDG *progress* is not necessarily slower.
14. Marshall and Cole 2010.
15. It is important to point out that these simple graphical patterns can be driven by more fundamental development factors, such as growth and institutions. The next section tackles some of these issues.
16. World Bank 2004.
17. A study (IDA/DECVP 2007) found the correlation between contemporaneous CPIA and growth to be weak and the correlation between CPIA and future growth to be strong. The CPIA measures the level of policies, not the change; and it focuses on actual implementation, not just introduction or announcement. It is therefore backward looking. The inclusion of the 1996 CPIA is an attempt to capture the policy achievements close to the reference year in 1990, and the 2009 index will include the more recent record. See appendix 1 for a discussion of the use of the CPIA index and other alternatives. See also the guide for CPIA in World Bank (2009).
18. A review of the determinants of MDGs is in chapter 3. See also Lay (2010) and Lofgren (2010) for extensive reviews on the determinants of education-related and health-related MDG indicators.
19. See, for example, Arbache, Go, and Page (2008).
20. See World Bank (2010).

References

Arbache, J., D. Go, and J. Page. 2008. "Is Africa's Economy at a Turning Point" In *Africa at a Turning Point? Growth, Aid and External Shocks,* ed. D. Go and J. Page, 14–86. Washington, DC: World Bank.

Bourguignon, F., A. Bénassy-Quéré, S. Dercon, A. Estache, J. W. Gunning, R. Kanbur, S. Klasen, S. Maxwell, J.P. Platteau, and A. Spadaro. 2008. "Millennium Development Goals at Midpoint: Where Do We Stand and Where Do We Need to Go?" European Report on Development, European Commission, Brussels.

Clemens, M. A., C. J. Kenny, and T. J. Moss. 2007. "The Trouble with the MDGs: Confronting Expectations of Aid and Development Success." *World Development* 35 (5): 735–51.

Collier, P., and S. A. O'Connell. 2006. "Opportunities and Choices." Explaining African Economic Growth, chapter 2 of synthesis volume. African Economic Consortium, Nairobi, Kenya:

Easterly, W. 2009. "How the Millennium Development Goals Are Unfair to Africa." *World Development* 37 (1): 26–35.

Ferreira, F., P. Leite, and J. Litchfield. 2008. "The Rise and Fall of Brazilian Inequality: 1981–2004." *Macroeconomic Dynamics* 12: 199–230.

Ferreira, F., P. Leite, and M. Ravallion. 2010. "Poverty Reduction without Economic Growth? Explaining Brazil's Poverty Dynamics 1985–2004." *Journal of Development Economics* 93 (1): 20–36.

Government of Brazil. 2009. "Comments of the Government of Brazil to the report of the Special Rapporteur on the Situation of Human Rights and Fundamental Freedoms of Indigenous Peoples," James Anaya. Presentation at the United Nations on July 9, 2009.

Harttgen, K., and S. Klasen. 2010. "Fragility and MDG Progress: How Useful Is the Fragility Concept." Working Paper 20, Robert Schuman Centre for Advanced Studies, European University Institute, Florence, Italy.

IDA/DECVP (International Development Association and Development Economics, Office of the Chief Economist). 2007. "Selectivity and Performance: IDA's Country Assessment and Development Effectiveness." IDA 15. Washington, DC.

Lall, S. 2000. "The Technological Structure and Performance of Developing Country Manufactured Exports, 1985–1998." Working Paper 44. Queen Elizabeth House, University of Oxford, Oxford, UK.

Lay, J. 2010. "MDG Achievements, Determinants and Resource Needs: What Has Been Learnt?" Policy Research Working Paper 5320, World Bank, Washington, DC.

Leo, B., and J. Barmeier. 2010. "Who Are the MDG Trailblazers? A New MDG Progress Index." Working Paper 222, Center for Global Development, Washington, DC.

Lofgren, H. 2010. "What Determines the Evolution of MDG Indicators? A Selective Review of the Literature." Unpublished manuscript, World Bank, Washington, DC.

Marshall, M., and B. Cole. 2010. *Global Report 2009: Conflict, Governance, and State Fragility.* Washington, DC: Center for Global Policy.

ODI (Overseas Development Institute). 2010. "Millennium Development Goals Report Card: Measuring Progress across Countries." London.

PBL (Netherlands Environmental Assessment Agency). 2008. *Towards a Global Integrated Sustainability Model: GISMO 1.0 Status Report.* Report 550025002. Bilthoven: Netherlands.

———. 2009a. *Beyond 2015: Long-Term Development and the Millennium Development Goals.* Bilthoven, Netherlands.

———. 2009b. *Growing within Limits. A Report to the Global Assembly 2009 of the Club of Rome.* Bilthoven, Netherlands.

———. 2011. "Scarcities in a Sea of Plenty: Global Resource Scarcities and Policies in the European Union and the Netherlands." Bilthoven, Netherlands.

Ravallion, M. 2009. "Why Don't We See Poverty Convergence?" Policy Research Working Paper 4974, World Bank, Washington, DC.

———. 2011. "A Comparative Perspective on Poverty Reduction in Brazil, China and India." *World Bank Research Observer* 26 (1): 71–104.

UNCTAD (United Nations Conference on Trade and Development). 2010. "Liner Shipping

Connectivity Index." Division on Technology and Logistics, Geneva, Switzerland.

Uwezo Tanzania. 2010. *Are Our Children Learning? Annual Learning Assessment Report Tanzania 2010.* Dar es Salaam, Tanzania.

World Bank. 2004. *Global Monitoring Report: Policies and Actions for Achieving the Millennium Development Goals and Related Outcomes.* Washington, DC.

———. 2007. *Global Economic Prospects 2007: Managing the Next Wave of Globalization.* Washington, DC.

———. 2009. "Country Policy and Institutional Assessments—2009 Assessment Questionnaire." Operations Policy and Country Services. Washington DC: World Bank.

———. 2010. *Global Monitoring Report 2010: The MDGs after the Crisis.* Washington, DC.

———. 2011. *World Development Report 2011: Conflict, Security and Development.* Washington, DC.

2

Economic Growth in Developing Countries

In chapter 1, economic growth is seen as critical to attaining the Millennium Development Goals (MDGs). Prospects for further progress on the MDGs should be seen in light of macroeconomic developments in emerging and developing economies, and in the global economic environment they face.

Economic recovery is proceeding along two tracks. Advanced economies are experiencing subdued growth with high unemployment, while many fast-growing emerging economies are seeing inflation pressures build amid some signs of overheating. Projections put annual global growth at about 4.5 percent in 2011 and 2012. But sustaining the global recovery demands divergent policy responses: in the advanced economies, redressing fiscal imbalances and repairing and reforming financial systems; in the emerging economies, facilitating external rebalancing and checking overheating pressures, in many cases allowing further exchange rate appreciation, and in some, more ambitious fiscal tightening.

Good policies among low-income countries contributed to strong growth before the crisis. The policy buffers established then also allowed for active countercyclical policies that softened the impact of the crisis and drove a relatively rapid return to pre-crisis growth rates. To substantially reduce poverty and meet the MDGs, however, low-income and other developing countries need to grow faster and to rebuild buffers so as to guard against future shocks. In addition to strong, well-designed policies in the countries themselves, international cooperation is required to restore a global economic environment conducive to poverty reduction and development and to provide adequate assistance, with special attention to the most vulnerable countries.

Economic recovery

Global economic activity has gathered pace, unevenly

The *World Economic Outlook* of the International Monetary Fund (IMF) estimates that after contracting by 0.5 percent in 2009, global GDP expanded by 5.0 percent in 2010, compared with the projection of 4.2 percent a year ago (table 2.1). The recovery is markedly uneven, however, with rates of growth in advanced market economies several percentage points less than those in

TABLE 2.1   Global output, 2007–14
annual percentage change

Region	2007	2008	2009	2010	Projections 2011	Projections 2012–14
World output	**5.4**	**2.9**	**−0.5**	**5.0**	**4.4**	**4.6**
Advanced economies	2.7	0.2	−3.4	3.0	2.4	2.5
Emerging and developing economies	8.8	6.1	2.7	7.3	6.5	6.6
Central and Eastern Europe	5.5	3.2	−3.6	4.2	3.7	3.9
Commonwealth of Independent States	9.0	5.3	−6.4	4.6	5.0	4.6
Developing Asia	11.4	7.7	7.2	9.5	8.4	8.5
Middle East and North Africa	6.2	5.1	1.8	3.8	4.1	4.5
Sub-Saharan Africa	7.2	5.6	2.8	5.0	5.5	5.7
Western Hemisphere	5.7	4.3	−1.7	6.1	4.7	4.0
Emerging economies	9.2	6.3	2.6	7.5	6.7	6.7
Other developing economies	7.2	6.0	5.2	6.2	6.1	6.4
Least developed countries (LDCs)[a]	9.0	6.9	5.2	5.3	6.1	6.4

Source: World Economic Outlook.
a. United Nations classification, a subset of developing countries.

emerging market and developing economies.[1] Although below the levels existing immediately before the crisis, per capita real growth rates in low-income countries remained positive even in the depths of the economic crisis in 2009, and they strengthened further in 2010 (figure 2.1).

Spurred by expanding inventories and fixed investments, global merchandise trade rose 13 percent in 2010, while industrial production also rebounded. Household spending firmed in many emerging market economies and in other countries with strong precrisis fundamentals. But in many advanced market economies, lower property values and stubbornly high unemployment reduced household wealth and incomes, while weaknesses in the financial system still constrain credit; together, these factors are restraining consumption. Exceptional policy stimulus helped advanced market economies achieve 3 percent growth in 2010—still a modest rate, considering that they are emerging from a deep recession.

Price inflation remains low in advanced economies, where unemployment is high and excess capacity is considerable, but is becoming a policy concern in some emerging market economies. Inflation rates in emerging market and some developing economies average about 6 percent, reflecting rising commodity prices and other factors. Most low-income countries do not yet seem to have experienced an increase in inflation.

FIGURE 2.1   Low-income economies' per capita growth remained positive in 2009, in contrast to elsewhere

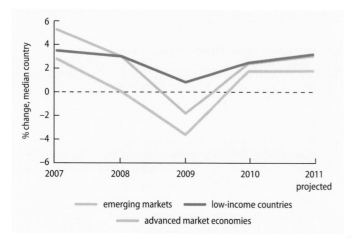

Sources: World Economic Outlook; IMF 2010a; IMF staff estimates.

Commodity prices have rebounded, leading to concerns over food price inflation

Together with other factors, economic recovery brought sharp increases in metals, food, and other commodity prices in 2010 (figure 2.2). This helped support a strong growth

FIGURE 2.2   **Economic recovery has taken many commodity prices sharply higher**

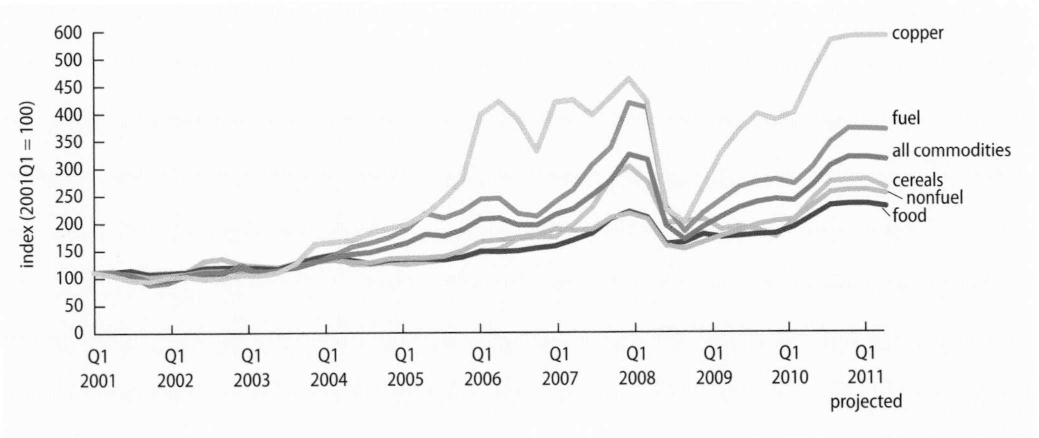

Sources: World Economic Outlook; IMF staff estimates.
Note: Indexes are in U.S. dollars. Data for 2011 are projected.

rebound among low-income commodity exporters. However, surging food prices are again sparking concerns over the affordability of food for the poorer segments of the population in some low- and lower-middle-income countries (box 2.1).[2] Food price increases are also adding to inflationary pressures in many emerging market economies, while in parts of Sub-Saharan Africa good harvests have muted food price increases. With continued economic recovery in 2011, overall commodity prices may rise further—though food price levels will depend greatly on weather patterns during the year.

Policy challenges remain for global financial stability, but most low-income countries weathered the crisis well

In advanced economies, leverage is still high, and balance sheet restructuring and regulatory reform are incomplete. The heightened sensitivity of financial markets to fiscal outlooks is leading to funding pressures in some markets. Differences in interest rates and growth prospects have spurred strong capital flows from advanced to emerging (and some developing) economies.

Emerging and developing countries' access to international financial markets has returned broadly to precrisis levels. After an uptick in mid-2010, the fall in international bond spreads toward 2006–07 levels suggests largely restored market access for sovereign borrowers and investment-grade corporations (figure 2.3). Market access for subinvestment-grade borrowers has also been substantially restored, though high-yield spreads remain well above those before the crisis—even if yields are now lower. Share prices have also increased (figure 2.4). Bank financing has continued to recover, notably to emerging markets in Asia and Latin America. With the protracted economic problems of emerging Europe, bank lending to them contracted modestly in 2010 (figure 2.5).

Improved financial regulation and crisis policy measures helped banking systems in most emerging and developing countries withstand the crisis well. The share of nonperforming loans did, however, increase somewhat further in 2010, as it did in advanced economies (figure 2.6). Banking sectors have also benefited from financial market resilience, including somewhat more stable exchange and interest rates. Even so, lingering concerns about systemic risks to bank and corporate solvency highlight the need to further strengthen the financial supervisory and institutional framework. To safeguard financial stability, the problems of impaired assets need to be addressed.

BOX 2.1   The global food price surge in 2010—causes and prospects

The IMF food price index has increased sharply since the middle of 2010 and has surpassed its prerecession peaks (left figure). (For the index's definition and methodology, see "IMF Primary Commodity Prices" at http://www.imf.org.) Price increases have been broad based and led by a surge in grain prices by 80 percent. Prices of key grains, including corn and wheat, have risen sharply to close to their 2008 peaks. For more income-elastic food groups, such as vegetable oils, meat, and seafood, prices are pushing past previous highs (right figure).

The catalyst for the recent food price rise has been a series of weather-related supply shocks to major grains. Wheat prices were the first to surge, as the improving supply picture reversed sharply in mid-2010. Drought and wild fires in the Russian Federation and Kazakhstan and heavy rain in Ukraine led to significant downward revisions in global production estimates. Corn prices began to rise as estimates of the 2010/11 U.S. harvest were progressively downgraded because of adverse weather during the summer months.

La Niña has contributed to adverse weather conditions around the Pacific Rim. Recent satellite evidence indicates that this is among the most intense La Niña episodes of the last 50 years and that its effects are likely to be close to their peak during the southern hemisphere summer. This has already affected rice harvests across Asia and food products typically not traded globally, such as local fruits and vegetables.

While supply has disappointed, demand for major food crops has remained robust, largely reflecting growth in emerging economies but also demand for biofuel feedstock. Many important food items are relatively income inelastic, but previous global recessions have been associated with lower demand growth. During the most recent recession, however, demand growth remained steady and has now risen to around 2.5 percent a year for the major crops. China and other emerging market economies account for 70–80 percent of demand growth during the past three years. The U.S. corn ethanol sector has rebounded from the 2008–09 crisis. Almost 40 percent of the 2010 U.S. corn crop is estimated to have been used as ethanol feedstock, an increase of 5 percentage points over the previous year.

Low global inventories and trade restrictions have exacerbated the price response to supply disappointments in recent quarters. Global food inventories were run down to very low levels in 2002–08 as demand picked up and the global supply response lagged. That response has now begun, most evident in the increase in acreage harvested; but stocks will likely only recover gradually. The imposition and extension of grain export restrictions by Russia and Ukraine in 2010 added to price volatility.

Output should recover quickly from recent supply shocks, and increased global acreage indicates that more normal weather conditions will bring large harvests in 2011. Weather-related supply shortfalls tend to be followed by sharp recoveries in output for many major crops, including wheat. This would ease market tightness and allow prices to decline modestly over the next 12 months, although they will remain high compared with 10–15-year averages. One important risk is that the La Niña weather pattern may adversely affect southern hemisphere harvests. More generally, food markets will remain vulnerable to more widespread supply shocks for as long as inventories are low. (See also related discussion in the trade section of chapter 5.)

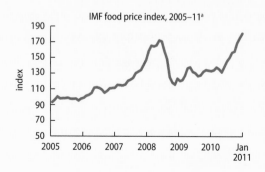

IMF food price index, 2005–11[a]

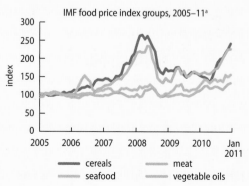

IMF food price index groups, 2005–11[a]

cereals   meat
seafood   vegetable oils

Source: International Monetary Fund.
a. U.S. dollar price index rebased at 2005 = 100. Data for 2011 are current as of February 2011.

FIGURE 2.3   Bond spreads and international bond issuance are virtually back to precrisis levels in emerging and developing countries

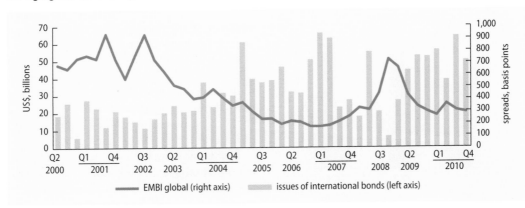

Sources: Dealogic; Bloomberg; IMF staff estimates.

FIGURE 2.4   Share prices, too, have bounced back

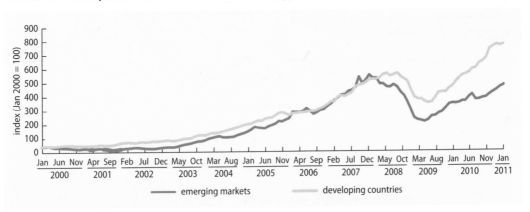

Sources: International Financial Statistics; IMF staff estimates.
Note: Prices are presented in local currency.

FIGURE 2.5   Emerging market bank financing continues to recover

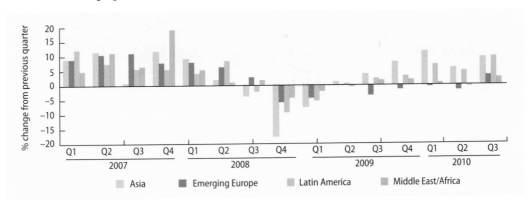

Sources: Bank for International Settlements; IMF staff estimates.
Note: Liabilities to BIS-reporting banks, adjusted for exchange rate changes. Changes are calculated as flow adjusted for exchange rate changes as a share of the stock in the previous quarter.

FIGURE 2.6 **Nonperforming loans in emerging and developing countries, 2003–10**

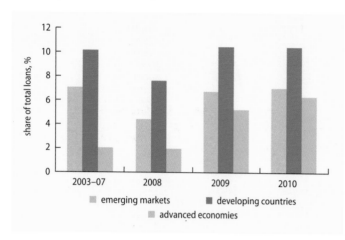

Sources: Global Financial Stability Report; IMF staff estimates.

Trade and capital flows have bounced back, into a changed picture

Globally, current account imbalances widened in 2010 after narrowing considerably in 2009 in the midst of the crisis (figure 2.7). They remain below the levels of 2004–08. A number of emerging market economies that experienced renewed surges in capital inflows in 2010 accumulated more foreign exchange reserves; the size of their current account surpluses did not fall and may have widened somewhat. After large swings in 2009, terms-of-trade changes in 2010 seem to have been relatively benign (figure 2.8). In emerging and low-income countries in 2010, levels of official reserves roughly kept pace with the rebound in trade, with only modest declines in the median ratio of reserves to imports and, for emerging economies, increasing somewhat relative to short-term external debt (figure 2.9).[3]

The crisis affected low-income countries mainly through export demand, foreign direct investment (FDI), and remittances, more than global interest rates or the terms of trade.[4] Exports from low-income countries contracted very sharply in late 2008 and early 2009. Critically, though, relative to previous crises, these countries had entered this crisis with lower external debt, narrower fiscal and current account deficits, and higher external reserves (figure 2.10). (See also chapter 1, regarding growth and these countries' progress toward reaching the MDGs.) These proved to be important policy buffers that could be drawn upon to help cushion the shock (see lower external debt, narrower fiscal and current account deficits, and higher external reserves below). By late 2010, monthly exports to the

FIGURE 2.7 **Global current account imbalances, 2000–11**

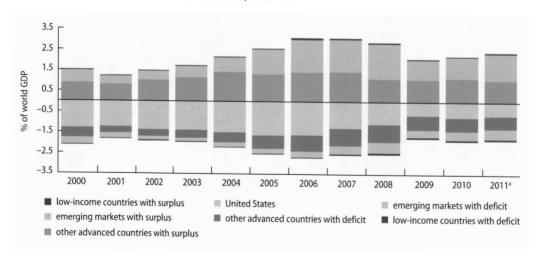

Sources: World Economic Outlook; IMF staff estimates.
Note: The global statistical discrepancy is not shown.
a. projected.

FIGURE 2.8   **Annual changes in terms of trade, by quintile group**

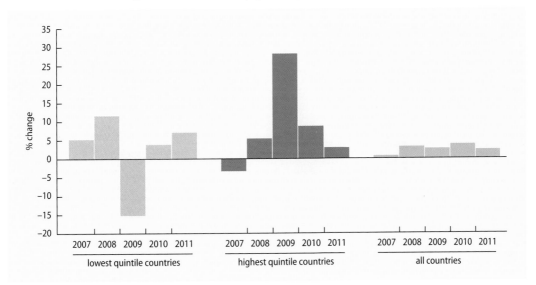

Sources: World Economic Outlook; IMF staff estimates.
Note: Quintile groups are based on the average (mean) of terms-of-trade changes in 2009 and 2010.

FIGURE 2.9   **Reserve levels broadly kept pace with the rebound in trade**

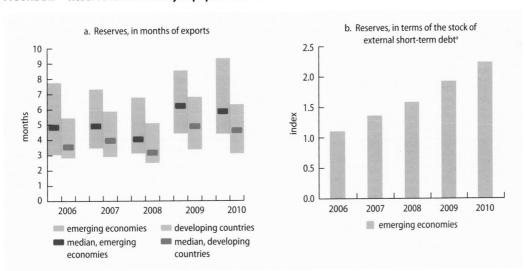

Sources: World Economic Outlook; IMF staff estimates.
Note: Bars represent the range between the 25th and 75th percentiles.

Sources: World Economic Outlook; IMF staff estimates.
a. The median ratio is shown. Stock of short-term external debt
includes amortization paid to official creditors.

Group of Twenty (G-20) countries approached their peak precrisis levels—but with interesting compositional shifts (box 2.2).

Despite important signs of a recovery in financial flows, the picture for emerging and developing countries is mixed. In aggregate, there was a sharp recovery in trade credit and strengthening in portfolio equity and bond flows in 2010, and modest increases in FDI flows.[5] However, (simple average) net

FIGURE 2.10 **Low-income countries' precrisis macroeconomic policy buffers were stronger than in earlier years**

[Figure: Bar chart comparing "previous crises" (light) and "2005–07" (dark) across five indicators: current account deficit adjusted for FDI/GDP (percent, left axis); fiscal deficit/GDP (percent, left axis); reserve coverage (months of imports, left axis); inflation (right axis); external public debt/GDP (right axis). Left axis 0–6, right axis 0–45 percent.]

Sources: World Economic Outlook; IMF staff estimates.

BOX 2.2   Low-income-country exports during the exit from the crisis: early evidence

Exports from low-income to G-20 countries recovered steadily in 2010, after a sharp fall in the second half of 2008 and early 2009.[a] Using three-month moving averages (non-seasonally adjusted), their exports grew from US$15 billion in January 2007 to US$25 billion in August 2008, fell to US$13 billion a month in early 2009, then reached US$22 billion in October 2010 (figure below, left).

Direction of trade

Of total low-income-country exports to G-20 countries, about two-thirds go to advanced market economies and one-third goes to emerging market economies (figure below, right).[b] But low-income-country exports to emerging market economies were growing more quickly before the crisis, fell less abruptly during the crisis, and in 2010 accounted for more than 40 percent of their export growth. Among exports to emerging market economies, however, China accounted for about one-third prior to the crisis, but nearly half by late 2010. While China accounted for about one-sixth of low-income-country export growth in the precrisis period, it accounted for one-quarter in 2010.

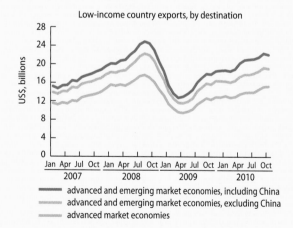

Low-income country exports, by destination

advanced and emerging market economies, including China
advanced and emerging market economies, excluding China
advanced market economies

Sources: Global Trade Atlas; IMF staff estimates.
Note: Based on three-month backward moving averages of imports reported by Argentina, Australia, Brazil, Canada, China, EU-27, India (estimated for July–October 2010), Indonesia, Japan, Republic of Korea, Mexico, Russian Federation, South Africa, Turkey, and the United States;

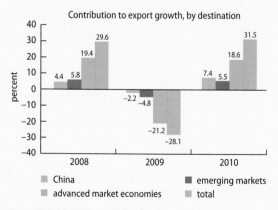

Contribution to export growth, by destination

China
advanced market economies
emerging markets
total

Sources: Global Trade Atlas; and IMF staff estimates.

BOX 2.2   (continued)

Product composition

Minerals constituted about two thirds of low-income-country exports prior to the crisis, followed by light manufactures such as textiles and clothing (figure below and at top right).ᶜ Exports of other ("heavy") manufactures were under 10 percent before the crisis but close to 15 percent by end-2010 (figure at bottom right). Minerals exports were the source of the greatest changes in exports and remain the largest export category. They accounted for three-quarters of pre-crisis low-income-country export growth (mainly fuel exports by oil exporters), but were also highly vulnerable in the downturn—nearly 90 percent of the export contraction in 2009 was in minerals. Minerals exports remained the largest export item with the highest contribution to export growth in the postcrisis period: in 2010, about two-thirds of low-income-country export growth was in mineral products.

Interestingly, the exit from the crisis is also seeing increased exports of heavy manufactures. These rose from March 2009, driven by exports to China. This reflects exports of chemical products, plastics, rubber, and metal products, mainly from Asian low-income-countries.

Aggregate low-income-country exports will remain sensitive to demand for minerals and other commodities, an area where continued strong growth in emerging markets will be important. But there is also tentative evidence that emerging market growth may be helping some low-income countries diversify their export composition.

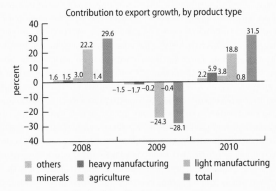

Contribution to export growth, by product type

Sources: Global Trade Atlas; IMF staff estimates.

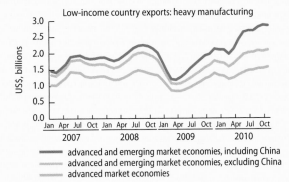

Low-income country exports: heavy manufacturing

advanced and emerging market economies, including China
advanced and emerging market economies, excluding China
advanced market economies

Sources: Global Trade Atlas; IMF staff estimates.
Note: Based on three-month backward moving averages of imports reported by Argentina, Australia, Brazil, Canada, China, EU-27, India (estimated for July–October 2010), Indonesia, Japan, Republic of Korea, Mexico, Russian Federation, South Africa, Turkey, and the United States.

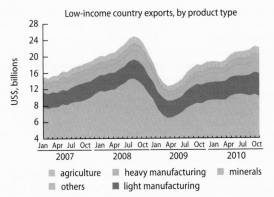

Low-income country exports, by product type

agriculture   heavy manufacturing   minerals
others   light manufacturing

Sources: Global Trade Atlas; IMF staff estimates.
Note: Based on three-month backward moving averages of imports reported by Argentina, Australia, Brazil, Canada, China, EU-27, India (estimated for July–October 2010), Indonesia, Japan, Republic of Korea, Mexico, Russian Federation, South Africa, Turkey, and the United States.

a. The analysis in this box is based on detailed bilateral monthly trade statistics provided for 19 of the G-20 countries under subscription by the Global Trade Information Service's Global Trade Atlas.

b. Countries are classified as follows: *advanced markets* refer to 32 countries included in *World Economic Outlook* classification 110; *low-income countries* refer to 71 countries eligible for the Poverty Reduction and Growth Trust; and *emerging markets* refer to all the countries in the sample that are neither advanced markets nor low-income countries.

c. Products are classified as follows: *agriculture* (HS codes 01–05 [animal and animal products] and 06–15 [vegetable products]), *minerals* (25–27 [mineral products]); *light manufactures* (16–24 [foodstuffs], 50–63 [textiles], and 64–67 [footwear/headgear]); *heavy manufactures* (28–38 [chemicals and allied industries], 39–40 [plastics/rubbers], 72–83 [metals], 84–85 [machinery/electrical], and 86–89 [transportation]); and *others*.

TABLE 2.2   Net financial flows
percent of GDP

Flows	2007	2008	2009	2010	2011 projection
Emerging market economies	12.0	10.4	8.1	8.0	7.9
Private capital flows, net	8.9	6.4	1.7	1.9	2.7
of which: private direct investment	5.3	4.8	3.5	3.3	3.0
private portfolio flows	1.2	−0.9	−0.9	0.5	0.2
Private current transfers	4.3	4.0	3.9	3.8	3.6
Official capital flows and transfers (net)	−1.2	0.0	2.4	2.3	1.6
Memorandum item:					
Reserve assets	−3.9	−1.7	−2.4	−2.0	−1.7
Developing countries	13.9	13.2	11.7	10.5	13.2
Private capital flows, net	3.4	1.6	0.8	−0.1	0.6
of which: private direct investment	7.0	6.6	5.4	5.6	5.8
private portfolio flows	−1.9	−1.6	−1.6	−1.5	−1.3
Private current transfers	3.9	3.9	3.9	4.1	4.1
Official capital flows and transfers (net)	6.5	7.7	7.0	6.5	8.5
Memorandum item:					
Reserve assets	−4.3	−2.3	−3.4	−2.9	−3.5
Least developed countries[a]	12.9	10.5	8.2	9.3	11.8
Private capital flows, net	−0.5	−4.3	−3.6	−3.2	−4.1
of which: private direct investment	6.1	5.8	4.6	5.3	5.4
private portfolio flows	−2.5	−2.4	−2.6	−2.5	−2.4
Private current transfers	1.9	2.0	2.2	2.5	2.3
Official capital flows and transfers (net)	11.4	12.9	9.6	10.0	13.5
Memorandum item:					
Reserve assets	−4.3	−2.2	−5.0	−4.5	−4.8
Fragile states[b]	14.7	6.2	0.1	1.8	10.3
Private capital flows, net	−1.5	−7.4	−8.8	−8.7	−6.4
of which: private direct investment	6.1	5.7	3.7	4.5	5.4
private portfolio flows	−1.2	−0.9	−0.9	−1.4	−1.8
Private current transfers	1.9	1.7	2.4	3.1	3.0
Official capital flows and transfers (net)	14.3	12.0	6.5	7.5	13.7
Memorandum item:					
Reserve assets	−4.3	−2.8	−7.6	−7.0	−9.9

Sources: World Economic Outlook; IMF staff estimates.
Note: Unweighted simple averages.
a. United Nations classification, a subset of developing countries.
b. World Bank classification, a subset of emerging and developing countries.

financial inflows, expressed relative to GDP, actually fell farther in 2010—suggesting that many recipient countries may not yet be sharing in these increases (table 2.2). Net financial flows to developing countries in 2011 are projected to reach 13 percent of GDP, near the average for 2007–08.

Inflows of FDI are lagging other signs of recovery, both in emerging market and developing countries (table 2.2),[6]although increases in workers' remittances to precrisis levels have partly offset this (table 2.3).[7]

Twin-track macroeconomic policies reflect the uneven economic recovery

In advanced and some emerging market economies, as the impact of fiscal stimulus wanes and active fiscal adjustment begins, highly supportive monetary policy remains important for a more vigorous recovery. But policy makers must address the social costs of continued high unemployment (including high youth unemployment in some countries) at the same time.[8] Most emerging economies

TABLE 2.3   **Inflows of international remittances**
US$, billions

Source of inflows	2003–07 annual average	2008 annual	2009 annual	2010 estimate	2011 projections
Emerging market economies	150.2	233.2	224.1	238.3	252.5
Developing countries	28.9	55.4	53.1	56.8	60.9
Least-developed countries[a]	12.8	22.9	24.2	25.9	27.9
Fragile states[b]	9.0	15.6	14.2	15.7	17.0

Sources: World Bank; IMF staff estimates.
Note: Remittances include workers' remittances, compensation of employees, and migrant transfers.
a. United Nations classification, a subset of developing countries.
b. World Bank classification, a subset of emerging and developing countries.

face different challenges, including incipient inflationary pressures and, often, a need to rebalance growth toward domestic sources. Accordingly, among developing countries and particularly among emerging market economies, the macroeconomic policy mix shifted notably in 2010. Following the combined monetary and fiscal loosening by most emerging market economies in the face of contracting global output in 2009, one-third undertook both monetary and fiscal tightening in 2010 (figure 2.11). As global conditions improved, developing countries also began to reverse their countercyclical policies.

Continued accommodative monetary policy in most advanced economies has been critical to alleviating the financial crisis and recession. In contrast, monetary conditions in most emerging and developing countries began to normalize in 2010, but remained too accommodative in many cases. While some 80 percent of emerging market economies undertook monetary policy loosening in 2009, only about one-third did so in 2010. Many developing countries continued with some monetary loosening (figure 2.12). Resumed strong growth in emerging market economies underpinned declining measures of

FIGURE 2.11   **Macroeconomic policy responses to the crisis vary**

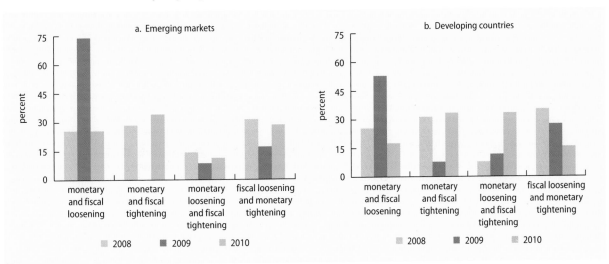

Sources: International Financial Statistics; IMF staff estimates.
Note: Fiscal conditions are defined based on annual change in government balance as a percent of GDP in 2008, 2009, and 2010. Monetary conditions are based on the change in the monetary conditions index; changes are calculated Q4 over Q4, except for 2010, which uses Q3. The monetary conditions index is a linear combination of nominal short-term interest rate and the nominal effective exchange rate (with a one-third weight for the latter).

FIGURE 2.12   **Monetary policy loosening**

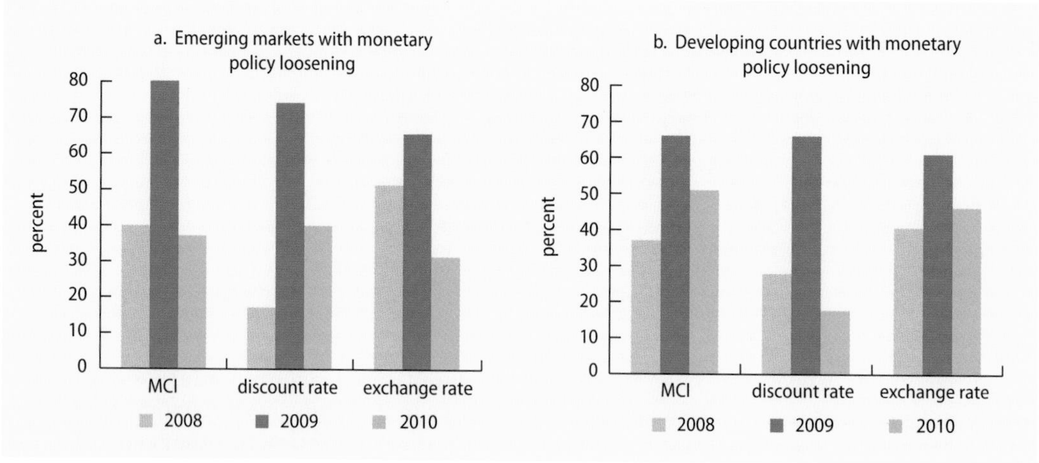

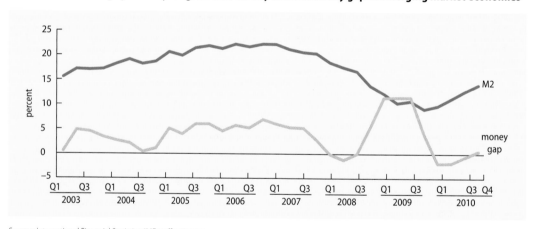

Sources: World Economic Outlook; IMF staff estimates.
Note: MCI = monetary conditions index. Monetary policy loosening is based on MCI calculations. MCI is a linear combination of nominal short-term interest rate and the nominal effective exchange rate (with a one-third weight for the latter).

FIGURE 2.13   **Average year-on-year growth in money and the money gap in emerging market economies**

Sources: International Financial Statistics; IMF staff estimates.
Note: The money gap is the difference between year-on-year growth rates of the monetary aggregate M2 and nominal GDP. The sample includes emerging market economies that have data on both for the whole sample period shown.

excess liquidity (such as growth of the money supply relative to nominal GDP), even as monetary aggregates expanded (figure 2.13).

Fiscal policy has begun to shift from supporting recovery to cutting deficits.[9] The average deficit among advanced economies fell by about 1 percentage point of GDP in 2010. But because this mainly reflected better growth and reduced financial sector support rather than narrower cyclically adjusted balances, the need remains for robust, specific fiscal consolidation plans. Among major emerging market economies, deficits fell modestly and cyclically adjusted deficits were broadly unchanged, suggesting that easy credit conditions may be discouraging the more rapid consolidation that could help dampen currency appreciation and inflationary pressures (figure 2.14).[10]

Low-income countries have also begun to reverse the unprecedented countercyclical fiscal response that helped soften the impact of the crisis. As in past downturns, fiscal revenue declined during the crisis. This time,

FIGURE 2.14   **Fiscal deficit, 2008–11**

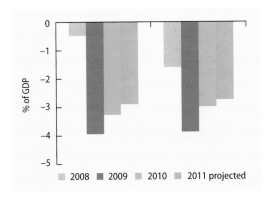

Sources: World Economic Outlook; IMF staff estimates.
Note: General government balance data from World Economic Outlook based on *Government Finance Statistics Manual 2001* definitions of fiscal balance.

FIGURE 2.15   **Low-income countries: fiscal balances and economic crises**

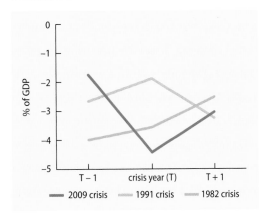

Sources: World Economic Outlook; IMF 2010a; IMF staff estimates.

however, most of these countries did not curtail spending—indeed, about half of them accelerated growth of real primary expenditures in 2009, undertaking a vigorous countercyclical fiscal response that required additional financing (figure 2.15).[11] As revenues grew in 2010, fiscal deficits declined by about 1 percentage point of GDP (more among Asian low-income countries), and low-income countries began to rebuild policy buffers, even as they broadly sustained rates of expenditure growth (figure 2.16).

The quality of low-income-country macroeconomic policies in 2010 was broadly in line with that in recent years

Monetary policy, fiscal policy, access to foreign exchange, and the consistency of macroeconomic policies are areas that IMF country desks judged strong in most countries in 2010 (figure 2.17).[12] Expenditure composition and public sector governance are seen as areas of relative weakness. Whether the result of an actual deterioration or because the global

FIGURE 2.16   **Real primary expenditure in low-income countries has increased in favor of public investment and social sectors**

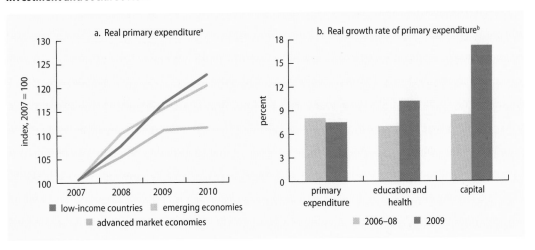

Sources: World Economic Outlook; IMF 2010a; IMF staff estimates.
a. Median.
b. Median.

FIGURE 2.17   **Macroeconomic policy quality in low-income countries remained little changed**

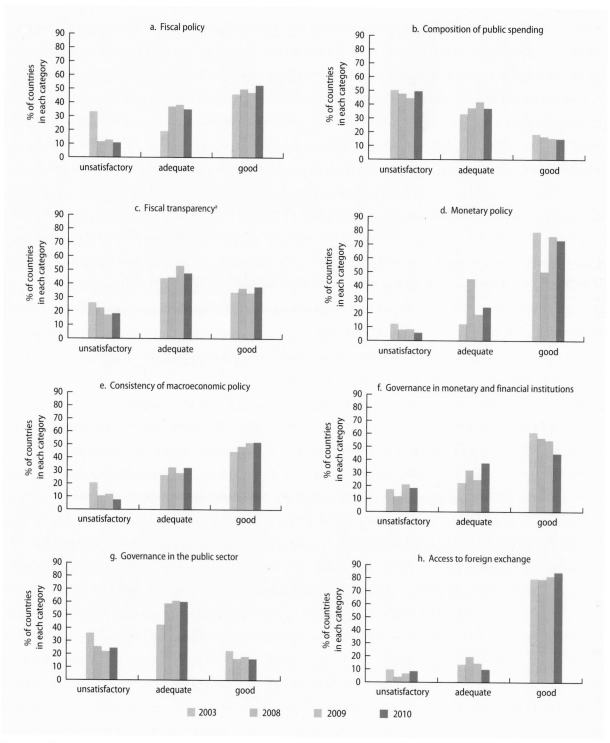

Source: IMF staff estimates.
a. Available from 2005.

crisis has enhanced awareness of the inherent risks, IMF teams appear to have become more concerned with the adequacy of low-income countries' financial sector governance.

Exiting from the crisis: achieving sustainable growth

Meeting the policy challenges in emerging market economies

Despite their impressive growth and declining poverty rates, emerging market economies remain home to many of the world's poor people. A continued strong and stable economic performance, complemented by targeted poverty-reduction policies, will help these countries meet the MDGs. In addition, as these economies have become important trade and financial partners for low-income countries, this performance will also contribute to those countries' MDG progress.

Fiscal balances improved in most emerging market economies in 2010, driven in part by higher growth. Their overall budget deficit in 2010 is projected at about 4 percent of GDP (around 0.75 percent of GDP lower than in 2009), in some cases partly the result of one-off receipts. Cyclically adjusted balances in the six largest economies were only marginally tighter in 2010, but an adjustment of around 0.5 percent of GDP is expected in 2011. Government debt rose during the crisis (especially in emerging Europe), but on average remains at less than 40 percent of GDP (below the average in advanced economies).

The policy challenges of the emerging economies involve overheating and strong capital inflows—issues quite different from those of other countries. (The advanced market economies, for example, must formulate and implement detailed fiscal consolidation plans to avoid unsustainable fiscal situations, even while they face sluggish growth and job creation.) For these economies, growth is generally strong and debt is manageable,[13] although many are at risk of overheating pressures associated with rapid credit growth, inflation, and possible asset

price bubbles. Robust domestic demand and the recovery of global output are leading to a rapid closure of output gaps, even as food and commodity prices have returned to precrisis peaks.[14] Inflationary expectations are rising and policy targets have been exceeded in a number of Asian and Latin American countries. Inflationary pressures could threaten some otherwise sound policy frameworks, but some countries' concerns about further currency appreciation are slowing their monetary policy responses. Strong capital inflows that exacerbate overheating pressures are complicating the policy response.

Timid policy responses to overheating would pose risks to the real economy and could derail growth prospects, especially in the large economies. Inadequate responses to large capital inflows could result in asset price overvaluations and an increased risk of a hard landing in credit and property markets, possibly triggering broader macroeconomic and financial instability (box 2.3). To lower risks of a hard landing, many emerging economies will need to tighten policies. This may include a further removal of monetary accommodation, further macroeconomic prudential tightening, and, often, exchange rate appreciation. Some will also need to tighten fiscal policies.

Tackling obstacles to growth in low-income countries

The crisis has set back progress toward the MDGs in many low-income countries, after an extended period of strong economic growth that had made substantial inroads into poverty. Although growth has since picked up and poverty rates are falling again, recovery at the projected pace will not make up the progress lost because of the crisis. To regain momentum, action is needed to boost growth, emphasizing growth patterns that benefit subnational regions and sectors where poor people are most numerous—and pushing ambitious microeconomic and sectoral reforms to promote access to social services and basic infrastructure.[15] Economic growth

---

BOX 2.3   Emerging market capital inflows: experience and challenges

Capital flows to emerging market economies have rebounded with the ebbing of the global financial crisis. The largest recipients are Asian and Latin American emerging market economies, South Africa, and Turkey. In several countries, net inflows are close to all-time highs; on a gross basis, however, total inflows to emerging markets have yet to reach their precrisis peak. Compared with other waves of inflows, the current episode is characterized by a predominance of volatile portfolio inflows. Gross inflows have reached 6 percent of GDP in only three quarters since the postcrisis trough; it took three years to reach a similar magnitude in the surge that preceded the global crisis. Portfolio inflows account, on average, for almost one-half of inflows (Brazil and the Republic of Korea are the top two recipients), much more than in the previous wave. Direct investment and cross-border bank lending are less predominant this time, reflecting lagging economic performance and impaired financial intermediation in advanced market economies.

The main pull and push factors behind the recent acceleration of capital flows from advanced to emerging economies are improved fundamentals and growth prospects in emerging market economies and loose monetary policy in advanced economies. From a structural perspective, the global crisis and the more recent jitters in Europe have exposed balance sheet vulnerabilities in advanced economies and appear to have triggered a gradual shift in the portfolio allocation of institutional investors toward emerging market economies, many of which are enjoying low debt, proven resilience to shocks, and improved ratings. From a cyclical perspective, the two-speed nature of the ongoing global recovery will likely keep interest rate differentials between emerging market and advanced economies wide for a prolonged period. Surging commodity prices are an additional cyclical force pushing capital toward commodity exporters, such as Brazil and Peru. In relative terms, more-liquid emerging markets are attracting larger inflows. All things considered, the stage seems set for the ongoing wave of inflows to be both large and persistent, bringing important investment and growth benefits to emerging market economies. However, inflows have tended to reverse suddenly and in a synchronized manner in the past, causing sharp currency depreciation and severe balance sheet dislocations. Emerging

market economies therefore face the challenge of absorbing the benefits of capital inflows while limiting the attendant macroeconomic and financial stability risks.

A close look at selected countries that have received large capital inflows provides useful insights regarding the effects of and policy responses to the recent episode of inflows (see the figure on the next page). These countries are facing large capital inflows mainly in the form of long-term portfolio debt flows, although commodity exporters also continue to enjoy large direct investment inflows. Despite significant accumulation of international reserves, real exchange rates in most cases have appreciated back to precrisis levels—although the degree of nominal appreciation has been less pronounced and more varied across countries. Surging portfolio inflows helped propel stock and bond prices especially in countries with shallower capital markets. While there are limited signs of bubbles so far, cyclical pressures are emerging, with credit to the private sector picking up strongly in some cases.

Macroeconomic policy responses to the current inflow episode have varied. On the monetary policy side, most countries have begun clawing back the easier monetary policy stance adopted during the global crisis. That said, countries have refrained from tightening aggressively, despite emerging inflationary pressures, out of fear that tightening would pull in more capital. The fiscal stance has also varied widely across countries, but most countries have yet to fully unwind the structural loosening adopted during the crisis, despite closing output gaps, implying a procyclical stance in many cases.

The countries under review have generally complemented macroeconomic policy with other measures to manage capital inflows. Such measures include taxes on certain inflows, minimum holding periods, and currency-specific reserve requirements. Recourse to these measures has been motivated by concerns about export competitiveness, financial stability, sterilization costs, and political constraints on fiscal policy. Many measures were designed to address specific risks associated with certain types of flows, such as their impact on certain asset markets or their short-term nature; and to guard against the risk of flow reversal. Evidence to date on their effectiveness in reducing targeted inflows is mixed, though in most cases currency

BOX 2.3   (continued)

appreciation has slowed or halted around the time of the introduction of the measures. Market participants have expressed concerns about policy and regulatory uncertainty and distortions from measures that go beyond macroeconomic policies. Even so, they consider the measures implemented so far to be "at the margin" and are likely to continue investing in countries where the positive structural story dominates.

The variety of policy responses adopted—and their potential multilateral implications—suggests the importance of developing a broadly accepted framework for countries with open or partially open capital accounts on policies to deal with capital inflows. Choosing appropriate responses can be challenging given the uncertainties associated with the causes and effects of the inflows and with possible policy reactions. Even so, a framework for considering appropriate macroeconomic and other policy responses to inflows can be beneficial. Primacy should be given to structural measures that increase the capacity of the economy to absorb capital inflows and prudential measures that enhance the resilience of the financial

system. Beyond this, when confronted with surging inflows, macroeconomic policies are appropriate tools—namely allowing the currency to strengthen, accumulating reserves, and/or rebalancing the monetary and fiscal policy mix.

Because they can potentially be used to avoid the necessary macroeconomic policy adjustments, measures designed to influence capital inflows (capital flow management measures or CFMs) could be used when appropriate macroeconomic conditions are in place—when the exchange rate is not undervalued, reserves are more than adequate, and the economy is overheating so that lowering policy rates would not be advisable. If these conditions exist but fiscal policy is pro-cyclical, CFMs could be used temporarily to complement fiscal tightening plans that are already in place, in view of the lags associated with the macroeconomic impact of fiscal consolidation. If CFMs are adopted, residency-based measures generally should be given lower priority, consistent with the general standard of fairness that countries expect from their participation in a multilateral framework.

Note: This box presents the main messages from IMF (2011b).

Capital Flows and Policy Responses in Selected Emerging Markets

	Magnitude of net inflows[a] Average in the last wave of inflows (% of GDP)	Composition of net inflows[a] Orange = Portfolio flows, Gold = Other flows, Green = FDI	Currency appreciation % change in the NEER from the trough since the crisis	Reserve increase Increase in % of GDP from the trough since the crisis	Monetary policy Change in policy rates in the recent wave	Inflation % year over year, average of last 6 months	Average during 2006–08	Real credit growth % year over year, average of last 6 months	Fiscal policy Change in cyclically adjusted fiscal stance between 2009–10	Capital flow management measures[b]
Brazil	6.2		38.4	6.0	⬆	5.0	(4.5)	12.9	⟨⟨⟸ ⟹⟩	Yes
Indonesia	2.6		19.4	7.4	⬆	6.2	(9.8)	9.2	⟹⟩ ⟨⟨⟸	Yes
Korea, Rep.	1.9		17.5	10.7	⬆	3.3	(3.2)	0.4	⟹⟩ ⟨⟨⟸	Yes
Peru	5.9		5.6	9.0	⬆	2.1	(3.2)	9.3	⟨⟨⟸ ⟹⟩	Yes
South Africa	6.6		41.4	2.6	⬇	3.6	(6.4)	−0.1	⟹⟩ ⟨⟨⟸	No
Thailand	5.0		9.3	22.3	⬆	3.1	(4.1)	4.3	⟨⟨⟸ ⟹⟩	Yes
Turkey	6.9		6.5	1.7	⬇	7.9	(9.6)	21.4	⟨⟨⟸ ⟹⟩	Yes

Sources: International Financial Statistics; Haver Analytics; GDS; IMF staff calculations.

a. Net inflows are defined as the sum of foreign direct investment, portfolio, and other investment balances. Calculations are made for the last wave of capital inflows (2009Q3–2010Q2).

b. Capital flow management measures (CFMs) refer to certain administrative, tax, and prudential measures that are part of the policy tool kit to manage inflows.

MAP 2.1   GDP: Economic growth in 2009 and 2010 has been uneven

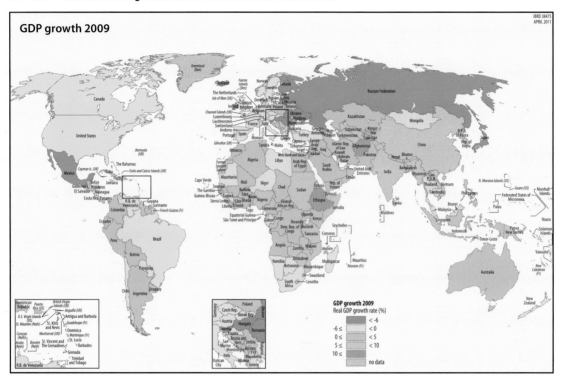

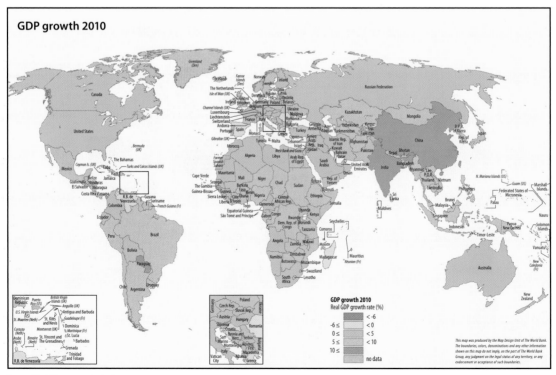

Source: World Economic Outlook.

MAP 2.2   Fiscal balance: Countries are diverging in their responses to fiscal challenges

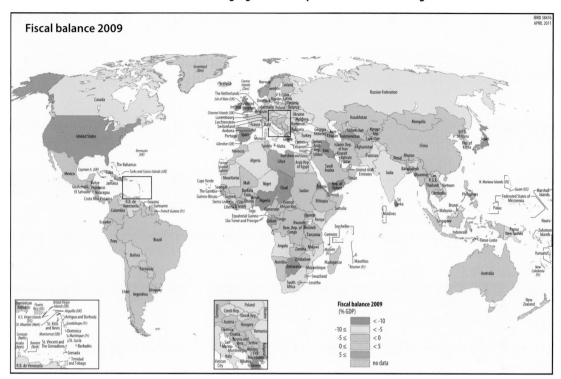

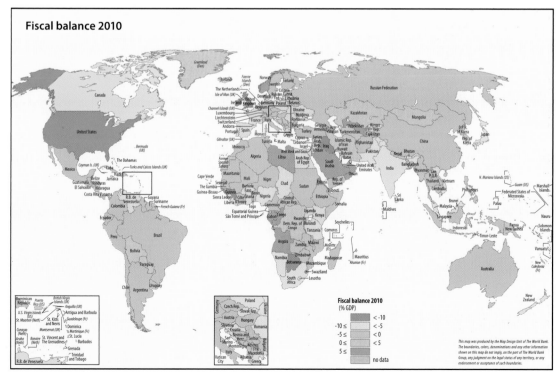

Source: World Economic Outlook.

in low-income countries must also be made more resilient so that progress is not derailed by future shocks.

To achieve accelerated and sustained growth, low-income countries will require much higher investment in infrastructure. By raising productivity and encouraging private investment, closing the present large infrastructure gap could substantially increase rates of per capita income growth.[16] The cost of addressing Sub-Saharan Africa's infrastructure needs is estimated at around $93 billion a year, equivalent to 15 percent of the region's GDP (or 22 percent of GDP for the region's low-income countries).[17] This raises the twin challenges of investing efficiently in infrastructure to get the biggest possible growth dividend and financing that investment in a sustainable manner.

Effective public investment management is critical to efficient investing. It begins with establishing strategic guidance to anchor government thinking and inform sector-level decisions, and with independent review and analysis of the feasibility of prospective projects. In later stages, project selection processes, budgeting, implementation, project evaluation, and audit are key.[18] A new index of the capacity of 71 developing countries (including 40 low-income countries) to appraise, select, implement, and evaluate infrastructure projects can guide public investment management reforms to areas in which they are needed most.[19] Although the index scores for many low-income countries indicate weak capacity throughout the process, this is not universal: Rwanda, for example, scores better than many lower-middle-income countries.

Financing more infrastructure spending presents its own challenges, beginning with debt sustainability. Infrastructure competes with existing priorities (such as social spending) and with the new demands of adapting to climate change.[20] Ongoing needs for large-scale grants and highly concessional loans for investment underscore the importance of donors meeting aid commitments, even as they face fiscal constraints at home. (See

chapter 5 for more discussion.) Given scarce concessional financing, however, low-income countries with moderate debt vulnerabilities and effective public finance institutions would be justified in borrowing on market terms to finance productive investments, within the limits of a sound debt management strategy.

Stronger domestic revenue mobilization has a key role in sustainable infrastructure financing. Tax revenue collections in low-income countries lag behind those of lower-middle-income countries by 6–8 percentage points of GDP. While low-income countries have large shares of hard-to-tax informal and small-scale agricultural sectors, such structural factors account for only part of the difference. Closing this gap will require long-term efforts. Experience suggests that vigorous reforms to tax policy and tax administration can raise revenue ratios by 1 percentage points in the first year and, if consistently pursued, by up to 5 percentage points over 10 years. Individual country circumstances vary, but tax policy reforms for a typical low-income country would emphasize broadening tax bases (such as for value added and corporate income taxes), increasing rates of certain environmental and excise taxes, and improving regional coordination on matters such as corporate taxes.[21] Tax policy reforms should be complemented by efforts to secure taxes from large and medium enterprises and wealthy individuals, and by other tax administration reforms.

Enhanced market access for low-income-country exports would also support higher growth and help meet the MDGs. Multilateral trade reform—especially by concluding the World Trade Organization Doha Round (see chapter 5)—would spur global trade and growth and foster a development-friendly global macroeconomic environment. Most critically for low-income countries, which need a stable global trading environment to export and to attract investment, the Doha Round would bring the added security of tightened World Trade Organization trade rules. Further actions by advanced countries and major emerging market economies to expand and improve trade preferences for the least-developed countries could further boost growth in the poorest countries.[22]

Making growth resilient in low-income countries

With policy buffers drawn down because of the global financial crisis, low-income countries now face the task of shoring up these buffers to boost resilience to future adverse shocks. A gradual consolidation of low-income countries' macroeconomic positions over the medium term is projected, with improving fiscal and current account balances, moderate inflation, generally adequate reserve positions, and declining debt paths. Almost three-fourths of low-income countries are seen improving their fiscal buffers over the next four years. But doing so will require disciplined fiscal and monetary policies, together with vigorous financial and real sector reforms.

One-third of the projected improvement in the primary balance would come from a cyclical recovery in revenues. The balance would come mainly from measures to boost underlying revenue performance and trim nonpriority spending, some of which are part of longer-term reform efforts initiated before the crisis. Additional donor support to countries with larger projected adjustments could help ease the burden of rebuilding fiscal buffers. With low-income countries' revenue-to-GDP ratios below potential, substantial and sustained increases in fiscal revenues (as outlined above) are critical to rebuilding buffers while making room for priority investments (figures 2.18 and 2.19).

For most low-income countries, medium-term debt dynamics are not a major concern as they rebuild fiscal buffers along the recovery path. For example, the median improvement in the primary balance is projected at 1.3 percentage points of GDP over five years. The share of countries with fiscal deficits in excess of 5 percent of GDP is projected to drop from almost half in 2009 to one-tenth by 2014. At the other end of the spectrum,

FIGURE 2.18   The overall debt outlook in low-income countries seems favorable as fiscal buffers are being rebuilt along with the recovery

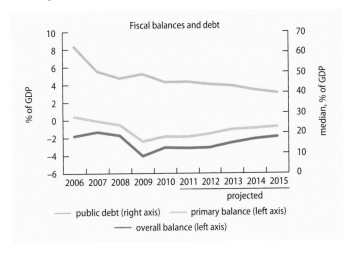

Source: IMF 2010a.

FIGURE 2.19   Low-income countries projected to cut real spending tend to have high deficits and debt

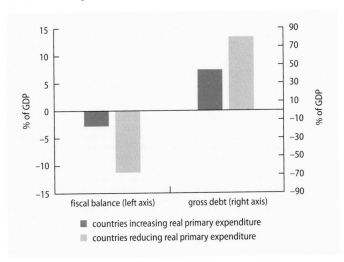

Source: IMF 2010a.
Note: The average for 2010 is shown.

almost half the low-income countries are expected to have fiscal deficits of below 2 percent of GDP by 2014, compared with one-quarter in 2009. As growth recovers and fiscal situations improve, the median public debt ratio would decline again: half the low-income countries would see public debt fall below 40 percent of GDP by 2015, while one-fifth would have debt exceeding 65 percent of GDP.

The global recovery is projected to boost demand for exports and strengthen current account balances, helping bolster reserve cushions. The projected improvement in the external environment would help maintain median reserve coverage at around the equivalent of four months of imports over the medium term, although country experience would differ: one in seven low-income countries would have reserve coverage exceeding six months of imports, while one in 20 would have less than two months.

Exchange rate policies should continue to be used to cushion the effect of future volatility where possible. Many low-income countries with fixed exchange rate regimes could benefit from somewhat faster accumulation of reserves. Conversely, some with floating rates appear to have built more than adequate reserve cushions; they could afford to raise spending (figures 2.20 and 2.21).

Most low-income countries can continue using monetary policy to support the recovery if the present moderate rates of inflation

FIGURE 2.21   Reserve cushions would not improve much among low-income countries with relatively low reserves

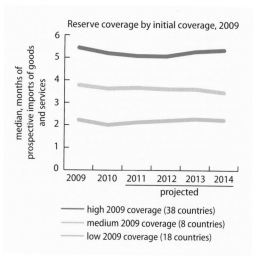

Reserve coverage by initial coverage, 2009

— high 2009 coverage (38 countries)
— medium 2009 coverage (8 countries)
— low 2009 coverage (18 countries)

Source: IMF 2010a.
Note: "Low" is defined as having less than three months of reserves coverage; "medium" as having more than three but less than four months of reserves coverage.

continue, but they must closely monitor the effects of commodity prices on their domestic inflation rates, given the risks associated with rising world prices for food and fuel. If these global shocks persist and feed through to local prices, monetary policy should accommodate the direct impact; however, it may need to be tightened in some cases to counter second-round effects.

The crisis has underscored the importance to low-income countries of adequate financial regulatory frameworks, effective supervision, and sound financial institutions. Supervisory authorities will need to ensure that credit standards do not deteriorate during times of strong credit growth. Regulatory frameworks should focus on the risks assumed by banks and the sources of their business growth to ensure that these are sustainable. Closer supervision is required to ensure that banks are complying with prudential regulations. In banks where financial strains have been significant, the balance sheet cleanup should proceed quickly—recognizing losses and having shareholders inject needed capital.

FIGURE 2.20   The current account balance is projected to improve gradually in low-income countries as exports rebound

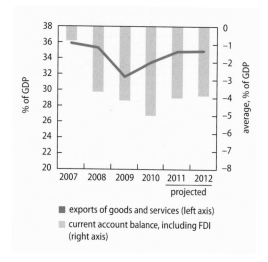

■ exports of goods and services (left axis)
■ current account balance, including FDI (right axis)

Source: IMF 2010a.

Developing domestic debt markets would help mobilize national savings and increase low-income country policy buffers, helping cushion the impact of the crisis. Low-income countries also have enormous investment needs that require financing. Although external financing has to remain a significant part of the financing mix, policies to mobilize domestic savings and develop domestic debt markets would broaden the range of available options.

Reforms that promote economic diversification also have an important role to play in managing macroeconomic volatility and fostering durable growth.[23] Such diversification is likely to involve further trade integration,

which will require both low-income countries and their trading partners to undertake further reforms of their trade regimes. Barriers in labor and product markets also impede the emergence of new sectors and the entry of new firms; addressing these barriers would promote diversification. To the extent that transformation in economic structures leads to social dislocation, it would be important to ensure that effective social safety nets are in place to protect vulnerable groups (see the discussion of indigenous peoples and socially excluded groups in chapter 4). Fragile states face special challenges (box 2.4; also see figure 1.7 and box 1.4 in chapter 1 and box 5.4 in chapter 5).

BOX 2.4   **Fragile states—experience and implications**[a]

Fragile states are generally off target to meet the MDGs. They are typified by poor initial conditions (left figure below), slow GDP growth (right figure below), and macroeconomic instability. These

characteristics contribute to a cycle of underdevelopment that reinforces political instability and conflict, with negative regional spillovers.

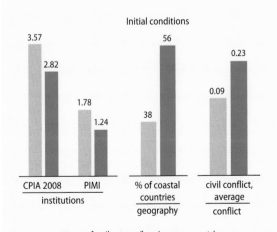

Source: IMF staff calculations.
Note: CPIA = Country Policy and Institutional Assessment; PIMI = public investment management index.

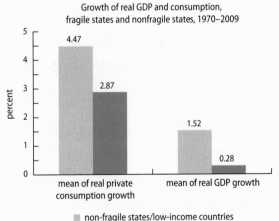

Source: IMF staff calculations.

continued

BOX 2.4 **Fragile states—experience and implications** (continued)

The quality of institutions (measured by the Country Policy and Institutional Assessment and by the index of public investment management mentioned above) tend to be considerably weaker in fragile states than in other low-income countries.[b] Fragile states are also characterized by lower levels of development and a much higher incidence of conflict.[c]

Slow real GDP growth
- During 1970–2009, average real GDP growth in fragile states was about one-fifth that of other low-income countries. The difference in the growth performance is especially apparent since the early 1990s.
- While the number of growth upswings was broadly similar, growth downswings are twice as frequent in fragile states.
- Output losses that follow economic and political shocks are larger and persist longer than in other low-income countries.

Macroeconomic instability
- Measured by high inflation, large debt-to-GDP ratios, and low international reserves, macroeconomic instability has been much higher in fragile states than in other low-income countries.

Implications for global policy
International organizations and development partners have recognized that the problems of fragile states present distinct challenges and warrant well-targeted approaches. Concerned about preserving peace and security in these countries and aware of the risk of spillovers to neighbors, they have made considerable efforts to develop effective paradigms for engagement.

Their key challenge for effective engagement is to devise strategies that recognize these states' capacity constraints, their large financing needs, and the need for prolonged engagement. Furthermore, given their multidimensional needs, fragile states would benefit from a well-coordinated and comprehensive strategy of assistance from the international community. This strategy should emphasize the paramount need to secure peace and security; the need to rebuild capacity and strengthen institutions through a common technical assistance strategy; and the design, scale, and timing of macroeconomic adjustment that can secure a virtuous cycle of development.

a. The IMF does not maintain a formal list of fragile states, and the analysis here uses the World Bank list.

b. The average Country Policy and Institutional Assessment score for fragile states in 2008 was 2.82, compared with 3.57 for nonfragile low-income countries.

c. This is indicated by lower per capita GDP and investment ratios and by weaker health and education indicators.

Boosting the impact of international support

To regain momentum toward the MDGs, international cooperation will be required on three fronts. First, low-income countries in particular will need a strong and stable global economic environment in which to continue growing. To secure such an environment, the advanced market economies need to repair and reform their financial systems and address their fiscal imbalances, and emerging market economies should adjust their macroeconomic policies to reorient growth domestically and to avoid possible overheating.

Second, actions are needed to help low-income countries achieve and sustain more rapid economic growth and restore their policy buffers. Inadequate infrastructure is one major challenge for growth. Addressing the infrastructure gap requires stronger public investment management systems and enhanced domestic revenue mobilization—areas where international organizations can offer policy advice and technical assistance. It also requires large-scale, highly concessional finance, underscoring the need for donors to meet aid commitments and to strengthen the overall effectiveness of aid. Another major challenge is to expand trade opportunities, particularly for the poorest countries. Key steps include completing the Doha Round and expanding and improving Aid for Trade.[24]

Third, fragile states lag farthest behind in reaching the MDGs, and they require additional support to help build institutions and move toward a virtuous circle of development, peace, and security.

Notes

1. Except where otherwise noted, this chapter distinguishes "advanced" and "emerging and developing" economies according to the IMF *World Economic Outlook* country classification. Within the latter group, "emerging economies" are those not eligible for the IMF Poverty Reduction and Growth Trust (PRGT) (see http://www.imf.org) and "low-income countries" (or "developing economies") are those eligible for the PRGT. The analysis in box 2.4 is based on the World Bank definition of fragile states. Least-developed countries are a subset of low-income countries, as defined by the United Nations.

2. The January 2011 *Global Economic Prospects* (World Bank 2011a) examines the poverty implications of higher food prices (box 6 of that volume) and explores links between financial markets and food prices, finding little evidence that investment-based demand has driven up prices (box 7).

3. In 2009, increases in the ratios of reserves to imports reflected the IMF special drawing rights (SDRs) allocation (see the factsheet on SDRs at http://www.imf.org) and 2009's sharp contraction in global trade.

4. IMF 2010a.

5. World Bank 2011a.

6. World Bank 2011b, table 2.

7. World Bank 2011b.

8. In addition to immediate income loss from not working—loss for society and for the individual—the considerable human costs of unemployment include long-lasting income loss, increased illness and mortality, and reduced

educational achievement and social cohesion (ILO-IMF 2010). Policy makers can take the following steps to improve employment opportunities (including where young adult unemployment runs high): establishing more flexible labor market regulations together with effective social safety nets; implementing programs to upgrade skills and better match them with the demands of labor markets; and strengthening the business environment (IMF 2010d).

9. IMF 2011c.

10. In addition to facilitating greater price stability, there is evidence that fiscal adjustment in emerging economies has typically helped promote income equality in the longer term. See IMF (2010b), appendix 3.

11. More than half of the additional deficit was financed domestically, including borrowing in domestic debt markets, central bank financing, or drawing down government deposits. External borrowing accounted for much of the rest, with the IMF financing a significant component.

12. IMF country desks were asked in January 2011 to assess the quality of macroeconomic policies in 2010 as unsatisfactory, adequate, or good.

13. Recovery has been very strong in emerging Asia and Latin America and more restrained in the Middle East and emerging Europe, where output in some countries remains well below precrisis levels.

14. Emerging and developing economies' export volumes grew 13 percent in 2010 and are expected to remain buoyant in 2011.

15. IMF 2010c.

16. Calderon (2009) estimates that by increasing the stock and quality of their infrastructure to that of Mauritius, Sub-Saharan low-income countries would raise their annual per capita income growth by more than 2 percentage points.

17. Briceno-Garmendia, Smits, and Foster 2008.

18. Rajaram et al. 2010.

19. Dabla-Norris et al. 2010.

20. Brumby and Verhoeven (2010) note that though government investment spending among low-income countries accelerated in 2009–10, fiscal consolidation pressures may reduce its growth over the next few years.

21. IMF 2011a.
22. Elborgh-Woytek, Gregory, and McDonald 2010.
23. Haddad, Lim, and Saborowski 2010.
24. Hoekman and Wilson 2010; see chapter 5 of this volume.

References

Briceno-Garmendia, C., K. Smits, and V. Foster. 2008. "Financing Public Infrastructure in Sub-Saharan Africa: Patterns, Issues, and Options." Africa Infrastructure Country Diagnostic Background Paper No. 15, World Bank, Washington, DC.

Brumby, J., and M. Verhoeven. 2010. "Public Expenditure after the Global Financial Crisis." In *The Day after Tomorrow: A Handbook on the Future of Economic Policy in the Developing World*, ed. O. Canuto and M. Giugale, 193–206. Washington, DC: World Bank.

Calderon, C. 2009. "Infrastructure and Growth in Africa." Policy Research Working Paper 4914, World Bank, Washington, DC.

Dabla-Norris, E., J. Brumby, A. Kyobe, Z. Mills, and C. Papageorgiou. 2010. "Investing in Public Investment: An Index of Public Investment Efficiency." Working Paper 11/37, International Monetary Fund, Washington, DC.

Elborgh-Woytek, K., R. Gregory, and B. McDonald. 2010. "Reaching the MDGs: An Action Plan for Trade." Staff Position Note 10/14, International Monetary Fund, Washington, DC.

Haddad, M., J. J. Lim, and C. Saborowski. 2010. "Managing Openness and Volatility: The Role of Export Diversification." Poverty Reduction and Economic Management Network, World Bank. *Economic Premise* 6 (March). http://siteresources.worldbank.org/INTPREMNET/Resources/EP6.pdf.

Hoekman, B., and J. Wilson. 2010. "Aid for Trade: An Action Agenda Looking Forward." Poverty Reduction and Economic Management Network, World Bank. *Economic Premise* 25 (August). http://siteresources.worldbank.org/INTPREMNET/Resources/EP25.pdf.

ILO-IMF (International Labour Organization-International Monetary Fund). 2010. "The Challenges of Growth, Employment and Social Cohesion." Paper prepared for the Joint ILO-IMF Conference in cooperation with the Office of the Prime Minister of Norway, Oslo, Norway, September 13.

IMF (International Monetary Fund). 2010a. "Emerging from the Global Crisis: Macroeconomic Challenges Facing Low-Income Countries." Washington, DC. http://www.imf.org/external/np/pp/eng/2010/100510.pdf.

———. 2010b. *Fiscal Monitor. Fiscal Exit: From Strategy to Implementation.* Washington, DC. http://www.imf.org/external/pubs/ft/fm/2010/fm1002.pdf.

———. 2010c. "Reaching the MDGs: Macroeconomic Prospects and Challenges in Low-Income Countries." Washington, DC. http://www.imf.org/external/np/exr/mdg/2010/091610.pdf.

———. 2010d. *Regional Economic Outlook: Middle East and Central Asia.* October. Washington, DC.

———. 2011a. "Revenue Mobilization in Developing Countries." February.

———. 2011b. "Recent Experiences in Managing Capital Inflows—Cross-Cutting Themes and Possible Policy Framework."

———. 2011c. "Strengthening Fiscal Credibility." *Fiscal Monitor Update* January. http://www.imf.org/external/pubs/ft/fm/2011/01/update/fmindex.pdf.

Rajaram, A., T. Minh Le, N. Biletska, and J. Brumby. 2010. "A Diagnostic Framework for Assessing Public Investment Management." Policy Research Working Paper 5397, World Bank, Washington, DC.

World Bank. 2010. *Global Monitoring Report: The MDGs after the Crisis.* Washington, DC.

———. 2011a. *Global Economic Prospects: Navigating Strong Currents.* Washington, DC.

———. 2011b. *Migration and Remittances Factbook, 2011.* Washington, DC.

Linking Spending and Outcomes: Some Lessons from Impact Evaluations in Education and Health

Education and health are key dimensions of many of the Millennium Development Goals (MDGs). As 2015 approaches, calls for greater development effectiveness are taking on increased urgency for two reasons: development assistance for health and education has risen to unprecedented amounts, but has not led to expected improvements in outcomes; and the global crisis has forced a reexamination of social spending.

This chapter highlights lessons about this disconnect between spending and outcomes derived from recent impact evaluations in health and education. Although designing the right approach to improving outcomes is complex and context dependent, a systematic evidence base generated through impact evaluations can provide useful guidance for policy makers. Furthermore, the body of these evaluations has grown tremendously in recent years. The base of impact evaluations is still far from complete, and much more work is needed; but some interesting findings have already begun to emerge.

Existing impact evaluations show that efforts aimed at improving access to education and health services have met with some success. However, it has been much more difficult to improve the quality of education and health services, which remain low in many developing countries. Hence, the disconnect between development spending and learning and health outcomes. The disconnect stems in part from the narrow focus on financing inputs, while ignoring other parts of the causal chain that links public spending to changes in outcomes. The causal chain shows that incentives facing both service providers and consumers are important mediating variables in the link between development spending and outcomes, and policies have often failed to sufficiently account for them. Not surprisingly, therefore, one of the strong lessons emerging from impact evaluations is that continuing to increase provision of traditional inputs will have only limited impact if issues of service delivery and consumer behavior are not addressed. As highlighted in the 2004 World Development Report: Making Services Work for Poor People, improving service delivery in health and education, in addition to increasing resources, is vital to reach many MDGs.

Although this chapter points to the limited impact of input provision, it does not question the need for additional financing because improving quality also requires resources. It

Girls from Lagos, Nigeria, are eager to get on the school bus.

71

is important to ensure that institutions provide services efficiently and responsively—and that their potential clients have the ability and desire to use services efficiently and hold service providers accountable for quality. And when quality and institutional arrangements improve, the returns to additional investments are also greater. This focus on institutional arrangements is consistent with the findings presented in chapter 1, which highlights policies and institutions in explaining the heterogeneity of MDG progress.

Disconnect between expenditure and outcomes

Budget allocations for health and education are at an all-time high in the developing world. Development assistance for health has quadrupled since 1990, peaking at $24 billion in 2008 (figure 3.1a). Health spending by developing-country governments has also peaked (albeit at a much lower level), nearly doubling to reach $240 million during 1995–2006. Similarly, development assistance for education has doubled since 2002, reaching a high of $10.8 billion in 2007 (figure 3.1b).

Despite these huge funding gains, progress toward development targets has been uneven. Lack of resources only partly explains many of the remaining gaps because links between spending and human development outcomes are weak,[1] and good policies and strong institutions are central to improving the productivity of education and health spending.

True, access to education and health services has expanded sharply in recent years. For example, basic immunization coverage in low-income countries increased by 20 percentage points during 2000–08.[2] Primary and secondary school enrollment rates have also improved, in some cases dramatically. But the quality (or outcomes) of education and health remains a grave concern. In education, this is made evident by the poor learning outcomes of school children.[3] Often, countries that spend more on primary education (compared with the level predicted by per capita income) generate on average only a small improvement in test scores (compared with scores predicted by per capita income) (figure 3.2). In India, even though most children of primary-school age were enrolled in school, 35 percent of them could not read a simple paragraph and 41 percent could not do a simple subtraction.[4]

FIGURE 3.1 **Government and donor spending on health and education is unprecedented**

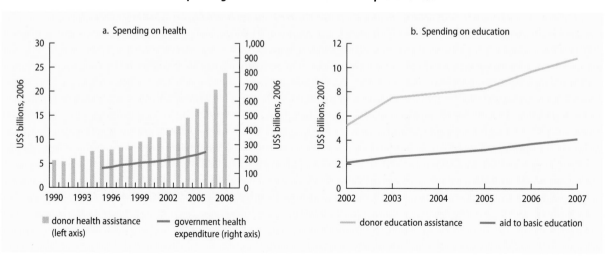

Sources: IHME 2010; OECD-DAC 2009, cited in UNESCO 2010.
Note: Includes all on-budget and off-budget health-related disbursements from bilateral donor agencies, grant-making and loan-making institutions, United Nations agencies, and nongovernmental organizations. Development assistance to education comes not only as direct allocations to the education sector but also through general budget support.

FIGURE 3.2   The relationship between expenditure and learning outcomes is weak

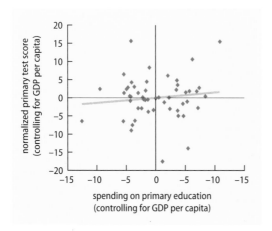

Source: Bruns, Filmer, and Patrinos 2011.
Note: The graph shows the deviation of normalized test scores from that predicted by GDP per capita against the deviation of public spending on primary education per student (relative to GDP per capita) from that predicted by GDP per capita.

FIGURE 3.3   There are wide differences in the share of public health spending going to the rich and the poor

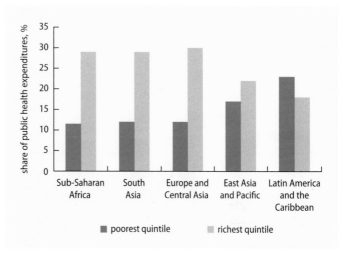

Source: Authors' calculations, based on data from Filmer 2003.

In health, basic immunization rates have expanded, but full immunization coverage—needed for the full impact on child mortality—is much lower.[5] Likewise, the global average attendance at a minimum of one prenatal visit is 78 percent, but attendance at four visits—needed for the full impact on maternal mortality—is around 48 percent.[6] Clinical competence may also be lacking (as in Senegal, where an assessment of service quality found that only 34 percent of cases were correctly diagnosed).[7]

So, more resources—even when increasing coverage—may not be enough to have a big effect on outcomes.

The disconnect between spending and outcomes partly reflects the failure of human development spending to reach poor people. Public spending on health and education is generally believed to be an effective means to reach the poor, but empirical evidence fails to support this assumption. Since the 1990s, numerous studies have found that public health spending is not concentrated among the poor and that the rich benefit disproportionately from public health subsidies.[8] Apart from Latin America and the Caribbean, the rich receive far greater benefits from public

health spending than do poor people (figure 3.3). In Sub-Saharan Africa, South Asia, and Europe and Central Asia, the incidence of health spending among the richest fifth of the populace was more than twice that of the poorest fifth.

So, what are some of the factors that cause the disconnect between public spending and changes in human development outcomes?

Understanding the disconnect

Calls for greater development effectiveness are implicitly calls to strengthen the links in the causal chain between spending on inputs and human development outcomes. Each link of the chain, if weak, can prevent increased public financial and physical resources from being translated into improvements in human development outcomes: the link between resources allocated and services and goods generated, between goods and services generated and consumption, and between consumption of goods and services and education outcomes (figure 3.4). The first link emphasizes supply-side factors, the third link demand-side factors. The middle link is the critical intermediate step where the demand-

FIGURE 3.4   Links between public expenditure and human development outcomes

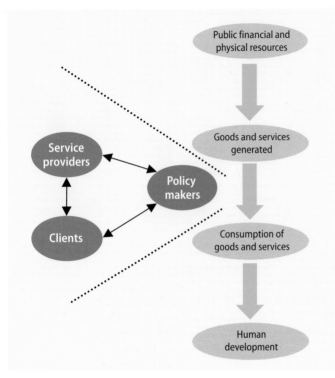

Sources: Adapted from Go 2010 and World Bank 2003.
Note: The service delivery triangle showing the interaction among clients, service providers, and policy makers has been adapted from the 2004 *World Development Report* (World Bank 2003). This diagram is a simplification of very complex relationships among spending, supply, service delivery, demand, and outcomes. There are nuances that are not captured here. One such nuance is that services provision implies use, whereas the generation of goods does not. Another is that different service providers (government, nongovernment, faith-based) have different motivations and incentives, so their interaction with clients and policy makers and the outcomes will be different. See, for example, Reinikka and Svensson (2010). Finally, incentives created by different financing arrangements (including prepayment mechanisms) and their impact on provider and consumer behavior are not fully captured here.

side and supply-side factors intersect for the delivery of health and education services.

On the supply side, inequitable resource allocation, lack of complementary inputs (both sectoral and cross-sectoral), and crowding out of private sector provision can weaken the link between public spending and the amount of goods and services generated. And the consumption of these goods and services will depend critically on the quality of service delivery, a crucial intermediate step where the results chain frequently breaks down. This can often be traced to poor incentives for service providers and low accountability. The weak service delivery link can also reinforce existing inequalities in human development outcomes because

the challenges of service delivery are often more pronounced in hard-to-reach areas and underserved populations.

The service delivery triangle in figure 3.4 outlines the relationships among different system actors. Citizens, especially poor people, who ultimately consume the education and health services generated by the public system are the clients. They have a direct relationship with frontline service providers, such as teachers in public schools and health care workers in public health facilities—the short route of accountability. Crucially, however, the service providers generally have no direct accountability to the consumers, unlike in a market transaction. Instead, they are accountable only to the government that employs them. The accountability route from consumers to service providers is therefore through the government—the long route. To hold service providers accountable for the quantity and quality of services provided, citizens must act through the government—a process that is difficult for poor people especially because they can seldom organize themselves and be heard by policy makers. Moreover, the government rarely has enough information—or indeed the mechanisms—to improve service provider performance.

Demand-side factors also mediate between public spending and human development outcomes. The lack of uptake from consumers resulting from the lack of demand, information, or other factors can undermine the positive impacts of public spending in health and education.

All this suggests that merely increasing the supply of human development inputs and services will not automatically improve human development outcomes. Thus it is that the pervasive approach in global resource mobilization efforts (that is, filling narrowly defined resource gaps through predominantly supply-side interventions without strengthening service delivery and consumer uptake) has limited impact.

What do impact evaluations say?

By understanding the causal pathways, practitioners can be better placed to improve development effectiveness and thus accelerate progress toward the MDGs (and secure more value for money).

Impact evaluations have emerged as an important tool to conduct such analyses. They assess the changes in the well-being of individuals that can be directly attributed to a particular project, program, or policy—and thereby provide robust and credible evidence on how a project has performed and what changes they have "caused." At a broader level, the information they generate can contribute to a systematic evidence base on the kinds of interventions that work. Rigorous, project-specific impact evaluations can also shed light on the broader functioning of the education and health systems and on general household behavior. They often have forced a rethinking of assumptions regarding human behavior (as illustrated in box 3.1) or brought to light unexpected impacts of certain types of development interventions (as illustrated in box 3.2).

Because of the explicit focus on causality, the main methodological requirement for an impact evaluation, and what sets it apart from other types of monitoring and evaluation, is the need for a credible counterfactual (that is, what the outcome for project beneficiaries would have been without the project).[9] Establishing a counterfactual retrospectively is hard. For this reason, it is best to design the impact evaluation alongside the program and to build it into the program.

Some caveats regarding impact evaluations need to be noted. Although extremely useful, impact evaluations cannot answer all development questions. Furthermore, the existing knowledge base of impact evaluations in education and health is far from complete. In many areas, the current evidence does not support as clear an answer as one would like. In others, it does not answer some key questions. The results of many individual impact evaluations cannot be generalized. In fact, the question of external validity of impact evaluations has been an important and often somewhat contentious one.[10] Formulating general recommendations from the conclusions of impact evaluations is often hampered by lack of comparability among

settings, different forms of the intervention, and varying levels of rigor in the evaluation. Also, very few impact evaluations inform us about the longer-term impact of programs or whether observed impacts persist after the program has ended. Another frequently heard critique of impact evaluations is that they do not focus enough on the reasons why certain projects work and others do not.[11] It has also been argued that impact evaluations do not lend themselves easily to distributional analysis because they are focused on estimating average treatment effects.[12] Finally, very few impact evaluations collect or report on program cost data; and this represents a missed opportunity to gain insights into efficiency, cost effectiveness, as well as longer-term financing issues such as sustainability.

Many of these objections can be resolved by expanding the base of rigorous impact evaluations on certain topics. Researchers should replicate successful models in different contexts to assess the extent to which programs work under varying circumstances. In addition, replicating interventions that have been successful in small-scale settings at a regional or national level will help contribute to knowledge of what works in the real world. In certain cases, such as incentives and accountability, there is a need to test various combinations and extensions of existing approaches. Conducting a series of related evaluations in a comparable setting with cross-cutting treatment designs generates considerable cost savings in data collection and allows cost-effectiveness comparisons across program variants. It is also important to collect cost and process data, data on intermediate outcomes, and good qualitative data to complement quantitative data. The World Bank's Development Impact Evaluation (DIME) initiative is encouraging the use of impact evaluations and promoting their integration into government programs (box 3.3).

Although this chapter focuses on impact evaluations, such evaluations are not the only source of evidence concerning effective interventions to advance the education and health MDGs. Other evaluation methods also contribute to this debate—such as mixed

BOX 3.1   Some impact evaluations have forced a rethinking of our assumptions about HIV/AIDS

Development interventions are often designed on the basis of certain assumptions, particularly for HIV/AIDS—an area where knowledge has grown by leaps and bounds, especially over the past decade. Impact evaluations have contributed to that learning, and some evaluations have shown how erroneous these assumptions can be. Here are a few examples.

Assumption: Promoting knowledge of HIV/AIDS will reduce risky behavior

Information and education campaigns have been the main focus of HIV/AIDS prevention campaigns. Although they have improved knowledge and self-reported behavior, their apparent impact on behaviors may actually be the result of a reporting bias fueled by the people's greater knowledge of what they would need to do to reduce their risk, rather than a reflection of substantial changes in actual behaviors. Two recent meta-analytic reviews show that only a small fraction of behavior change interventions had an impact on HIV or other sexually transmitted infections.[a] Information needs to be better targeted and packaged to have an impact on actual behavior. Nor is *more* information necessarily better. Consider a program that sent text-message reminders concerning adherence to antiretroviral treatment: weekly reminders improved adherence, daily reminders did not. People got habituated to them or perhaps considered them intrusive.

Assumption: More HIV testing will lead to declines in risky behavior

HIV testing is one of the key policy responses to the HIV/AIDS epidemic in Africa, but there is little rigorous evidence on how individual sexual behavior responds to testing. Impact evaluations from East Africa produce three findings.[b] First, individuals surprised by an HIV-positive test are more than five times more likely to contract a sexually transmitted infection than are members of a similar untested control group, indicating an increase in risky sexual behavior. Second, individuals who believed they were at high risk for HIV have a 60 percent decrease in their likelihood of contracting a sexually transmitted infection following an HIV-negative test, indicating safer sexual behavior. Third, when HIV tests

agree with a person's belief of HIV infection, there is no statistically significant change in contracting a sexually transmitted infection. Using the distribution of beliefs of HIV infection and prevalence from the study, the evaluation finds the overall number of HIV infections to increase by 25 percent when people are tested, compared with when they are unaware of their status—an unintended consequence of testing.

Assumption: It is usually stigma that prevents people from picking up HIV test results

It is often argued that getting people to learn their HIV status is crucial for fighting HIV/AIDS, but that stigma and fear of obtaining a positive result create a major barrier preventing people from picking up their results at testing centers. An impact evaluation in Malawi found, however, that small incentives and deadlines were enough to induce people to do this.[c] Distance to the center was also a key determinant of attendance. These findings suggest that procrastination and the inconvenience of travel, rather than stigma, explain much of the problem.

Assumption: People who test positive will reduce their risky behavior

Although people can behave altruistically once they know they are HIV-positive, they may also show disinhibition behavior because they have less to lose when engaging in risky behavior. A recent study in Mozambique[d] found that risky sexual behaviors increase in response to the perceived changes in risk associated with greater access to antiretroviral therapy. So, scaling up access to antiretroviral therapy without prevention programs may not be optimal if the objective is to contain the disease because people would adjust their sexual behavior in response to the perceived changes in risk.

a. McCoy, Kangwende, and Padian 2009; Mavedzenge, Doyle, and Ross 2010.
b. Weinhard et al. 1999; Gong 2010.
c. Thornton 2005.
d. De Walque, Kazianga, and Over 2010.

BOX 3.2   Spillovers and unintended effects can be important

Impact evaluations have helped highlight positive spillovers of certain types of human development interventions. In Kenya, providing deworming drugs at treatment schools lowered the incidence among nontreated children as a result of a fall in transmission rates.[a] Spillover effects are also shown to be strong in the provision of AIDS antiretroviral treatment. Also in Kenya, children's weekly hours of school attendance increased more than 20 percent within six months of initiating antiretroviral treatment for any adult household member.[b] For boys in treatment households, these increases closely followed their reduced supply of paid labor. Similarly, young children's short-term nutritional status—measured as weight for height—also improved dramatically.

Although Mexico's conditional cash transfer (CCT) program Opportunidades/*Progresa* targeted poor children, school participation also increased among children above the poverty cutoff.[c] Scholarship programs for girls have demonstrated positive externalities for boys' school participation and teachers' attendance.[d]

Some projects, however, may have unintended negative consequences. For example, increasing the availability of affordable antimalarial drugs—as with artemisinin-based combination therapy, the only remaining effective class of first-line antimalarial drugs—may result in increased resistance of the malaria parasite to those drugs and overtreatment of individuals not infected with malaria who are presumptively diagnosed (and the resultant negative health outcomes because the true cause of illness remains untreated). There are also concerns over the sustainability of the subsidy (as a result of inefficient targeting). Cohen, Dupas, and Schaner (2010) confirmed the fears of overtreatment and showed that subsidized access to malaria rapid diagnostic tests substantially reduced these unintended consequences. Another example of a negative spillover effect is that some CCT programs show that, in some contexts, parents compensate for the reduction in labor market work of one child (the CCT beneficiary who is required to attend school) by increasing the hours worked by other siblings.[e]

a. Miguel and Kremer 2004.
b. Zivin, Thirumurthy, and Goldstein 2006.
c. Lalive and Cattaneo 2006; Bobonis and Finan 2009.
d. Kremer, Miguel, and Thornton 2009.
e. Barerra-Osorio, Linden, and Urquiola 2007; Filmer and Schady 2009.

methods, objectives-based approaches, qualitative methods, and theories of change.

This chapter draws especially on the body of knowledge emerging from impact evaluations in the areas of health and education. Even though we have restricted the scope of this discussion to health and education, it is important to recognize that impact evaluations are also generating valuable policy-relevant evidence in the areas of other MDGs (such as water and sanitation)[13] that are not discussed here. In synthesizing the evidence on health and education, we have restricted ourselves to the more rigorous empirical work that has relied on a viable identification strategy (that is, the counterfactual is reliable) and produced causal links between interventions and impacts—something that traditional monitoring and evaluation does not always accomplish. Acknowledging that not all rigorous evidence comes from impact evaluations alone, we focus only on them, partly because of limitations of space and partly because a lot of evidence coming from impact evaluations is fairly recent and highlights how evidence-based decision making can be operationalized (for examples, see boxes 3.1 and 3.2). As noted, the evidence base from impact evaluations in health and education sectors is still evolving and, at this stage, remains very far from complete. In light of that, the chapter refrains from making any explicit policy recommendations or engaging in detailed policy discussions.

BOX 3.3   The DIME initiative

There are several initiatives in the World Bank to improve the quality of evidence to inform development practice. One example is the Development Impact Evaluation (DIME) initiative. Created in 2005 in the Office of the Chief Economist, DIME was relaunched in 2009 as a broad-based, decentralized effort to mainstream impact evaluation in the Bank. The objective is to improve the quality of the Bank's operations, strengthen country institutions for evidence-based policy making, and generate knowledge in 15 development areas.

With 185 completed studies and 280 active studies in 85 countries, the World Bank is attempting to enhance and expand knowledge of the *what* and the *how* of economic development by delivering precise estimates of the cause-effect relationship between policy action and outcomes.

The DIME approach centers on three aspects, in a dramatic shift in the practice of evaluation. First, DIME has been moving the evaluation practice from external and ex post evaluations toward internal, prospective, and operationally driven evaluations that are externally validated through the use of state-of-the-art methods. This framework promotes a results-based model and allows governments to own and set the research agenda, thus receiving just-in-time advice on their most-pressing operational questions and genuinely transforming the way they make decisions for their programs.

Second, DIME builds teams that combine both operational and technical expertise. This ensures that researchers work in close collaboration with project teams from the planning stage onward to sustain a process of prospective and operationally driven knowledge generation. In this model, the project and research teams work together to embed a learning agenda in the project design.

Third, DIME organizes impact evaluations around development areas and offers tailored programmatic and strategic support. Cross-country events develop regional communities of practice around certain sub-themes, and teams share knowledge and experience going beyond the impact evaluation agenda. This ensures that all studies share a coherent and strategic research agenda and that the results are policy relevant and are disseminated to a wide audience of practitioners. DIME sponsors 15 thematic impact evaluation programs: access to infrastructure, active labor market programs, agriculture adaptations, conditional cash transfers, early childhood development, education service delivery, energy mitigation, health systems and results-based financing, HIV/AIDS, finance and private sector growth, forestry adaptations, institutional reform, local development, malaria, and water resource management adaptations.

Source: Legovini 2010.

Efforts to help improve access have met with some success, but some questions remain

Reducing schooling costs has helped increase school enrollment

The driving focus of education policy making in developing countries has been a push to increase enrollments in primary and secondary schools. Interventions that reduce the out-of-pocket costs of schooling have been particularly successful.[14] The reduction in schooling costs can take many direct or indirect forms. For instance, providing free uniforms and textbooks and building more classrooms in rural Kenya had a strong impact on total years of schooling completed.[15] Similarly, school feeding interventions have increased school participation in a variety of settings.[16]

A rich evidence base also shows the positive role of financial incentives in promoting school participation in a variety of contexts. This evidence includes the evaluation of Mexico's conditional cash transfer (CCT) program that documented the efficacy of CCTs as a mechanism for encouraging enrollment and attendance.[17] These results have been replicated by many other researchers in many other countries.[18] In fact, evidence from CCT programs in nine other countries (Bangladesh, Cambodia, Chile, Colombia, Ecuador,

MAP 3.1   The maternal mortality rate is declining only slowly, even though the vast majority of deaths are avoidable

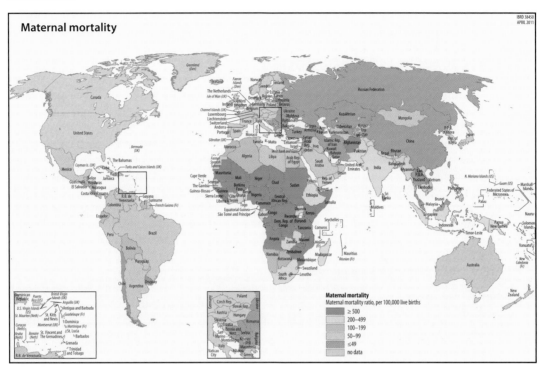

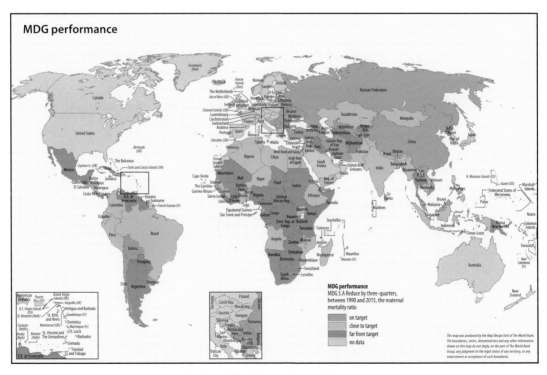

Source: World Bank staff calculations based on data from the World Development Indicators database.

Honduras, Nicaragua, Pakistan, and Turkey) has consistently demonstrated significant impacts of these programs on school enrollment in the initial years of program operation. Reducing user fees can similarly increase enrollment.[19] However, few of these programs have been around long enough to determine whether the impact is a short-term effect of a novel project or is more lasting. In addition, the higher enrollments induced by these programs were not accompanied by increased achievement.[20]

Some impact evaluations have shown that improving school quality does not seem to be a major inducement for increasing school participation.[21] Indeed, interventions improving the quality of education have, on average, generated no changes in participation.[22] But much more evidence on this question is needed before the results can be generalized.

Health input provision programs have to grapple with uptake issues

All provision programs deal with the central issue of how to get citizens to take up the inputs and services they offer. In developing countries, health facilities are not always accessible to poor, rural, and remote communities. Other modes of delivery, such as school-based and community-based health interventions, have been popular. But we are only beginning to learn how well such programs work and under what conditions.

Impact evaluations have shown that schools can be an effective mode of delivery for health input provision and can address some uptake challenges because the families do not have to be persuaded. Some (but not all) school feeding programs have improved children's nutritional intake[23] and health. A recent study has shown improvements in anthropometric outcomes of the younger siblings of students who receive take-home rations.[24]

Other school-based health programs have also shown positive impacts. School-based mass treatment with inexpensive deworming drugs in Kenya (where the prevalence of intestinal worms among children is very high) improved health not only among treated students but also among untreated students at treatment schools and among untreated students at nearby nontreatment schools, thanks to reduced disease transmission.[25] Also in Kenya, school-based intermittent preventive treatment helped reduce anemia prevalence.[26] The delivery of such treatment was estimated to cost $2 per child treated per year, and the estimated cost per anemia case averted was $30. This type of intervention would be especially cost effective in areas with high rates of malaria transmission.[27]

Cheap telecommunication technologies can address uptake, especially in resource-limited settings. An intervention in Kenya used text messages to remind antiretroviral therapy patients to adhere to the treatment guidelines—an important goal, given concerns of widespread drug resistance when adherence is poor. Weekly reminders increased the percentage of participants achieving 90 percent adherence to the therapy by approximately 13–16 percent, compared with no reminder.[28] They also reduced the frequency of treatment interruptions.

Community-based interventions have also become more popular, particularly as complements to facility-based care, linking communities with facilities-based services. Despite showing great promise, community health worker programs have had mixed results, as reflected in the findings of one of the few rigorous impact evaluations of such programs in Ethiopia. The Ethiopian program significantly increased the proportion of children fully immunized and the proportions of children and women using insecticide-treated bednets for malaria protection. But the effect on prenatal and postnatal care was rather limited, as was the impact on the incidence and duration of diarrhea among children under 5 years of age.[29]

Because community-based interventions often come as a package comprising input provision, information, advocacy, and other components, it is hard to untangle the impacts of the different components. Impact evaluations may be useful in this; but, so far, their number is quite limited. A meta-analysis of health literature found that clean delivery had the most pronounced effect on reducing maternal mortality. In comparison, building community support and advocacy groups, involving other family members through community mobilization, or training community health workers and traditional birth attendants had little or no impact on reducing maternal mortality. But community interventions affected perinatal mortality through different channels: community support groups, advocacy through group sessions, and family involvement in care were especially effective in reducing perinatal deaths. Family involvement in care also showed a positive impact in reducing stillbirths. Additional impact evaluations are needed to confirm these findings.

Other programs have tried to deal with the uptake issue by combining demand-side and supply-side interventions. An impact evaluation of an immunization program in India shows that whereas pure supply-side improvements were associated with increases in immunization, uptake rates were much higher when supply-side improvements were combined with modest demand-side incentives in kind.[30] There are few comparative studies of the relative impact on demand-side stimulation versus supply-side responses. For one of the few CCTs that combined interventions on both sides—Nicaragua's *Red de Proteccion Social*—the impact evaluation was unable to untangle the demand-side and supply-side effects.[31]

Cost sharing does not necessarily improve the efficiency of health input subsidies

Many practitioners argue that for some types of health inputs (particularly those requiring the recipient to follow a treatment regime to see health benefits), cost sharing can improve the efficiency of the input subsidy.[32] In this long-standing debate, others contend that cost sharing dampens demand, especially among the poor.

In Zambia, households paying a higher price for a water treatment product were more likely to report treating their drinking water two weeks later.[33] Likewise, controlled studies in several countries record improvements in the use of services among poor people

after copayments increased the transparency and accountability of providers to poor clients.[34] In contrast, an impact evaluation in Kenya finds that cost sharing does not seem to improve targeting of insecticide-treated bednets for malaria prevention to those in greatest need, and that women who pay for their bednets are no more likely to use them than are those who receive them free.[35] Cost sharing also dampens demand considerably, with uptake dropping by 75 percent when the price of bednets increases from zero to $0.75 (from a 100 percent subsidy to an 88 percent subsidy).

Another impact evaluation in Kenya shows that introducing a small cost-sharing component into a school-based deworming program dramatically reduced the uptake of deworming medication and raised little revenue, relative to administrative costs. Nor did the user fees help target treatment to the sickest students.[36] Interestingly, one study shows that uptake is particularly sensitive to price at prices close to zero.[37] In other words, uptake is found to be highly sensitive to having a positive price, but there is less evidence that it is sensitive to variation within the positive price range.

These findings suggest the need for more research, particularly to establish optimal levels of subsidization for different health inputs.[38]

CCT programs have often been effective in reaching the poor

CCTs have traditionally been designed to target poor people, so it is not surprising that a number of CCT programs have reduced poverty. But the impact varies, and there is still not much clarity about the conditions under which CCTs will be most effective in reducing poverty. *Red de Proteccion Social* in Nicaragua and *Familias en Accion* in Colombia show strong effects on poverty, whereas *Programa de Asignacion Familiar* in Honduras and *Oportunidades/Progresa* in Mexico had significant but more modest effects. Some of the larger CCTs from Brazil, Jamaica, and Mexico have also shown an impact on poverty at the national level.

But the CCTs in Cambodia and Ecuador did not affect median consumption or reduce national poverty.[39]

In Ecuador, cash transfers improved cognitive outcomes for the poorest children but not for children somewhat better off.[40] In poor households, child work is a major cause of school-age children dropping out of school. Reduced child work by CCT beneficiaries has been found in Brazil, Cambodia, Ecuador, Mexico, and Nicaragua. In Cambodia, for example, the average child receiving the transfer was 10 percentage points less likely to work for pay. Results on this have been mixed, however, and more research is needed to understand work's impact on siblings—especially if the number of CCTs targeting individual children increases.

Despite being more likely to adopt improved child care practices, the worst-off households in Mexico had greater difficulties translating these improvements into improved nutritional outcomes—largely because of the lack of complementary inputs among poorly educated mothers, poor access to safe water, and poorer quality nutrients.[41]

Incentives do not need to be large

Some impact evaluations have shown that small benefits can often be enough to incentivize the desired change in behavior, and increasing the total size of the transfer has only small marginal effects on service uptake or behavior. In Cambodia, giving a child $45 quarterly to stay in school proved as effective as giving $60.[42] Similarly, in Malawi, the school participation effects of giving a household $5 were not significantly different from giving $10. "[T]he key parameter in setting benefit levels is the size of the elasticity of the relevant outcomes to the benefit level."[43]

Elasticity also varies across the type of behavior being incentivized. In southwest Tanzania, the group receiving $60 had reductions of sexually transmitted infections, but the $30 group had the same infection rate as the control group that received no payments. Not surprisingly, the program was more effective for people from poorer and rural areas.

Whether cash transfers should be "conditioned" on certain behaviors is context specific

Although CCTs have shown some positive impacts on schooling and other outcomes,[44] unconditional cash transfers have also improved child health and increased school participation.[45] So, development practitioners and policy makers have become very interested in whether the programs should be conditioned on certain behaviors or not.

A study shows that some households in Mexico and Ecuador did not realize that the cash transfers they were getting were conditional on school attendance; and, for these households, school enrollment was significantly lower than for those who thought that the transfers were conditional.[46]

In Malawi, the effect of conditioning differed for different outcomes. For school participation of adolescent girls, the impact of the transfers was significantly greater when they were conditioned on school attendance than when not so conditioned. But they had little effect on the likelihood of teenage pregnancies or marriages, while unconditional cash transfers were very effective in delaying marriage and childbearing.[47] Therefore, the answer to the question of whether cash transfers should be conditioned on certain behaviors appears to be context specific—but, again, more research is needed on the subject.

Providing information can be a highly cost-effective way to change behavior

An impact evaluation from Madagascar shows that providing information to youths about returns to schooling improved children's school performance and attendance in the first few months following the intervention.[48] Similarly, providing information on returns to schooling to boys in eighth grade increased average years of schooling in the Dominican Republic, although the program did not have an impact on the poorest students.[49]

Providing information to adults has also shown some promising results. In India, informing households that their drinking water is contaminated increases the probability that they start purifying their water.[50] In Bangladesh, informing households that the water in their wells has an unsafe concentration of arsenic raises the probability that they will switch to another well.[51] But information provision alone does not change consumer behavior in all contexts. A study from Kenya shows that providing consumers information about the mortality and morbidity from malaria or about the financial gains from avoiding malaria infection had no impact on the uptake of malaria control devices.[52] Similarly, evidence from the United States has shown that information alone is usually ineffective in changing risky health-related behavior.[53]

The experience with translating information and knowledge into HIV risk-reducing behavior change has had mixed results, as the AIDS literature suggests.[54] There are, however, some impact evaluations of behavioral interventions that have shown a reduction in risky sexual behavior.[55] In western Kenya, for example, female students were warned about the high HIV prevalence rates among older men and they responded by dramatically reducing the number of teenage childbirths with older men. Similarly, helping girls stay in school by giving them a free school uniform reduced teen pregnancy at a relatively low cost ($12 per girl) when compared to the cost per teenage childbirth averted ($750). Providing abstinence-only information about teenage sexual behavior had no impact on the likelihood of risky behavior. But providing detailed information on the risk of HIV led to a 28 percent decrease in the likelihood that girls started childbearing within a year—thus suggesting a reduction in unprotected sex among those girls.[56]

Despite improvements in access, it has been very difficult to improve learning and health outcomes

Providing increased traditional schooling inputs has often been ineffective in improving learning outcomes

Attempting to fill narrowly defined resource gaps in schooling by increasing the provision of traditional inputs has not been very successful for improving learning outcomes. Traditional inputs that have been tested on this dimension include textbooks, school meals, blackboards and other visual aids (like flip charts), teacher training, and even smaller class sizes.[57] Some of these studies are discussed below.

Some example of such studies include one in Kenya that found that providing textbooks to students did not raise average test scores; it raised only the scores of the best students.[58] Also in Kenya, introducing complementary learning aids such as flip charts to schools had no impact on student performance.[59] Similarly, school feeding interventions have had little or no impact on student performance.[60] The Bolivian Social Investment Fund had a significant impact on school infrastructure but not on education outcomes within the evaluation period.[61] An extra teacher in rural Indian nonformal education centers did not significantly improve test scores (although this was not measured with great precision).[62] And, contrary to expectations, some studies have shown that simply reducing pupil–teacher ratios does little for student performance.[63]

In recent years, education practitioners have experimented with nontraditional inputs—mostly those to fill gaps left by teachers—and technology-based inputs emerge as promising. A Nicaraguan program of radio instruction for students finds strong positive impacts on mathematics performance.[64] Computer-assisted learning in urban India increased test scores in mathematics.[65] In another program in Indian schools, an electronic machine or flash card–based activities (to help teach English) increased test scores in English.[66] Computers failed, however, to improve student performance in a program in Colombia.[67]

Newer approaches toward remedial education for poor-performing students have also shown promise. A reading intervention in rural India that gave four days of training to community volunteers with grade-10 or grade-12 educations to enable them to teach children how to read significantly improved reading.[68]

CCTs help increase the uptake of services, but their impact on health and learning outcomes is mixed

A positive impact on health care utilization (such as children's visits to health centers) was reported in Honduras, Jamaica, Mexico, Nicaragua, and Paraguay (but not in Chile).[69] Out of seven studies reporting immunization results, significant and sizable impacts on full immunization coverage (an intermediate outcome) were found only in Nicaragua and Turkey.[70] In Mexico, however, the impact was small and not significant—results ascribed to the already high immunization rate at baseline (above 90 percent).

The impact of CCTs on health and nutritional outcomes is also mixed. One of the few studies that reported health impacts was Mexico's *Oportunidades/Progresa,* where children under 3 who received CCTs were 22 percent less likely to report an illness episode in the previous four weeks than were the children in the comparison group. Children young enough to be exposed to the program for 24 months were 40 percent less likely to be reported ill—a finding that suggests the program generated cumulative health benefits. Conversely, no effect on child height was reported among children of any age in Brazil, Ecuador, Honduras, and Nicaragua;[71] and, in Colombia, among children ages 3–7 years.[72] Where studies have reported positive institutional impacts, the impacts have been larger among younger children (that is, younger at the time of the baseline survey—in particular, younger than 2 years at baseline). One of the few CCTs that addressed maternal health outcomes, *Janani Surksha Yojana* in India, had a small impact on the uptake of prenatal care; a large, positive impact on institutional deliveries; and a smaller effect on home delivery with a skilled birth attendant. There was also some evidence of a lower probability of perinatal and neonatal deaths, but not of maternal deaths.[73]

Although the positive impact of CCTs in expanding access to education is well documented,[74] evidence on the impact of educational transfers (in-kind or cash transfers) on learning outcomes is not as encouraging.[75]

One example is a small cash transfer program in Malawi's Zomba district, where the transfers improved school enrollment and attendance but did not significantly improve learning variables (which included a self-report on English literacy and a teacher's evaluation of student progress).[76] The lack of any discernible effect on learning outcomes (despite large impacts on school enrollment) may partly be caused by their drawing lower-ability students back to school.[77]

In a similar vein, CCTs have had a positive impact on the uptake of growth monitoring services.[78] But the impact on growth indicators has been mixed, and the positive impacts were generally modest.[79] CCTs in Colombia, Mexico, and Nicaragua were accompanied by a substantial positive impact on linear growth,[80] although no impact was found in Brazil[81] or Honduras.[82] Nonetheless, despite the difficulty of cross-study comparisons (because of differences in age groups, exposure, and program design), it can be concluded that programs with larger cash transfers (such as those in Colombia, Mexico, and Nicaragua, where transfers represented 15–25 percent of total household expenditures) tend to have the largest impact. Younger age groups are likely to benefit more (consistent with the nutrition literature), and the effects are larger for height than for weight indicators.[83]

Only three of the CCT program evaluations (Honduras, Mexico, and Nicaragua) looked at the impact on micronutrient status. In Mexico, after one year, beneficiary children had higher mean hemoglobin levels and significantly lower rates of anemia than did nonbeneficiaries.[84] But nearly half the children under 1 year were still anemic after one year of exposure to the intervention. No effect was found for the older children, and no differences were observed for other micronutrients (such as iron, vitamin A, and zinc). The modest impacts on micronutrient status were ascribed to low use or uptake of the fortified foods (Mexico)[85] and supplements (Nicaragua),[86] sharing foods with other beneficiary household members, overdilution of the product, and program design weaknesses.[87]

MAP 3.2   Each year of a girl's education reduces, by as much as 10 percent, the risk of her children dying before age five

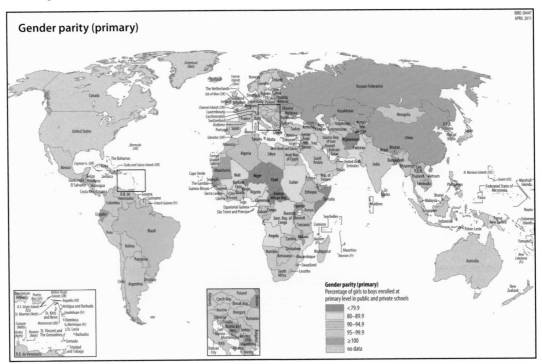

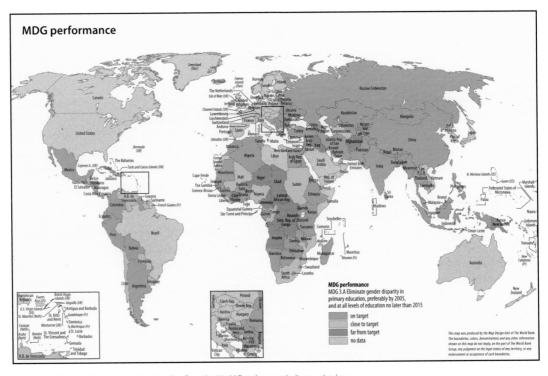

Source: World Bank staff calculations based on data from the World Development Indicators database.

Nutritional improvements are expected to flow from the increased consumption arising from the income effect of the cash transfer and the better practices (such as breastfeeding, proper weaning, growth monitoring, and consumption of nutritious foods) that arise from health education during growth monitoring. The relative contribution of health education to each of these practices has not been assessed. The majority of impact evaluations have found that CCTs may disproportionately affect the consumption of particular items, such as food. It has been hypothesized that CCTs increase the bargaining power of women within the household, and that this drives the greater food expenditure.[88] There is also some evidence of changes in diet composition. Not only do households increase dietary diversity, but they also shift toward higher-quality sources of calories. In Nicaragua, households that receive transfers from the *Atencion a Crisis* program spend significantly less on staples and more on animal protein, fruits, and vegetables.[89]

Identifying the reasons for increased use of health or education services is complicated. Sometimes it rises because services are physically more accessible. This is likely the case for such low-cost health services as bednets and treatment for sexually transmitted infections where the nonservice costs of use—particularly transport and perhaps facility search costs—are a larger share of cost to the consumer than is the service cost. In education, a crucial element is always likely to be the opportunity cost to households (the loss in earnings from sending children). A further reason for increased uptake is that use is linked to finance, and thus it improves the providers' incentive to increase the quantity of services.[90]

Intervening early in a child's life can produce strong impacts

Evidence suggests that education and health programs targeting young children can have strong impacts on overall human development outcomes. Some of the most compelling evidence for this comes from Guatemala, where nutritional intervention and micronutrient supplementation before 3 years of age showed beneficial effects on schooling, reading, and intelligence tests in adulthood (25–42 years).[91] Some evaluations show significant improvements in cognitive and learning outcomes among children who benefited from CCT programs before they entered school.[92] At every level of income, households with young children receiving the cash transfers were more likely to read, tell stories, and sing to their children and to have books, paper, and pencils for them to use at home.[93] This is an important result because early cognitive development was a strong predictor of school attainment in Brazil, Guatemala, Jamaica, the Philippines, and South Africa, even after controlling for wealth and mother's education.[94]

Children who qualify for CCTs benefit most from schooling at an early age. In Ecuador, most children at age 3 in the sample were only modestly behind the reference population on a test of cognitive development.[95] By age 6, however, when they entered first grade, children in the two poorest deciles of the national distribution of wealth were almost three standard deviations behind where they should be—and have almost no chance of catching up. Remedial investments targeting them therefore need to make equity–efficiency tradeoffs; investments in early childhood are more likely to avoid such tradeoffs.[96] Similarly, the results reported above on the impact of nutrition programs on growth and micronutrient status suggest larger impacts among small children. Despite this evidence, there is some debate over which age group CCTs should target to ensure that school-age children also benefit.[97]

Service delivery often fails the poor

A recent study reports results from surveys in which enumerators made unannounced visits to primary schools and health clinics in Bangladesh, Ecuador, India, Indonesia, Peru, and Uganda. They recorded whether they found teachers and health workers in the facilities.[98] On average, about 19 percent of teachers and 35 percent of health workers were absent, and many teachers and health workers in their facilities were not working. Across Indian government-run schools, only 45 percent of teachers assigned to a school were engaged in teaching at any given time. In Ghana, Morocco, Tunisia, and the Brazilian state of Pernambuco[99] the instructional time teachers allocated to learning tasks ranged from 78 percent in Tunisia to 39 percent in Ghana.

Observational data for a sample of doctors in New Delhi, India, showed differences between the levels of expertise and quality of care provided among private doctors who serve the rich and the poor. Poorer patients receive low-quality advice and spend a fair amount of money on unnecessary (and often substandard) drugs. Wealthier patients get better advice, both because they see more competent providers and because their providers put in more effort.[100]

Why are incentives weak and accountability low among service providers in developing countries? One reason is the highly centralized and bureaucratic education and health systems. Hiring, salaries, and promotion decisions are made at the center, determined largely by educational qualifications and seniority, with almost no scope for performance-based pay. Governments find it difficult to monitor the performance of health workers, especially those providing highly discretionary services such as clinical care. Furthermore, teachers and health workers are typically organized interest groups that can be politically influential. These factors imply that disciplinary action for poor performance is rare and that teachers and health workers are almost never fired. In addition, asymmetric information between client and provider (especially strong for health services) makes accountability difficult.

These problems are almost never addressed through the long route of accountability—through political pressure that consumers exert on the government. One possible reason poor performance of service providers is not on the political agenda: providers are an organized interest group, and clients, particularly in health, are diffuse. Those who are poor enough to use public schools and public clinics have less political power than do middle-class teachers and health workers. In many countries, even those moderately well off send their children to private schools and use private clinics. Even when part of the population chooses private providers instead of public ones, public money keeps flowing into public schools and hospitals. Hence, the cycle of weak accountability and weak incentives continues.

New approaches are being designed to improve the critical link of service delivery

As seen in figure 3.4, service delivery is the link between generation and consumption of goods and services. Empirical evidence from microeconomic studies has shown that this link is often weak in developing countries—an important reason why public spending on inputs and demand-side interventions does not translate into commensurate human development outcomes. What explains the service delivery weaknesses?

The following issues stand out: inequitably low allocations to services reaching low-income groups, leaks of funding between central ministries and frontline providers, and failures of frontline providers such as teachers and doctors to perform effectively. Impact evaluations have highlighted and explored solutions on the last of those three points.[101] It has been argued that frontline service providers' weak incentives and low accountability in developing countries often translates into ineffective service delivery.[102] New service delivery approaches attempt to solve the incentive and accountability issues while reducing the need for (onerous) monitoring by the government and the citizenry. These approaches can be classified under three headings: information for accountability, greater citizen accountability and autonomy in service provision, and pay for performance.[103]

Information to increase accountability can be effective in some contexts

To hold their service providers accountable, poor people need information on their rights and on how well their service providers are performing. Furthermore, availability of information on service delivery performance provides the means to monitor progress. In recent years, programs have been designed to provide citizens with this information in the hope that it will enable them to hold service providers accountable. This has been easier to do in education than in health because of the nature of the services.[104]

Citizen report cards provide clients with simple information on how well local service providers are doing. In Pakistan, providing parents with report cards containing information about the relative performance of children and schools in the village (including private schools) improved student performance in public schools and lower-quality private schools and reduced fees at higher-quality private schools.[105]

Elsewhere, impact evaluations of similar programs have shown less direct results. For example, a Liberian program that publicized to parents the results of an early-grade reading assessment and showed teachers how to prepare quarterly report cards for parents showed very little impact on learning after two years. But when the information on student reading skills was combined with intensive teacher training, student performance improved dramatically.[106] Similarly in Chile, publicizing rankings of school quality by region did not appear to affect school performance.[107]

A large information campaign in Uganda used school display boards and newspapers to provide information to parents and communities on the exact amount of operational funding each school could expect and the date when the funding transfer to the school would be made. The campaign was associated with a sharp reduction in the leak of school grants expenditures.[108] The researchers also documented that schools in districts with higher media exposure experienced greater increases in enrollments and higher test scores on the primary-school exit exam than did schools in districts with lower media exposure.

Another dimension of information for accountability, tested in two studies in India,

yielded mixed results. In both studies, villagers were provided with information about their rights and responsibilities for education provision and oversight. One part of the country showed no impact from providing information alone,[109] and a different part of the country showed some impact on student learning through improved service provision by teachers.[110]

It seems clear that, although providing information for accountability to citizens may be important, it is ineffective to simply give communities information on school quality without also increasing their ability to take action.

Greater citizen accountability and autonomy in service provision show promise

Parents and community leaders have information about local service providers and local service delivery that centralized systems tend to ignore. Involving them in decision making with system actors (teachers, head teachers, doctors, and nurses) can better align spending with local needs. Greater autonomy and accountability of local service delivery can increase incentives to adopt proven successful practices; evaluate the effectiveness of home-grown initiatives; and build a sense of commitment, ownership, and pride. But there are also risks, including limited information, narrow interests, elite capture, and inadequate representation of the disadvantaged. Increasingly, development practitioners are experimenting with ways to increase the autonomy of local stakeholders in service provision. Again, this model has been evaluated more in education than in health.

One way to increase accountability is to give local communities resources and training to manage service provision, an approach tried in school-based management programs that give local communities decision-making power and resources for school management. Studies show a positive impact on how schools are managed and how teachers, head-teachers, and parents interact, but they reveal no consistent improvement in student performance.

For example, school-based management in Mexico has a positive impact on teacher behavior and school management,[111] but little impact on student performance.[112] A similar program in Nepal showed a significant impact on access and equity; the impact on school governance measures was mixed, with regional variation in outcomes; and there was no evidence that the changes were associated with improvements in learning outcomes.[113]

There has been considerable work on hospital autonomy and the impacts of decentralized management on hospital performance, but the analyses have rarely had any controlled or quasi-experimental design to control for a counterfactual. This is partly because hospital autonomy is usually implemented with many other management reforms, making it difficult to isolate autonomy from management capacity and system improvements.

Another approach is to give clients more control over service providers. In western Kenya, giving parents stronger oversight over teachers improved student performance when combined with other reforms. And the effect on student performance of hiring extra teachers can be greater when school committees are given training on how to supervise and manage teachers; the effect was largest among the students assigned to a contract teacher (as opposed to a civil servant). In India, local communities' hiring of contract teachers (who were younger and less qualified) at lower salaries than those received by regular teachers by improved student performance.[114] But very little is known about the long-term effects of contract teachers, and such a system is unlikely to be sustainable over a long period.

Again, the evidence on school-based management is inconclusive. More impact evaluations are needed, particularly on the pathways that translate this kind of decentralization into better school quality.

Pay for performance holds great promise, but more evidence is needed

Performance-based bonuses that reward schools and teachers for improving student outcomes have been introduced in diverse settings (such as India, Israel, and Kenya), and all have positive impacts on student learning

outcomes. In some cases (such as in India),[115] individual bonuses led to larger improvements in student outcomes, whereas group bonuses had lower implementation costs. That suggests some cost–benefit trade-offs between the two. In Chile's National System of School Performance, group bonuses also yielded quite modest impacts. In more detail, one evaluation of the system found a modest cumulative positive effect on student achievement for schools that had a higher probability of winning the bonus,[116] and a positive effect on student test scores.[117]

Some evaluations suggest uncertainty about the duration of benefits. In Kenya, group-based incentives for teachers improved student performance but the gains were short-lived.[118] Other settings suggest that the targets are important. In the Brazilian state of Pernambuco, during the first year, schools with more ambitious targets made significantly larger test score gains than did similarly performing comparison schools assigned lower targets. In the second year—with controls for schools' 2008 test results and other school characteristics—schools that barely missed the threshold for getting the bonus in 2008 improved more than schools that barely achieved it. It appears that both higher targets and barely missed bonus achievement created incentives that had a positive effect on school motivation and performance.[119]

Two other evaluated programs rewarded teachers for attendance. One allowed school heads in rural Kenya to give individual teachers bonus pay for regular attendance (measured by unannounced random visits).[120] But they simply distributed the full bonus to all teachers, regardless of attendance. The inability or unwillingness of the head teacher to enforce the performance bonus to reward regular attendance explained the lack of impact on attendance as well as the absence of change in teacher pedagogy, pupil attendance, or pupil test scores.

A program in rural India, however, produced very different results.[121] In randomly selected rural schools run by nongovernmental organizations, a schedule of monthly teacher bonuses and fines based on attendance was monitored with daily date-stamped and time-stamped photographs. The maximum bonus for a teacher with no days absent was about 25 percent of a month's salary. The program had a dramatic effect on teacher absenteeism over three years. Although there were no observed changes in teachers' classroom behavior and pedagogy (other than greater presence), student test scores and rates of graduation to the next level of education rose significantly. The program was also quite cost effective.

In health care, paying for performance is designed to provide financial rewards for providers who increase service delivery and improve the quality of care. To date, the experience has been promising, but there is little evidence from evaluations using credible comparison groups—in fact, a recent review of the literature finds methodological limitations that constrain the ability to interpret the results as causal impacts of pay for performance.[122] Several studies without comparison groups found increases in service delivery indicators, such as immunization and attended deliveries (as in Haiti),[123] and in the number of curative consultations and institutional deliveries (as in early pilot programs in Rwanda).[124]

A quasi-experimental study in Cambodia found service delivery improvements among contracted providers, but the providers received significantly more resources than did the control groups—suggesting that it was potentially the additional resources (the resource effect) rather than pay for performance (the incentive effect) that explained these findings.[125] This raises an important policy issue: if pay for performance achieves its results from increased financial resources rather than incentives, the same results could be achieved from an increase in traditional inputs, and there would be no reason to incur the administrative costs associated with pay for performance.

The only impact evaluation in a low-resource setting that has been able to separate the incentive effect from the resource effect is a recent one of the Rwanda health center pay-for-performance program targeting maternal and child health outcomes. The incentive effect was isolated from the resource effect by increasing comparison facilities' budgets by the average payments made to the treatment facilities. The evaluation shows the greatest impact on those services that had the highest payment rates (institutional deliveries) and that needed the lowest provider effort (preventive care visits by young children).[126] Financial performance incentives improved both the use and quality of health services.

Future directions

Development practitioners need to do much more rigorous empirical work—particularly, impact evaluations—to come closer to answering critical questions of development effectiveness. But the start has been promising. Indeed, a recent review of CCTs concludes that no new research is needed on whether households—particularly, poor households—respond to conditions or incentives.[127]

Other questions remain unresolved or underaddressed—for example, the size of the incentive and its influence on the size of the impact,[128] complementary supply-side interventions or investments, payment frequency, means of payment, and other features of program design (such as how frequently conditions should be monitored, the gender of the cash transfer recipient, and whether to penalize noncomplying households).

A systematic base of impact evaluations of different interventions, in different contexts, will go a long way in moving toward evidence-based decision making and in making public spending more effective to close the remaining gaps in education and health outcomes in developing countries. Some topics, such as maternal mortality, are underrepresented in the impact evaluation literature—a critical shortcoming given that this coincides with the MDG that is least likely to be achieved. Also needed is more work on designing impact evaluations that have a basis in theory and provide useful information on whether and why programs work.

The evidence suggests that service delivery for education and health is weak in developing countries. But very little is known about the best ways to measure and strengthen this critical link in the results chain. Exploring new and different approaches to measure and improve service delivery is one of the most promising areas for future work—especially, comparative evaluations that assess alternative models of implementation.

Cost and cost effectiveness should be an explicit part of evaluation design. There rarely is discussion of the costs to achieve particular impacts. What magnitude of impact justifies the cost, or is it impact at any cost? Information to implement at scale is often missing, with no indication of the institutional investments to feasibly implement smaller experiments at scale. This lack of information on program costs and investments hampers decision making and implementing at scale.

More work is also needed on the political economy surrounding the use of empirical evidence to inform policy. Should donors invest more in impact evaluation and intervention design to improve political incentives and government interventions? How can governments be encouraged to pursue policies that strengthen service delivery (by improving the incentives of providers, among other things)? Some evidence on these issues is emerging. For example, enabling less-educated people in Brazil to use electronic voting technologies increased their political participation, shifted public spending toward public health care, improved service use by less-educated mothers, and thus reduced low-weight births.[129] Public spending on primary education rose in Africa when countries moved to greater multiparty competition.[130] A similar association between electoral competition and education spending has been found in Indian states.[131] But mobilizing communities may have little impact on public provider accountability if communities are severely constrained in taking public action.[132]

Interest is growing in demand-side financing approaches and more explicit use of incentives for service providers to improve performance. On the demand side, the massive increase in CCTs has improved human development outcomes. Similarly, vouchers received increased prominence in health and education. On the supply side, performance-based financing and pay for performance

have improved the performance of service delivery units in education and health.

Policy makers are realizing that continuing to spend ever-greater funds on health and education without quality improvements will neither bring their countries closer to the MDGs nor greatly improve human development outcomes among poor people. More supply-side subsidies for health and education services are not always the answer. The problems of supply-side dominance are, among others, weak targeting of the poor, lack of consumer choice, absence of links between provider payment and performance, weak incentives for service quality, and weak accountability to consumers. Supply-side effects have dominated planning—and too many multilateral development banks, including the World Bank, are guilty of this. Resource-needs projection models too often ignore the evidence suggesting a tenuous relationship between increased health expenditure and outcomes.

The stronger and more explicit focus on incentives in the health and education literature is encouraging. The modest human development results do not stem from a shortage of technical solutions. But a principal finding of this review is that simply increasing the size of interventions may not be enough to make adequate progress. Even where access and use have been expanded, human development outcomes have not necessarily improved (as the experience with CCTs suggests). Establishing appropriate incentives for suppliers and consumers, ensuring adequate provision of services to meet demand, ensuring that suppliers are accountable to consumers for the quality of service, and providing sufficient resources to poor consumers are all necessary to have an appreciable impact on human development outcomes.

Notes

1. See, for example, Filmer, Hammer, and Pritchett (1998) and Burnside and Dollar (1998). Baldacci, Guin-Siu, and de Mello (2002) conclude that the links between outcomes and public spending are stronger for education than for health. Gupta,

Verhoeven, and Tiongson (2003) disaggregated the impact on the outcomes of the poor, and found (as did Bidani and Rivallion [1997]), that the poor have worse health outcomes than the nonpoor and that public spending has a larger impact on the health outcomes of the poor than the nonpoor.

2. "Basic immunization" here refers to diphtheria, pertussis, and tetanus vaccination. Median coverage in low-income countries increased from 62 percent to 81 percent between 2000 and 2008 (WHO 2010).

3. Hanushek and Woessmann 2008.

4 Pratham Organization 2005.

5. WHO 2008. Full immunization refers to basic immunization plus measles and polio vaccination.

6. WHO 2010.

7. World Bank/AERC 2010.

8. See, for example, Van de Walle (1995), Castro-Leal et al. (1999), Mahal et al. (2000), Sahn and Younger (2000), and O'Donnell et al. (2007).

9. A complete discussion of impact evaluation methodologies can be found in Gertler et al. (2010).

10. See, for example, Rodrik (2008), Ravallion (2009), Deaton (2009), Sims (2010), and Angrist and Pischke (2010).

11. Deaton 2009.

12. Ibid.

13. See Kremer and Zwane (2007) for a review of water and sanitation literature on preventing diarrheal diseases.

14. Kremer and Holla 2009.

15. Kremer, Moulin, and Namunyu 2003.

16. Vermeersch and Kremer 2004; Kazianga, de Walque, and Alderman 2009; Meng and Ryan 2010; Powell et al. 1998.

17. Schultz 2004.

18. See, for example, Cardoso and Souza (2004), Levy and Ohls (2007), Barrera-Osorio et al. (2008), and Filmer and Schady (2008).

19. Barrera-Osorio, Linden, and Urquiola 2007; Borkum 2009.

20. Hanushek 2008.

21. See the review in Kremer and Holla (2009).

22. It should be noted that a recent study (not an impact evaluation) from Egypt (Hanushek, Lavy, and Hitomi 2008) has shown that school dropout decisions are very responsive to the quality of the school.

23. Afridi 2007; Jacoby, Cueto, and Pollitt 1996

24. Kazianga, de Walque, and Alderman 2009.

25. Vermeersch and Kremer 2004.

26. Clarke et al. 2008.

27. Temperley et al. 2008.

28. Pop-Eleches et al. 2011.

29. Admassie, Abebaw, and Woldemichael 2009.

30. Banerjee et al. 2010.

31. Regalía and Castro 2009.

32. For a detailed review of this debate, see Kremer and Holla (2008).

33. Ashraf, Berry, and Shapiro 2007.

34. World Bank 2003.

35. Cohen and Dupas 2010.

36. Kremer and Miguel 2007.

37. Ibid.

38. In this regard, the vast body of health financing and, specifically, the health insurance literature (although not explicitly captured in this chapter) is an important source of information.

39. Fiszbein and Schady 2009.

40. Paxson and Schady 2007.

41. Barber and Gertler 2010.

42. Filmer and Schady 2009.

43. World Bank 2009, p. 182.

44. Schultz 2004; de Janvry, Final, and Sadoulet 2006; Filmer and Schady 2010.

45. Edmonds and Schady 2009; Edmonds 2006; Case, Hosegood, and Lund 2005; Duflo 2003.

46. de Brauw and Hoddinott 2008; Schady and Araujo 2008.

47. Baird, McIntosh, and Özler 2011.

48. Nguyen 2008.

49. Jensen 2010.

50. Jalan and Somanathan 2008.

51. Madajewicz et al. 2007.

52. Dupas 2009.

53. Downs, Loewenstein, and Wisdom 2009; Davis et al. 2009.

54. Bertrand et al. 2006; Medley et al. 2009.

55. Duflo et al. 2006.

56. Dupas 2006, 2009.

57. For a full review, see Kremer and Holla (2009).

58. Glewwe, Kremer, and Moulin 2007. The authors argue that problems with the education system as a whole constrained the impact of increasing inputs. For example, textbooks are written in English (most students' third language) and many students could not use them effectively. More generally, the curriculum in Kenya and in many other developing countries tends to be oriented toward academically strong students.

59. Glewwe et al. 2004.

60. Vermeersch and Kremer 2004; Kazianga, de Walque, and Alderman 2009.
61. Newman et al. 2002.
62. Banerjee et al. 2005.
63. Duflo, Dupas, and Kremer 2007; Kremer, Moulin, and Namunyu 2003; Banerjee et al. 2005; Banerjee et al. 2007.
64. Jamison, Searle, Galda, and Heyneman 1981.
65. Banerjee et al. 2007.
66. He, Linden, and MacLeod 2007.
67. Barrera-Osorio and Linden 2009.
68. Banerjee et al. 2010.
69. Chile (Galasso 2006); Honduras (Morris et al. 2004); Jamaica (Levy and Ohls 2007); Mexico (Gertler and Boyce 2001); Nicaragua (Maluccio and Flores 2005); Paraguay (Soares, Ribas, and Hirata 2008).
70. Nicaragua (Barham and Maluccio 2008); Turkey (Ahmed et al. 2007).
71. Nicaragua (Macours, Schady, and Vakis 2008); Honduras (Hoddinott 2008); Brazil (Morris et al. 2004); Ecuador (Paxson and Schady 2008).
72. Attanasio et al. 2005.
73. The increase in institutional deliveries and a smaller increase in home delivery with a skilled birth attendant suggest that part of the increase in the number of births in facilities resulted from shifting births that otherwise would have occurred at home with a skilled attendant (Lim et al. 2010).
74. Among others, see Schultz (2004), Cardoso and Souza (2004), Levy and Ohls (2007), Barrera-Osorio et al. (2008), and Filmer and Schady (2008).
75. Miguel and Kremer 2004; Glewwe, Kremer, and Moulin 2007.
76. Baird et al. 2010.
77. Filmer and Schady 2009.
78. Growth monitoring services include weighing children at regular intervals during the first few years after birth and tracking growth against expected growth at a given age.
79. Mexico (Behrman and Hoddinott 2001; Gertler 2004; and Rivera et al. 2004); Colombia (Mesnard 2005); Nicaragua (Maluccio and Flores 2005); Colombia (Attanasio et al. 2005).
80. Rivera et al. 2004; Attanasio et al. 2005; Maluccio and Flores 2005.
81. Morris et al. (2004).
82. Caldés, Coady, and Maluccio 2006.
83. It is curious that weighing and growth monitoring featured so prominently in the CCTs because the epidemiologic evidence of the impact of growth monitoring on nutritional outcomes is weak. This may explain the mixed findings. "Available evidence on growth monitoring was not sufficient to support its use alone (without adequate nutrition counseling and referrals) as an essential nutrition support" (Bhutta et al. 2008, p. 429). See also Roberfroid et al. (2005); Garner et al. (2000); and Ashworth, Shrimpton, and Jamil (2008).
84. Rivera et al. 2004; Gertler 2004.
85. Behrman and Hoddinott 2001.
86. Adato and Roopnaraine 2004.
87. Leroy, Marie, and Verhofstadt 2009.
88. Schady and Rosero 2008.
89. Macours, Schady, and Vakis 2008.
90. Other ways are available to increase incentives facing providers by changing the way in which budgets or provider payments are structured. Thus, although improving incentives may be a useful side effect of voucher systems, it may be quite a costly option.
91. Behrman and Hoddinott 2001.
92. Ecuador (Paxson and Schady 2008); Nicaragua (Macours, Schady, and Vakis 2008).
93. Macours, Schady, and Vakis 2008.
94. Grantham-McGregor et al. 2007.
95. Paxson and Schady 2008.
96. This is consistent with the conclusion reached by Cunha and Heckman (2010), as well as a recent World Bank publication on early childhood development (Alderman 2011).
97. Worldwide, a worrying dropout occurs in the transition to secondary school. Attanasio et al. (2005) argue that eliminating the funding transfers to children in grade six and below and using those resources to increase the size of the transfer to children in grade seven and beyond would double school participation among the older children, with no effect on school participation by younger ones.
98. Chaudhury et al. 2006.
99. Abadzi 2009.
100. Das and Hammer 2005.
101. A detailed discussion is in *World Development Report 2004* (World Bank 2003).
102. World Bank 2003.
103. This classification comes from the recent work on school accountability done by Bruns, Filmer, and Patrinos (2011).
104. The most important differences between education and health services are because of information asymmetry and the relative infrequency of contact between health providers and their patients.

105. Andrabi, Das, and Khwaja 2009.
106. Piper and Korda 2010.
107. Mizala, Romaguera, and Urquiola 2007.
108. Reinikka and Svensson 2005, 2006; Björkman 2006; Björkman and Svensson 2009.
109. Banerjee et al. 2010.
110. Pandey et al. 2010.
111. Banerjee et al. 2010.
112. Skoufias and Shapiro 2006; Gertler, Patrinos, and Rubio-Codina 2006.
113. Chaudhury and Parajuli 2010.
114. Muralidharan and Sundararaman 2009; Goyal and Pandey 2009.
115. Muralidharan and Sundararaman 2009.
116. Mizala, Romaguera, and Urquiola 2007.
117. Gallego 2008.
118. Glewwe, Ilas, and Kremer 2003.
119. Ferraz and Bruns forthcoming.
120. Kremer and Chen 2001.
121. Duflo, Hanna, and Ryan 2010.
122. Eldridge and Palmer 2009.
123. Eichler et al. 2007.
124. Meessen, Kashala, and Musango 2007; Meessen et al. 2006; Soeters, Habineza, and Peerenboom 2006.
125. Schwartz and Bhushan 2004.
126. Basinga et al. 2010.
127. Gaarder, Glassman, and Todd 2010.
128. Filmer and Schady (2009), in the context of education enrollment, conclude that there are diminishing returns to the size of incentives.
129. Fujiwara 2010.
130. Stasavage 2005.
131. Khemani 2010.
132. Banerjee et al. 2010.

References

Abadzi, H. 2009. "Instructional Time Loss in Developing Countries: Concepts, Measurement, and Implications." *World Bank Research Observer* 24 (2): 267–90.

Adato, M., and T. Roopnaraine. 2004. "Sistema de evaluación de la Red de Protección Social de Nicaragua: Un análisis social de la 'Red de Protección Social' (RPS) en Nicaragua." International Food Policy Research Institute, Washington, DC.

Admassie, A., D. Abebaw, and A. Woldemichael. 2009. "Impact Evaluation of the Ethiopian Health Services Extension Programme." *Journal of Development Effectiveness* 1 (4): 430–49.

Afridi, F. 2007. "Child Welfare Programs and Child Nutrition: Evidence from a Mandated School Meal Program in India." *Journal of Development Economics* 92 (2): 152–65.

Ahmed, A., M. Adato, A. Kudat, D. Gilligan, and R. Colasan. 2006. "Interim Impact Evaluation of the Conditional Cash Transfer Program in Turkey. Final Report." International Food Policy Research Institute, Washington, DC.

Alderman, H., ed. 2011. *No Small Matter: The Impact of Poverty, Shocks, and Human Capital Investments in Early Childhood Development.* Washington, DC: World Bank.

Andrabi, T., J. Das, and A. Khwaja. 2009. "Report Cards: The Impact of Providing School and Child Test Scores on Educational Markets." Unpublished manuscript, World Bank, Washington, DC.

Angrist, J. D., and J. Pischke. 2010. "The Credibility Revolution in Empirical Economics: How Better Research Design Is Taking the Con Out of Econometrics" *Journal of Economic Perspectives* 24 (2): 3–30.

Ashraf, N., J. Berry, and J. M. Shapiro. 2007. "Can Higher Prices Stimulate Product Use? Evidence from a Field Experiment in Zambia." Working Paper 13247, National Bureau of Economic Research, Cambridge, MA.

Ashworth, A., R. Shrimpton, and K. Jamil. 2008. "Growth Monitoring and Promotion: Review of Evidence of Impact." *Maternal and Child Nutrition* 4 (Suppl 1): 86–117.

Attanasio, O., E. Battistin, E. Fitzsimmons, A. Mesnard, and M. Vera-Hernández. 2005. "How Effective Are Conditional Cash Transfers? Evidence from Colombia." Briefing Note 54, Institute for Fiscal Studies, London.

Baird, S., E. Chirwa, C. McIntosh, and B. Özler. 2010. "The Short-Term Impacts of a Schooling Conditional Cash Transfer Program on the Sexual Behavior of Young Women." *Health Economics* 19: 55–68.

Baird, S., C. McIntosh, and B. Özler. 2011. "Cash or Condition? Evidence from a Cash Transfer Experiment." Policy Research Working Paper 5259, World Bank, Washington, DC.

Baldacci, E., M. Guin-Siu, and L. de Mello. 2002. "More on the Effectiveness of Public Spending on Health Care and Education: A Covariance Structure Model." Working Paper WP/02/90, International Monetary Fund, Washington DC.

Banerjee, A. V., R. Banerji, E. Duflo, R. Glennerster, and S. Khemani. 2010. "Pitfalls of

Participatory Programs: Evidence from a Randomized Evaluation in Education in India." *American Economic Journal: Economic Policy* 2 (1): 1–30.

Banerjee, A., E. Duflo, S. Cole, and L. Linden. 2007. "Remedying Education: Evidence from Two Randomized Experiments in India." *Quarterly Journal of Economics* 122 (3): 1235–64.

Banerjee, A., E. Duflo, R. Glennerster, and D. Kothari. 2010. "Improving Immunisation Coverage in Rural India: Clustered Randomised Controlled Evaluation of Immunisation Campaigns With and Without Incentives." *British Medical Journal* 340 (1): c2220.

Banerjee, A., S. Jacob, and M. Kremer, with J. Lanjouw, and P. Lanjouw. 2005. "Promoting School Participation in Rural Rajasthan: Results from Some Prospective Trials." Unpublished manuscript, Massachusetts Institute of Technology, Cambridge, MA.

Barber, S. L., and P. J. Gertler. 2010. "Empowering Women: How Mexico's Conditional Cash Transfer Program Raised Prenatal Care Quality and Birth Weight." *Journal of Development Effectiveness* 2 (1): 51–73.

Barham, T., and J. Maluccio. 2008. "The Effect of Conditional Cash Transfers on Vaccination Coverage in Nicaragua." Health and Society Working Paper HS2008-01, Institute of Behavioral Science, University of Colorado, Boulder, CO.

Barrera-Osorio, F., M. Bertrand, L. L. Linden, and F. Perez-Calle. 2008. "Conditional Cash Transfers in Education: Design Features, Peer and Sibling Effects Evidence from a Randomized Experiment in Colombia." Policy Research Working Paper 4580, World Bank, Washington, DC.

Barrera-Osorio, F., and L. L Linden. 2009. "The Use and Misuse of Computers in Education: Evidence from a Randomized Experiment in Colombia." Policy Research Working Paper 4836, World Bank, Washington, DC.

Barrera-Osorio, F., L. L Linden, and, M. Urquiola. 2007. "The Effects of User Fee Reductions on Enrollment: Evidence from a Quasi-Experiment." Working Paper, Columbia University, New York.

Basinga P., P. J. Gertler, A. Binagwaho, A. Soucat, J. Sturdy, and C. Vermeersch. 2010. "Paying Primary Health Care Centers for Performance in Rwanda." Policy Research Working Paper 5190, World Bank, Washington, DC.

Behrman, J., and J. Hoddinott. 2001. "An Evaluation of the Impact of *Progresa* on Pre-school child Height." Discussion Paper 104, International Food Policy Research Institute, Washington, DC.

Bertrand, J. T., K. O'Reilly, J. Denison, R. Anhang, and M. Sweat. 2006. "Systematic Review of the Effectiveness of Mass Communication Programs to Change HIV/AIDS-related Behaviors in Developing Countries." *Health Education Research* 21 (4): 567–97.

Bhutta, Z., T. Ahmed, R. Black, S. Cousens, K. Dewey, E. Giugliani, B. Haider, B. Kirkwood, S. Morris, H. P. S. Sachdev, and M. Shekar. 2008. "What Works? Interventions for Maternal and Child Undernutrition and Survival." *Lancet* 371: 417–40.

Bidani, B., and M. Ravallion. 1997. "Decomposing Social Indicators Using Distributional Data." *Journal of Econometrics* 77 (1): 125–39.

Björkman, M. 2006. "Does Money Matter for Student Performance? Evidence from a Grant Program in Uganda." Working Paper 326, Institute for International Economic Studies, Stockholm University, Sweden.

Björkman, M., and J. Svensson. 2009. "Power to the People: Evidence from a Randomized Experiment of a Community-based Monitoring Project in Uganda." *Quarterly Journal of Economics* 124: 734–69.

Bobonis, G., and F. Finan. 2009. "Neighborhood Peer Effects in Secondary School Enrollment Decisions." *Review of Economics and Statistics* 91 (4): 695–716.

Borkum, E. 2009. "Can Eliminating School Fees in Poor Districts Boost Enrollment? Evidence from South Africa." Discussion Paper 0910-06, Columbia University, New York.

Bruns, B., D. Filmer, and H. A. Patrinos. 2011. *Making Schools Work: New Evidence on Accountability Reforms.* Washington, DC: World Bank.

Burnside, C., and D. Dollar. 1998. "Aid, the Incentive Regime, and Poverty Reduction." Policy Research Working Paper 1937, World Bank, Washington, DC.

Caldés, N., D. Coady, and J. Maluccio. 2006. "The Cost of Poverty Alleviation Transfer Programs: A Comparative Analysis of Three Programs in Latin America." *World Development* 34 (5): 818–37.

Cardoso, E., and A. Souza. 2004. "The Impact of Cash Transfers on Child Labor and School Attendance in Brazil." Working Paper 04-W07,

Department of Economics, Vanderbilt University, Nashville, TN.

Case, A., V. Hosegood, and F. Lund. 2005. "The Reach and Impact of Child Support Grants: Evidence from KwaZulu-Natal." *Development Southern Africa* 22: 467–82

Castro-Leal, F., J. Dayton, L. Demery, and K. Mehra. 1999. "Public Social Spending in Africa: Do the Poor Benefit?" *World Bank Research Observer* 14 (1): 49–72.

Chaudhury, N., J. Hammer, M. Kremer, K. Muralidharan, and F. H. Rogers. 2006. "Missing in Action: Teacher and Health Worker Absence in Developing Countries." *Journal of Economic Perspectives* 20 (1): 91–116.

Chaudhury, N., and D. Parajuli. 2010. "Giving It Back: Evaluating the Impact of Devolution of School Management to Communities in Nepal." Unpublished manuscript, World Bank, Washington, DC.

Clarke, S. E., M. C. H. Jukes, K. Njagi, L. Khasakhala, B. Cundill, J. Otido, C. Crudder, B. Estambale, and S. Brooker. 2008. "Effect of Intermittent Preventive Treatment on Health and Education in Schoolchildren: A Cluster-Randomised, Double-Blind, Placebo-Controlled Trial." *Lancet* 372: 127–38.

Cohen, J., and P. Dupas. 2010. "Free Distribution or Cost-Sharing? Evidence from a Randomized Malaria Prevention Experiment." *Quarterly Journal of Economics* 125 (1): 1–45.

Cohen, J., P. Dupas, and S. Schaner. 2010. "Prices, Diagnostic Tests and the Demand for Malaria Treatment: Evidence from a Randomized Trial." Working Paper, Harvard University, Cambridge, MA.

Cunha, F., and J. Heckman. 2010. "Investing in Our Young People." Working Paper 16201, National Bureau of Economic Research, Cambridge, MA.

Das, J., and J. Hammer. 2005. "Money for Nothing: The Dire Straits of Medical Practice in Delhi, India." Policy Research Paper 3669, World Bank, Washington, DC.

Davis, K. C., M. C. Farrelly, P. Messeri, and J. Duke. 2009. "The Impact of National Smoking Prevention Campaigns on Tobacco-Related Beliefs, Intentions to Smoke and Smoking Initiation: Results from a Longitudinal Survey of Youth in the United States." *International Journal of Environmental Research and Public Health* 6 (2): 722–40.

Deaton, A. 2009. "Instruments of Development: Randomization in the Tropics, and the Search for the Elusive Keys to Economic Development." Working Paper 14690, National Bureau of Economic Research, Cambridge, MA.

de Brauw, A., and J. Hoddinott. 2008. "Must Conditional Cash Transfer Programs Be Conditioned to Be Effective? The Impact of Conditioning Transfers on School Enrollment in Mexico." Discussion Paper 757, International Food Policy Research Institute, Washington, DC.

de Janvry, A., F. Finan, and E. Sadoulet. 2006. "Can Conditional Cash Transfer Programs Serve as Safety Nets in Keeping Children in School and from Working When Exposed to Shocks?" *Journal of Development Economics* 79: 349–73.

de Walque, D., H. Kazianga, and M. Over. 2010. "Antiretroviral Therapy Awareness and Risky Sexual Behaviors: Evidence from Mozambique." Policy Research Working Paper 5486, World Bank, Washington, DC.

Downs, J. S., G. Loewenstein, and J. Wisdom. 2009. "Strategies for Promoting Healthier Food Choices." *American Economic Review* 99 (2): 159–64.

Duflo, E. 2003. "Grandmothers and Granddaughters: Old-Age Pension and Intrahousehold Allocation in South Africa." *World Bank Economic Review* 17: 1–25.

Duflo, E., P. Dupas, and M. Kremer. 2007. "Peer Effects, Pupil-teacher Ratios, and Teacher Incentives." Unpublished manuscript, Harvard University, Cambridge, MA.

Duflo, E., P. Dupas, M. Kremer, and S. Sinei. 2006. "Education and HIV/AIDS Prevention: Evidence from a Randomized Evaluation in Western Kenya." Policy Research Working Paper 4024, World Bank, Washington, DC.

Duflo, E., R. Hanna, and S. Ryan. 2010. "Incentives Work: Getting Teachers to Come to School." Unpublished manuscript, University of Chicago, Chicago, IL.

Dupas, P. 2006. "Relative Risks and the Market for Sex: Teenagers, Sugar Daddies, and HIV in Kenya." Unpublished manuscript, Dartmouth College, Hanover, NH.

———. 2009. "Do Teenagers Respond to HIV Risk Information? Evidence from a Field Experiment in Kenya." Working Paper 14707, National Bureau of Economic Research, Cambridge, MA.

Edmonds, E. V. 2006. "Child Labor and Schooling Responses to Anticipated Income Shock in

South Africa." *Journal of Development Economics* 81: 386–414.

Edmonds, E. V., and N. Schady. 2009. "Poverty Alleviation and Child Labor." Working Paper 15345, National Bureau of Economic Research, Cambridge, MA.

Eichler, R., P. Auxila, A. Uder, and B. Desmangles. 2007. "Performance-Based Incentives for Health: Six Years of Results from Supply-Side Programs in Haiti." Working Paper 121, Center for Global Development, Washington, DC.

Eldridge, C., and N. Palmer. 2009. "Performance-Based Payment: Some Reflections on the Discourse, Evidence and Unanswered Questions." *Health Policy and Planning* 24 (3): 160–66.

Ferraz, C., and B. Bruns. Forthcoming. "Incentives to Teach: The Effects of Performance Pay in Brazilian Schools." World Bank, Washington, DC.

Filmer, D. 2003. "The Incidence of Public Expenditure on Health and Education." Background Note for *World Development Report 2004*, World Bank, Washington, DC.

Filmer, D., J. Hammer, and L. Pritchett. 1998. "Health Policy in Poor Countries: Weak Links in the Chain?" Policy Research Working Paper 1874, World Bank, Washington, DC.

Filmer, D., and N. Schady. 2008. "Getting Girls into School: Evidence from a Scholarship Program in Cambodia." *Economic Development and Cultural Change* 56: 581–617.

———. 2009. "Are There Diminishing Returns to Transfer Size in Conditional Cash Transfers?" Policy Research Working Paper 4999, World Bank, Washington, DC.

———. 2010. "Does More Cash in Conditional Cash Transfer Programs Always Lead to Larger Impacts on School Attendance?" *Journal of Development Economics*.

Fiszbein, A., and N. Schady. 2009. *Conditional Cash Transfers: Reducing Present and Future Poverty*. Washington DC: World Bank.

Fujiwara, T. 2010. "Voting Technology, Political Responsiveness, and Infant Health: Evidence from Brazil." Department of Economics, University of British Columbia, Vancouver. http://grad.econ.ubc.ca/fujiwara/jmp.pdf.

Gaarder, M., A. Glassman, and J. Todd. 2010. "Conditional Cash Transfers and Health: Unpacking the Causal Chain." *Journal of Development Effectiveness* 2 (1): 6–50.

Galasso, E., and N. Umapathi. 2007. "Improving Nutritional Status through Behavioral Change: Lessons from Madagascar." Policy Research Working Paper 4424, World Bank, Washington, DC.

Garner, P., R. Panpanich, S. Logan, and D. Davis. 2000. "Is Routine Growth Monitoring Effective? A Systematic Review of Trials." *Archives of Diseases in Childhood* 82: 197–201.

Gertler, P. J. 2004. "Do Conditional Cash Transfers Improve Child Health? Evidence from *Progresa*'s Control Randomized Experiment." *American Economic Review* 94 (2): 336–41.

Gertler, P. J., and S. Boyce. 2001. "An Experiment in Incentive-Based Welfare: The Impact of *Progresa* on Health in Mexico." Royal Economic Society Annual Conference 2003, No. 85.

Gertler, P. J., S. Martinez, P. Premand, L. B. Rawlings, and C. M. J. Vermeersch. 2010. *Impact Evaluation in Practice*. Washington, DC: World Bank.

Gertler, P. J., H. A. Patrinos, and M. Rubio-Codina. 2006. "Empowering Parents to Improve Education: Evidence from Rural Mexico." Policy Research Working Paper 3935, World Bank, Washington, DC.

Glewwe, P., N. Ilas, and M. Kremer. 2003. "Teacher Incentives." Working Paper 9671, National Bureau of Economic Research, Cambridge, MA.

Glewwe, P., M. Kremer, and S. Moulin. 2007. "Many Children Left Behind? Textbooks and Test Scores in Kenya." Working Paper 13300, National Bureau of Economic Research, Cambridge, MA.

Glewwe, P., M. Kremer, S. Moulin, and E. Zitzewitz. 2004. "Retrospective vs. Prospective Analyses of School Inputs: The Case of Flip Charts in Kenya." *Journal of Development Economics*, 74: 251–68.

Go, D. 2010. "Global Monitoring Report 2011 Approach Paper." Unpublished manuscript, World Bank, Washington, DC.

Gong, R. 2010. "HIV Testing and Risky Sexual Behavior." Job Market Paper, PhD Candidate, University of California-Berkeley, Berkeley, CA.

Goyal, S., and P. Pandey. 2009. "How Do Government and Private Schools Differ? Findings from Two Large Indian States." South Asia Human Development Sector Report No. 30, World Bank, Washington, DC.

Grantham-McGregor, S., Y. B. Cheung, S. Cueto, P. Glewwe, L. Richer, B. Trupp, and the International Child Development Steering Group. 2007. "Developmental Potential in the First 5

Years for Children in Developing Countries." *Lancet* 369: 60–70.

Gupta, S., M. Verhoeven, and E. Tiongson. 2003. "Public Spending on Health Care and the Poor." *Health Economics* 12: 685–96.

Hanushek, E. A. 2008. "Incentives for Efficiency and Equity in the School System." *Perspektiven der Wirtschaftspolitik* 9 (Special Issue): 5–27.

Hanushek, E. A., V. Lavy, and K. Hitomi. 2008. "Do Students Care about School Quality? Determinants of Dropout Behavior in Developing Countries." *Journal of Human Capital* 1 (2): 69–105.

Hanushek, E. A., and L. Woessmann. 2008. "The Role of Cognitive Skills in Economic Development." *Journal of Economic Literature* 46 (3): 607–68.

He, F., L. Linden, and M. MacLeod. 2007. "Teaching What Teachers Don't Know: An Assessment of the Pratham English Language Program." Unpublished manuscript, Columbia University, New York.

Hoddinott, J. 2008. "Nutrition and Conditional Cash Transfer (CCT) Programs." Unpublished manuscript, International Food Policy Research Institute, Washington, DC.

IHME (Institute for Health Metrics and Evaluation). 2010. "Financing Global Health 2009: Tracking Development Assistance for Health." University of Washington, Seattle, WA.

Jacoby, E., S. Cueto, and E. Pollitt. 1996. "Benefits of a School Breakfast Program among Andean Children in Huaraz, Peru." *Food and Nutrition Bulletin* 17 (1): 54–64.

Jalan, J., and E. Somanathan. 2008. "The Importance of Being Informed: Experimental Evidence on Demand for Environmental Quality." *Journal of Development Economics* 87 (1) 14–28.

Jamison, D., B. Searle, K. Galda, and S. Heyneman. 1981. "Improving Elementary Mathematics Education in Nicaragua: An Experimental Study of the Impact of Textbooks and Radio on Achievement." *Journal of Educational Psychology* 73 (4): 556–67.

Jensen, R. 2010. "The (Perceived) Returns to Education and Demand for Schooling." *Quarterly Journal of Economics* 125 (2): 515–48.

Kazianga, H., D. de Walque, and H. Alderman. 2009. "Educational and Health Impacts of Two School Feeding Schemes: Evidence from a Randomized Trial in Rural Burkina Faso." Policy Research Working Paper 4976, World Bank, Washington, DC.

Khemani, S. 2010. "Political Economy of Infrastructure Spending in India." Policy Research Working Paper 5423, World Bank, Washington, DC.

Kremer, M. E., and D. Chen. 2001. "Interim Report on a Teacher Incentive Program in Kenya." Unpublished manuscript, Harvard University, Cambridge, MA.

Kremer, M., and A. Holla. 2008. "Pricing and Access: Lessons from Randomized Evaluations in Education and Health." Unpublished manuscript, Harvard University, Cambridge, MA.

———. 2009. "Improving Education in the Developing World: What Have We Learned from Randomized Evaluations?" *Annual Review of Economics* 1: 513–45.

Kremer, M., and E. Miguel. 2007. "The Illusion of Sustainability." *Quarterly Journal of Economics* 112 (3): 1007–65.

Kremer, M., E. Miguel, and R. Thornton. 2009. "Incentives to Learn." *Review of Economics and Statistics* 91 (3): 437–56.

Kremer, M., S. Moulin, and R. Namunyu. 2003. "Decentralization: A Cautionary Tale." Unpublished manuscript, Harvard University, Cambridge, MA.

Kremer, M., and A. P. Zwane. 2007. "What Works in Fighting Diarrheal Diseases in Developing Countries? A Critical Review." *World Bank Research Observer* 22:1–24.

Lalive, R., and A. Cattaneo. 2006. "Social Interactions and Schooling Decisions." Discussion Paper 2250, Institute for the Study of Labor (IZA), Bonn, Germany.

Legovini, A. 2010. "Development Impact Evaluation Initiative: A World Bank–Wide Strategic Approach to Enhancing Development Effectiveness" Unpublished manuscript, World Bank, Washington, DC.

Leroy, J. L., R. Marie, and E. Verhofstadt. 2009. "The Impact of Conditional Cash Transfer Programmes on Child Nutrition: A Review of Evidence Using a Programme Theory Framework." *Journal of Development Effectiveness* 1: (2) 103–29.

Levy, D., and J. Ohls. 2007. "Evaluation of Jamaica's PATH Program: Final Report." Mathematica Policy Research, Washington, DC.

Lim, S., L. Dandona, J. Hoisington, S. James, M. Hogan, and E. Gakidou. 2010. "India's Janani Suraksha Yojana, a Conditional Cash Transfer Programme to Increase Births in Health Facilities: An Impact Evaluation." *Lancet* 375: 2009–23.

Macours, K., N. Schady, and R. Vakis. 2008. "Cash Transfers, Behavioral Changes, and the Cognitive Development of Young Children: Evidence from a Randomized Experiment." Policy Research Working Paper 4759, World Bank, Washington, DC.

Madajewicz, M., A. Pfaff, A. van Geen, J. Graziano, I. Hussein, H. Monotaj, R. Sylvi, and H. Ahsan. 2007. "Can Information Alone Change Behavior? Response to Arsenic Contamination of Groundwater in Bangladesh." *Journal of Development Economics* 84 (2) 731–54.

Mahal A., J. Sing, F. Afridi, V. Lamba, A. Gumber, and V. Selvaraju. 2000. "Who Benefits from Public Health Spending in India?" National Council for Applied Economic Research, New Delhi.

Maluccio, J., and R. Flores. 2005. "Impact Evaluation of a Conditional Cash Transfer Program: The Nicaraguan *Red de Protección Social*." Research Report 141, International Food Policy Research Institute, Washington, DC.

Mavedzenge, S., A. Doyle, and D. Ross. 2010. "HIV Prevention in Young People in Sub-Saharan Africa: A Systematic Review." Infectious Disease Epidemiology Unit, London School of Hygiene and Tropical Medicine, London.

McCoy, S., R. Kangwende, and N. Padian. 2009. "Behavior Change Interventions to Prevent HIV among Women Living in Low and Middle Income Countries." Synthetic Review 008, International Initiative for Impact Evaluation, New Delhi, India.

Medley, A., C. Kennedy, K. O'Reilly, and M. Sweat. 2009. "Effectiveness of Peer Education Interventions for HIV Prevention in Developing Countries: A Systematic Review and Meta-Analysis." *AIDS Education and Prevention* 21 (3): 181–206.

Meessen, B., J. P. Kashala, and L. Musango. 2007. "Output-Based Payment to Boost Staff Productivity in Public Health Centres: Contracting in Kabutare District, Rwanda." *Bulletin of the World Health Organization* 85 (2): 108–15.

Meessen, B., L. Musango, J. P. Kashala, and J. Lemlin. 2006. "Reviewing Institutions of Rural Health Centres: The Performance Initiative in Butare, Rwanda." *Tropical Medicine & International Health* 11 (8): 1303–17.

Meng, X., and J. Ryan. 2010. "Does a Food for Education Program Affect School Outcomes? The Bangladesh Case. *Journal of Population Economics* 23 (2): 415–47.

Mesnard, A. 2005. "Evaluation of the *Familias en Acción* Program in Colombia: Do Conditional Subsidies Improve Education, Health and Nutritional Outcomes?" Institute for Fiscal Studies, London.

Miguel, E., and M. Kremer. 2004. "Worms: Identifying Impacts on Education and Health in the Presence of Treatment Externalities." *Econometrica* 72 (1): 159–217.

Mizala, A., P. Romaguera, and M. Urquiola. 2007. "Socioeconomic Status or Noise? Trade-offs in the Generation of School Quality Information." *Journal of Development Economics* 84: 61–75.

Morris, S., P. Olinto, R. Flores, E.A.F. Nilson, and A. C. Figueiró. 2004. "Conditional Cash Transfers Are Associated with a Small Reduction in the Weight Gain of Preschool Children in Northeast Brazil." *Journal of Nutrition* 134: 2336–41.

Muralidharan, K., and V. Sundararaman. 2009. "Teacher Performance Pay: Experimental Evidence from India." Working Paper 15323, National Bureau of Economic Research, Cambridge, MA.

Newman, J. L., M. Pradhan, L. B. Rawlings, G. Ridder, R. Coa, and J. L. Evia. 2002. "An Impact Evaluation of Education, Health, and Water Supply Investments by the Bolivian Social Investment Fund." *World Bank Economic Review* 16 (2): 241–74.

Nguyen, T. 2008. "Information, Role Models and Perceived Returns to Education: Experimental Evidence from Madagascar." Working Paper, Massachusetts Institute of Technology, Cambridge, MA.

O'Donnell, O., E. van Doorslaer, R. Rannan-Eliya, A. Somanathan, S. Adhikari, D. Harbianto, C. Garg, P. Hanvoravongchai, M. Huq, A. Karan, G. Leung, C. W. Ng, B. R. Pande, K. Tin, K. Tisayaticom, L. Trisnantoro, Y. Zhang, and Y. Zhao. 2007. "The Incidence of Public Spending on Healthcare: Comparative Evidence from Asia." *World Bank Economic Review* 21 (1): 93–123.

OECD-DAC (Organisation for Economic Co-operation and Development-Development Assistance Committee). 2009. International Development Statistics: Online Databases on Aid and Other Resource Flows. Paris, France. http://www.oecd.org/dac/stats/idsonline.

Paxson, C., and N. Schady. 2007. "Cognitive Development among Young Children in Ecuador:

The Roles of Wealth, Health, and Parenting." *Journal of Human Resources* 42 (1): 49–84.

———. 2008. "Does Money Matter? The Effects of Cash Transfers on Child Health and Development in Rural Ecuador." Unpublished manuscript, World Bank, Washington, DC.

Piper, B., and M. Korda. 2010. "EGRA Plus: Liberia. Program Evaluation Report. Draft." RTI International, Research Triangle Park, NC.

Pop-Eleches C., H. Thirumurthy, J. P. Habyarimana, J. G. Zivin, M. P. Goldstein, D. de Walque, L. Mackeen, J. Haberer, S. Kimaiyo, J. Sidle, D. Ngare, and D. R. Bangsberg. 2011. "Mobile Phone Technologies Improve Adherence to Antiretroviral Treatment in a Resource-Limited Setting: A Randomized Controlled Trial of Text Message Reminders." *AIDS* 25 (6): 825–34.

Powell, C. A., S. P. Walker, S. M. Chang, and S. M. Grantham-McGregor. 1998. "Nutrition and Education: A Randomized Trial of the Effects of Breakfast in Rural Primary School Children." *American Journal of Clinical Nutrition* 68: 873–79.

Pratham Organization. 2005. "Annual Status of Education Report." Pratham Resource Center, Mumbai, India.

Ravallion, M. 2009. "Evaluation in the Practice of Development." *World Bank Research Observer* 24 (1): 29–53.

Regalía, F., and L. Castro. 2009. "Nicaragua: Combining Demand- and Supply-Side Incentives." In *Performance Incentives for Global Health—Potential and Pitfalls*, ed. R. Eichler, R. Levine, and the Performance-Based Incentives Working Group, 215–35. Washington, DC: Center for Global Development.

Reinikka, R., and J. Svensson. 2005. "Fighting Corruption to Improve Schooling: Evidence from a Newspaper Campaign in Uganda." *Journal of the European Economic Association* 3 (2-3): 259–67.

———. 2006. "The Power of Information: Evidence from a Newspaper Campaign to Reduce Capture of Public Funds." World Bank, Washington, DC; Institute for International Economic Studies, Stockholm University, Sweden.

———. 2010. "Working for God? Evidence from a Change in Financing of Nonprofit Health Care Providers in Uganda." *Journal of the European Economic Association* 8 (6): 1159–78.

Rivera, J. A., D. Sotres-Álvarez, J.-P. Habicht, T. Shamah, and S. Villalpando. 2004. "Impact of the Mexican Program for Education, Health, and Nutrition (*Progresa*) on Rates of Growth and Anemia in Infants and Young Children: A Randomized Effectiveness Study." *JAMA* 291 (21): 2563–70.

Roberfroid, D., P. Kolsteren, T. Hoerée, and B. Maire. 2005. "Do Growth Monitoring and Promotion Programs Answer the Performance Criteria of a Screening Program? A Critical Analysis Based on a Systematic Review." *Tropical Medicine & International Health* 10: 1121–33.

Rodrik, D. 2008. "The New Development Economics: We Shall Experiment, But How Shall We Learn?" Unpublished manuscript, John F. Kennedy School of Government, Harvard University, Cambridge, MA.

Sahn, D., and S. Younger. 2000. "Expenditure Incidence in Africa: Microeconomic Evidence." *Fiscal Studies* 21 (3): 321–48.

Schady, N., and M. C. Araujo. 2008. "Cash Transfers, Conditions, and School Enrollment in Ecuador." *Economía* 8 (2): 43–70.

Schady, N., and J. Rosero. 2008. "Are Cash Transfers Made to Women Spent Like Other Sources of Income?" *Economics Letters* 101 (3): 246–48.

Schultz, T. P. 2004. "School Subsidies for the Poor: Evaluating the Mexican *Progresa* Poverty Program." *Journal of Development Economics* 74 (1): 199–250.

Schwartz, J. B., and I. Bhushan. 2004. "Improving Equity in Immunization through a Public-Private Partnership in Cambodia." *Bulletin of the World Health Organization* 82: 661–67.

Sims, C.A. 2010. "But Economics Is Not an Experimental Science." *Journal of Economic Perspectives* 24 (2): 59–68.

Skoufias, E., and J. Shapiro. 2006. "Evaluating the Impact of Mexico's Quality Schools Program: The Pitfalls of Using Nonexperimental Data." Policy Research Working Paper 4036, World Bank, Washington, DC.

Soares, F. V., R. Ribas, and G. I. Hirata. 2008. "Achievements and Shortfalls of Conditional Cash Transfers: Impact Evaluation of Paraguay's Tekopora Program." International Poverty Center, Brasilia, Brazil.

Soeters, R., C. Habineza, and P. B. Peerenboom. 2006. "Performance-Based Financing and Changing the District Health System: Experience from Rwanda." *Bulletin of the World Health Organization* 84 (11): 884–89.

Stasavage, D. 2005. "Democracy and Education Spending in Africa." *American Journal of Political Science* 49 (2): 343–58.

Temperley, M., D. H. Mueller, J. Kiambo Njagi, W. Akhwale, S. E. Clarke, M. C. H. Jukes, B. B. A. Estambale, and S. Brooker. 2008. "Costs and Cost-Effectiveness of Delivering Intermittent Preventive Treatment through Schools in Western Kenya." *Malaria Journal* 7: 196–207.

Thornton, R. 2005. "The Demand for and Impact of HIV Testing: Evidence from a Field Experiment." Unpublished manuscript, Harvard University, Cambridge, MA.

UNESCO (United Nations Educational, Scientific, and Cultural Organization). 2010. *Education for All Global Monitoring Report 2010: Reaching the Marginalized.* Oxford, UK: Oxford University Press.

Van de Walle, D. 1995. "The Distribution of Subsidies through Public Health Services in Indonesia, 1978–87." In *Public Spending and the Poor: Theory and Evidence,* ed. D. Van de Walle and K. Neads, 226–58. Washington, DC: World Bank.

Vermeersch, C., and M. Kremer. 2004. "School Meals, Educational Achievement, and School Competition: Evidence from a Randomized Evaluation." Policy Research Working Paper 3523, World Bank, Washington, DC.

Weinhard, L. S., M. P. Carey, B. T. Johnston, and N. L. Bickham. 1999. "Effects of HIV Counseling and Testing on Sexual Risk Behavior: A Meta-Analytic Review of Published Research, 1985–1997." *American Journal of Public Health* 89 (9): 1152–63.

WHO (World Health Organization). 2008. *WHO Recommendations for Routine Immunization.* Geneva, Switzerland. http://www.who.int/immunization/policy/WHO_EPI_Sum_tables_Def_200713.pdf.

———. 2010. *World Health Report. Health Systems Financing: The Path to Universal Coverage.* Geneva, Switzerland.

World Bank. 2003. *World Development Report 2004: Making Services Work for Poor People.* Washington, DC.

World Bank/AERC (African Economic Research Consortium). 2010. "Service Delivery Indicators: Pilot in Education and Health in Africa." World Bank, Washington, DC.

Zivin J., H. Thirumurthy, and M. Goldstein. 2006. "AIDS Treatment and Intrahousehold Resource Allocations: Children's Nutrition and Schooling in Kenya." Working Paper 12689, National Bureau of Economic Research, Cambridge, MA.

Assisting Indigenous and Socially Excluded Populations

As we approach 2015 and come closer to meeting the Millennium Development Goals (MDGs) targets, the remaining challenges take on increased urgency. One of these is reaching out to the last and most difficult groups to reach—vulnerable populations with tenuous connections to the modern state and its economy.

Indigenous groups tend to have deeper poverty, less access to education, and worse health outcomes than the general population. In some rapidly growing economies, particularly in Asia, indigenous groups have enjoyed reductions in poverty at a pace comparable to general society. In other countries, particularly in Latin America, slow growth has slowed the pace of poverty reduction for indigenous groups, and targeted programs have made only a limited contribution. There is an urgent need for research to improve the availability and reliability of data on human development among indigenous groups—and to determine what kinds of programs have improved their welfare and in what contexts.

This chapter documents the poverty, education, and health of vulnerable and indigenous groups, highlighting their progress—and the remaining gaps. It also reviews countries that are off track in meeting the MDGs mainly because they have large vulnerable populations and countries on track that have off-track population groups. It also touches on the impact of the modern world on small, largely isolated groups, highlighting the need for sensitivity in dealing with them.

Last in heading down the home stretch

The last groups to be helped in countries are invariably in areas difficult to reach, are usually vulnerable, and have a tenuous connection to the modern state and its economy. Coming from minority ethnic groups and indigenous populations (box 4.1), they tend to speak a language different from the majority.[1] Whereas data coverage is a perennial challenge, MDG indicators for ethnic minorities and indigenous peoples are (with some exceptions) worse than population averages.

Poverty is higher among indigenous peoples than in the general population

As the global development community looks for ways to meet the MDG of halving (from its 1990 level) the share of people in poverty by 2015, it cannot ignore the plight of the world's indigenous peoples (box 4.1). They make up 4 percent of the global

From helmet to turban, hats worn by women and children give distinctive touches to each group of Hmong.

BOX 4.1   Who are indigenous peoples?

"Indigenous peoples" has no widely accepted definition. The World Bank's position is that "because of the varied and changing contexts in which indigenous peoples live and because there is no universally accepted definition of indigenous peoples, World Bank policy does not define the term. Indigenous peoples may be referred to in different countries by such terms as 'indigenous ethnic minorities,' 'aboriginals,' 'hill tribes,' 'minority nationalities,' 'scheduled tribes,' or 'tribal groups'" (World Bank Operational Directive 4.10).

The United Nations has not adopted a definition but has developed a modern understanding of the term based on a variety of characteristics: self-identification at the individual level and accepted by the community as their member; historical continuity with precolonial or presettler societies; a strong link to territories and surrounding natural resources; a distinct social, economic, or political system; a distinct language, culture, and belief system; individuals who form nondominant groups within society; and those who resolve to maintain and reproduce their ancestral environments and systems as distinctive peoples and communities.[a]

Moreover, evidence is growing that joining together under a common identity as indigenous peoples is fairly new and has accompanied a process among some groups of "reclaiming" identity.

With few exceptions, MDG indicators for indigenous groups across Asia are worse than all-population indicators. Under-five mortality rates for the Nepalese Janajati are distributed around the national level, but as a whole are below (that is, better than)

the national level. In India, however, infant mortality among the scheduled tribes is uniformly higher (worse) than the national average, and water deprivation rates both exceed and fall short of their national levels. Among the Hill Tribes in Thailand; the Kammu and Leu in the Lao People's Democratic Republic; and the Hmong, Muong, and BaNa in Vietnam, these rates are the worst in the region. The lowest female literacy rates are found among the Hmong in Lao PDR and Vietnam. And the existence of vulnerable groups who fare much worse than the general population is hardly unique to developing countries. In Australia and New Zealand, all indicators for Aborigines and Maori are worse than national averages.

Data coverage is far more limited in Africa, making overarching conclusions difficult. In many cases, available data do not cover core groups widely considered to be indigenous because of their small size (for example, the Ogiek in Kenya). The existing data show that under-five mortality rates tend to be highest among West African groups (such as the Fulani and Tuareg) and lowest among the Masai and Ethiopian groups. These last two groups also experience the highest rates of water deprivation. Education indicators are uniformly worse; even in countries with higher literacy (such as Namibia), the male literacy rate for San males is less than half that of the national sample; and for females, it is less than one third.

Source: Hall and Patrinos 2011.
a. UN 1981.

population—nearly 300 million—but they account for about 10 percent of the world's poor; and nearly 80 percent of them are in Asia.

Turning the situation around will require widespread and sustainable economic growth and poverty reduction, along with strategies to address multiple sources of disadvantage to reach those who need—and are willing to accept—special assistance.

One-third of indigenous people are poor.[2] Among the majority of countries with disaggregated data, poverty rates exceed 50 percent (table 4.1). Although the majority of indigenous people come from China and India, the indigenous poor are slightly more evenly distributed, largely owing to their strikingly low poverty rate in China. In other countries, indigenous peoples have disproportionately high poverty rates.

TABLE 4.1   **Poverty rates, latest year available**

Country/data year	Poverty head count (% poor)	
	Indigenous	Nonindigenous
Democratic Republic of Congo/2005	84.8	71.7
Mexico/2008	80.6	45.3
Ecuador/2006	78.0	46.6
Guatemala/2006	74.8	36.2
Gabon/2003	70.1	32.7
Bolivia/2006	69.3	46.0
Peru/2005	62.3	35.0
Vietnam/2006	52.3	10.3
Lao PDR 2002	50.6	25.0
Brazil/2002	48.0[a]	23.0[b]
India/2004	43.8	22.7
Chile/2006	15.2	9.1
China/2002	5.4	3.5

Source: Hall and Patrinos 2011.
Note: Head count poverty rates are national.
a. Refers to whites and "black/brown" (African origin).
b. Refers to whites (Telles 2007). Head count poverty rates are national.

A sizable poverty gap remains for indigenous people in global terms, ranging from small in China to significant in Vietnam.[3] The gap has even been increasing over time.

Research from Latin American countries with large indigenous populations—Bolivia, Ecuador, Guatemala, and Peru—shows a sticky persistence of (nonimproving) poverty rates for indigenous peoples over time. Progress used to be limited in Mexico as well, but poverty rates there have been falling over the last decade, especially between 2004 and 2008.[4] This may be the first period in history that the indigenous population in Mexico has seen an improvement. More important, analysis in Mexico shows that the difference in poverty rates between indigenous and nonindigenous peoples has been declining mostly as a result of explained or observable factors: education and access to services, the policy-driven variables, are important.

Chile has also seen reductions in indigenous poverty in recent years. But other countries in Latin America have not been so successful. Guatemala reduced poverty rapidly until recently; but even when poverty declined for the population as a whole, progress among indigenous people was much slower.

Similar trends were seen in Bolivia, Ecuador, and Peru. Indeed, for most countries in Latin America with a sizable indigenous population, there is almost no progress in poverty reduction for the indigenous population—even in countries where the nonindigenous population is making progress.

By contrast, poverty rates, even among indigenous people, have declined sharply in emerging Asia—notably, China, India, and Vietnam (figure 4.1). China's progress is remarkable: in 1981, it had one of the world's highest proportions of people living in poverty—84 percent. By 2005, that had fallen to 16 percent.[5] Even better, China's ethnic minorities' poverty rates declined faster than did the nonminority rates.

India and Vietnam also showed significant declines: although not as dramatic as China's, overall, the declines were much more robust for India's minorities, scheduled castes, and tribes and for Vietnam's ethnic minorities. But despite the rapid decline in poverty among indigenous people in Vietnam, their poverty rates remain much higher than those for the nonindigenous population; and the gap has widened slightly since the early 1990s.

Vulnerable groups receive less schooling and underperform in school

As with poverty, indigenous people are also disadvantaged in education, as in access to schooling (table 4.2). To varying degrees in nearly all countries, educational progress has lagged because of indigenous, low-income, gender, or disability status. Leaving such groups at the fringes of the education system will eventually impede a country's ability to develop. Even in India, despite its success in rapidly reducing poverty for the whole population (including significantly for the scheduled tribes, or Adivasi [literally "original inhabitants"]), this minority population accounts for a fourth of the poorest wealth decile. Education indicators tell a similar story, with improvements but large and persistent differences. Scheduled tribe children lag far behind when it comes to educational attainment above the primary level.[6]

FIGURE 4.1   Progress is mixed in reducing the poverty of indigenous groups

poverty rate over time

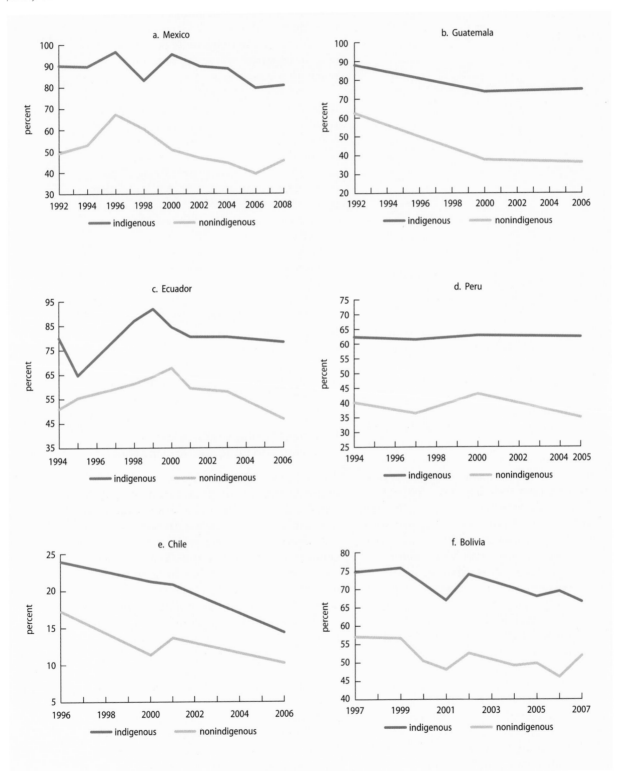

FIGURE 4.1   (continued)

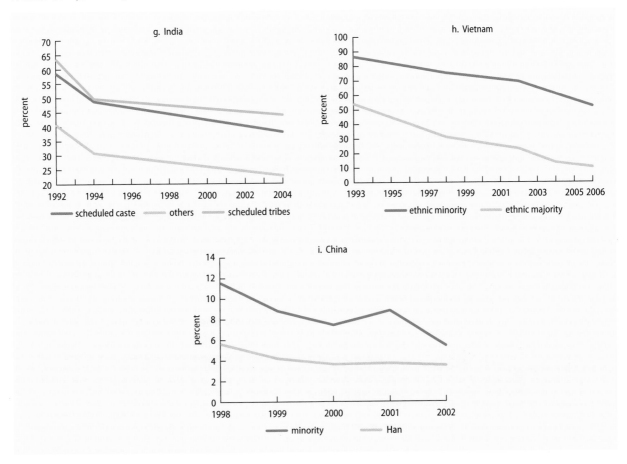

Source: Hall and Patrinos 2011.

TABLE 4.2   Years of schooling, latest year available

Country	Indigenous	Nonindigenous
China/2002	8.2	8.9
Peru/2001	6.4	8.7
Mexico/2008	6.3	8.6
Bolivia/2002	5.9	9.6
Brazil/2002	4.6[a]	6.6[b]
Ecuador/2006	4.3	6.9
Guatemala/2006	2.5	5.7

Source: Hall and Patrinos 2011.
Note: See box 1.5 for more information about Brazil.
a. Refers to whites and "black/brown" (African origin).
b. Refers to whites (Telles 2007).

Not only do vulnerable groups receive less schooling; they also tend to achieve less. In addition to poor starting conditions, insufficient inputs, and ineffective teaching, vulnerable groups are likely to experience discrimination that manifests in different ways (including self-perceptions and stigma).

Stigma is sometimes internalized, as an experimental investigation into the impact of caste on test scores in India demonstrated.[7] Children ages 11 and 12 were chosen at random from a low caste and three high castes and were given a series of puzzles to solve. When caste was not announced to the children, it had no bearing on the initial score or on the improvement in score registered in subsequent test rounds. But when caste was announced before the test, the scores for low-caste children fell dramatically, by 14–39 percent (figure 4.2). These findings confirm how much social identities are a product of

FIGURE 4.2   Test results show how stigma can be internalized

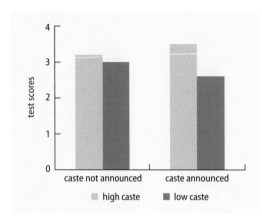

Source: Hoff and Pandey 2004.

history, culture, and personal experience, creating pronounced educational disadvantages through their effects on individual expectations.

Global evidence also shows how identity can limit development. A fractionalization data set compiled by Alesina and colleagues measures the degree of ethnic, linguistic, and religious heterogeneity in various countries.[8] It can be used to test the effects of

FIGURE 4.3   Heterogeneity has a negative effect on test scores

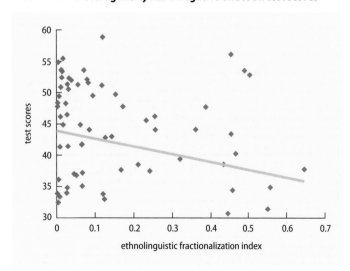

Source: World Bank staff calculations using data from Alesina et al. 2003 and Schlotter 2010.

fractionalization on the quality of institutions and economic growth. The data show just how heterogeneous many developing countries are, but they do not show that a high degree of heterogeneity produces negative outcomes. Fractionalization has been shown to slow the progress on many of the MDGs.[9] Although fractionalization is not correlated with schooling progress, there is an indication of a negative effect of heterogeneity on test scores (figure 4.3).

Both the global and Indian examples underscore the need to be careful in developing appropriate learning materials and environments for minorities. Although some of the self-perceptions and stigma will take time to address, these more immediate lessons for promoting rights and accountabilities can be used now.

Indigenous peoples live shorter lives everywhere

The *World Health Report 2010* states, "income is not the only factor influencing [health] service coverage. In many settings, migrants, ethnic minorities and indigenous people use [health] services less than other population groups, even though their needs may be greater."[10]

Indigenous peoples therefore deserve special attention. They live shorter lives and are in worse health than their nonindigenous compatriots almost everywhere. In seven Latin American countries, the proportion of indigenous women receiving antenatal care or giving birth at health facilities was much lower than for nonindigenous women.[11] Such inequality is one of the causes of the disparity in maternal health outcomes between the two populations. African-American women in the same countries also gave birth at health facilities less frequently and had poorer maternal health outcomes than other women.

Such health inequalities are not unique to low-income countries. Australia, Canada, and New Zealand show variations in access to health services between the two populations, frequently linked to distance and

MAP 4.1   Almost nine million children still die each year before they reach their fifth birthday

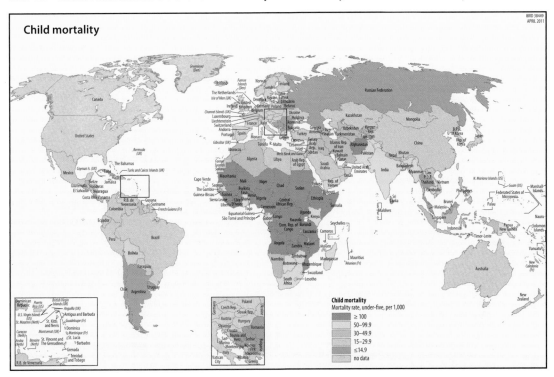

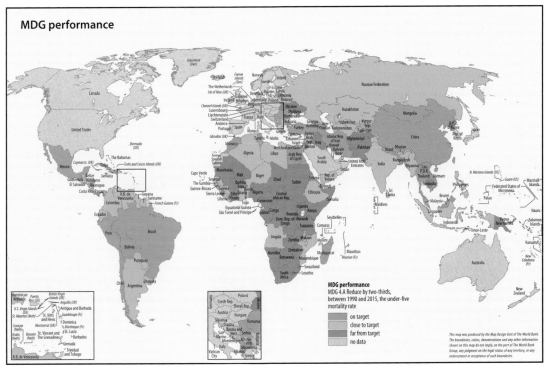

Source: World Bank staff calculations based on data from the World Development Indicators database.

FIGURE 4.4   **Both poor and rich countries show gaps in life expectancy**

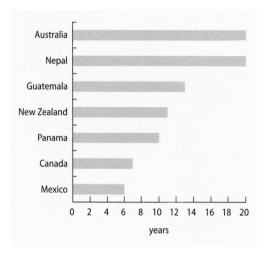

Source: UN 2009, p. 159.
Note: The figure shows the difference in years of life expectancy between indigenous and nonindigenous groups in each country.

transportation costs. Some rich countries also show gaps in life expectancy (figure 4.4).

Further evidence of insufficient attention to the needs of minority groups is seen in Europe, where the largest and most disadvantaged group, Roma, lags far behind the continent's majority population (box 4.2).

Gender is a key dimension

Gender is a key dimension in the social indicators of indigenous or otherwise excluded groups. Although both boys and girls in these groups are significantly underrepresented in school and lag on other important indicators, girls are particularly disadvantaged. Disturbingly, out-of-school girls from indigenous populations make up a large portion of total population of out-of-school girls in developing countries.[12]

BOX 4.2   **The Roma of Europe**

The Roma, or "Gypsies," are a Romani subgroup of about 7 million to 9 million people living primarily in Central and Eastern Europe. They are poorer than the general population: in some countries, Roma poverty rates are more than 10 times those of non-Roma.[a] And they are more likely to fall into poverty and stay poor. They also form a large proportion of youth and the potential labor force in these countries. But their low level of education means that European Union economies are losing hundreds of millions of euros annually in production and fiscal contributions.

Lower-bound annual estimates of productivity losses for Bulgaria, the Czech Republic, Romania, and Serbia total more than €2 billion, and there are similar estimates of €860 million in fiscal losses.[b] Using other Roma population estimates, the economic losses for the four countries combined amount to €5.7 billion annually, and the fiscal losses are €2 billion annually.[c] The annual fiscal gains from bridging the employment gap are much larger than the total cost of investing in public education for all Roma children—by factors of 7.7 in Bulgaria, 7.4 in the Czech Republic, 3.3 in Serbia, and 2.4 in Romania.

European governments and others have made a political commitment to improve Romani socioeconomic status and social inclusion under the aegis of the Decade of Roma Inclusion 2005–15. The initiative brings together governments and intergovernmental and nongovernmental organizations as well as Romani civil society to help ensure progress toward improving the welfare of Roma and to review such progress transparently and quantifiably. It commits governments to focus on education, employment, health, and housing while taking into account poverty, discrimination, and gender bias.

The Open Society Foundation documents the progress that countries are making at the halfway point for the 4.5 million Roma in participating countries.[d] Unfortunately, a lack of data remains the biggest obstacle in any assessment, as shown in the table on the next page. But even these patchy data allow one to see, for example, that the infant mortality rate among Roma is two or three times as high as that among the general population.

BOX 4.2   The Roma of Europe (continued)

Roma progress on selected indicators

Country	Year	Poverty (%)[a]	Primary education completion rate		Infant mortality rate (per 1,000 live births)	
			General (%)	Among Roma (%)	General	Among Roma
Albania	2005		Insufficient data	14.0	16.0	No data
	Most recent	78	Insufficient data	Insufficient data	13.0	No data
Bosnia and Herzegovina	2005		Insufficient data	No data	Insufficient data	No data
	Most recent	27	Insufficient data	No data	13.0	No data
Bulgaria	2005		Insufficient data	28.3	10.4	25.0
	Most recent	46	Insufficient data	31.6	8.6	25.0
Croatia	2005		95.0	No data	5.7	25.1
	Most recent	10	101.0	No data	4.5	11.5
Czech Republic	2005		102.0	No data	3.4	No data
	Most recent	45	93.2	No data	2.7	No data
Hungary	2005		95.0	76.4	6.2	No data
	Most recent	9	96.7	No newer data	5.6	No data
Macedonia, FYR	2005		96.0	50.8	12.8	Insufficient data
	Most recent	33	92.0	No data	10.8	Insufficient data
Montenegro	2005		91.1	9.2	9.5	No data
	Most recent	27	No newer data	20.0	7.5	No data
Romania	2005		No data	31.8	15.0	Insufficient data
	Most recent	66	No data	19.8	11.0	No data
Serbia	2005		95.0	22.7	8.0	25.0
	Most recent	57	99.5	No data	6.7	No newer data
Slovak Republic	2005		94.0	No data	7.2	No data
	Most recent	n.a.	No newer data	No data	5.9	No data

Source: OSI 2010; poverty estimates from the World Bank.
Note: n.a. = not available.
a. Percent of Roma living in households below $4.30 per day (purchasing power parity), expenditure based.

What works for Roma inclusion

Increasing the number of high school graduates would give the current generation of young Roma a better chance in the labor market and would improve school readiness to boost the chances of the next generation entering the classroom with the same skills as non-Roma. International experience suggests that investments in early childhood development and improvements in school attendance and completion are the most promising interventions to break the intergenerational transmission of social exclusion.[e]

Such interventions can be for supply (such as explicit desegregation efforts, teacher training, and school grants) and for demand (such as Roma mediators and conditional cash transfer programs).

a. Ringold, Orenstein, and Wilkens 2005.
b. De Laat 2010; World Bank 2010.
c. De Laat 2010; World Bank 2010.
d. OSI 2010.
e. See, for example, Heckman (2006); Kremer, Miguel, and Thornton (2009); and Patrinos (2007).

Sub-Saharan Africa has about 23 million girls out of school, 75 percent from excluded groups; South Asia has 23 million and 67 percent; the Middle East and North Africa have almost 5 million and 90 percent; Eastern Europe and Central Asia have 1.5 million and 90 percent (including rural populations in Turkey); and Latin America has 1.5 million—almost all from excluded groups. In aggregate, 71 percent of out-of-school girls in developing countries are from excluded groups.[13] In India, tribal women fare the worst: even among younger age cohorts (ages 15–21 in 2005), they attain an average of just four years of education, three years less than nontribal women.[14] In Lao PDR, non-Lao-Tai women receive significantly less education than non-Lao-Tai men or Lao-Tai of both sexes. For example, 34 percent of rural non-Lao-Tai girls had never attended school in 2002–03, compared with 6 percent of Lao-Tai girls.[15]

Indigenous groups and the MDGS

Some countries that are off track to reach one or more of the MDGs have large indigenous populations, although their presence may not be the only reason for this shortfall. Even some on-track countries have these populations; thus, when data are disaggregated, they are off track in the sense that although the country may reach all (or most) of the MDGs, but has significant segments of the population that are off track (or seriously off track). Indigenous people get little attention in country reports designed to monitor progress in meeting the goals (box 4.3).

Off-track countries—minority groups are lagging severely

Many of the off-track countries are in Africa.[16] And some of them are off track because of the severe lack of progress of their minority groups. Nigeria, for example, has three major tribes—the Igbo, Hausa, and Yoruba—more than 200 ethnic groups, and more than 500 indigenous languages and dialects. It would be important to use disaggregated data on these subgroups to investigate the link between minority groups and the failure to achieve the MDGs—not just for Nigeria, but more generally.

BOX 4.3   **Vulnerable groups deserve more attention in MDG country reports**

A review of 50 MDG country reports found that ethnic or linguistic minorities are mentioned in only 19, and the inequalities experienced by religious minorities are mentioned in only 2. An additional 10 reports mention only indigenous peoples, without identifying any other minority groups.

The mentions of minorities vary widely, with some reports providing a good range of information and disaggregated data under several MDGs. In other cases, minorities are mentioned only in the background section describing the national population and without particular attention to their situation in relation to the MDGs. Minorities are mentioned most frequently in connection with Goal 2 on universal primary education.

Attention to indigenous peoples, in general, is significantly higher than attention to nonindigenous marginalized minorities. Although attention to gender issues in many MDG country reports is positive, there is very little consideration of discrimination experienced by minority women or of targeted policies for them.

Minorities are virtually absent from the MDG country reports from donor countries. None of those reports considers minorities under any of the eight goals, and only the reports for Nepal and Vietnam give sufficient attention to indigenous peoples. Nor do any reports indicate any consultation with indigenous peoples or consistently provide disaggregated data for them.

Sources: UN 2010a; Hartley 2008.

TABLE 4.3   Status of indigenous groups relative to the MDGs, selected African countries

Country/data year/group	Under-five mortality (per 1,000 live births)	Water deprivation (% of households)	Nutrition deprivation (% of children)	Literacy rate (% of males)	Literacy rate (% of females)	Net primary enrollment (% of boys)	Net primary enrollment (% of girls)	Households in sample (n)
Cameroon/2004	148	29	13	80	65	81	78	10,462
Peulh	170	21	11	43	19	60	55	387
Pygmy	160	54	54	17	10	65	100	18
Fulfulde	192	26	18	27	13	57	49	1,632
Niger/2006	218	28	29	28	12	44	29	7,660
Peul	204	38	33	5	5	17	19	350
Tuareg	204	52	30	17	5	30	29	635
Mali/2006	215	6	16	37	17	46	39	12,998
Peulh	229	4	16	31	16	38	35	1,400
Tanachek	194	20	17	28	11	41	28	815
Guinea/2005	188	59	15	44	16	58	49	6,282
Peulh	171	61	12	40	14	56	45	2,228
Senegal/2005	135	11	5	54	35	58	58	7,407
Poular	137	13	8	44	29	56	56	1,990

Source: Computed from demographic and health surveys in MacDonald forthcoming.

Demographic and health surveys show the frequent considerable disadvantage in belonging to an indigenous group in some low-income African countries (table 4.3). In Cameroon, the Peulh and the Fulfulde (a large minority) are doing poorly on adult literacy and net primary enrollment. Niger's Peul and Tuareg face inequalities, even though the national population is far off track. Mali is nationally so far off track that there is seeming equality, with all groups performing poorly.

Groups left behind in countries otherwise performing well

Indigenous people in on-track middle-income countries are also being left behind. A few examples will suffice. Mexico, a middle-income country and an Organisation for Economic Co-operation and Development member, is on track to meet most of the MDGs. But under-five mortality for indigenous groups is at 52 per 1,000 live births—almost twice the 27 for nonindigenous groups. In addition, the poorest municipalities, heavily populated by indigenous peoples, have poor indicators for poverty and access to education and health. The worst-performing municipalities have a Human Development Index similar to those in poorer African countries: the community with

the lowest index in Mexico, the Metlatonoc, is at about the same level as Angola and Malawi. Perhaps it is not surprising that 98 percent of the population there is indigenous.[17]

India is also on track to meet the MDGs, but the scheduled tribes are largely off track. Although educational enrollment rates are fairly high for all groups, scheduled tribes suffer from high under-five mortality, poor access to water and sanitation, nutrition deprivation, and low levels of adult literacy.[18] Ecuador's under-five mortality is almost twice as high among indigenous people, at 138 per 1,000 live births versus 77 per 1,000 for nonindigenous groups.[19] Vietnam, a star performer in economic growth and poverty reduction, does very well on the MDGs overall and its ethnic minorities are generally progressing, although some are seriously off track for adult literacy.[20] Although indigenous groups in Vietnam have seen rapid declines in poverty, their poverty rates remain some 40 percentage points higher than those for the rest of the population.

Lessons from progress—and from stagnation

As we approach 2015, the daunting challenge of reaching the last of the excluded groups becomes apparent. They have a tenuous connection to the modern economy, likely speak a language different from the majority, and typically are an ethnic minority. Where such groups make up a sizable proportion of the population, the solution requires rapid, broad-based economic growth and poverty reduction. But even that may not be enough to address multiple sources of disadvantage from centuries of political and social exclusion. Instead, a direct effort at empowerment is required, using targeted approaches and enforcing political and social rights.

Growth is essential for poverty reduction

In some Asian countries, rapid poverty reduction and the relative gains of minority groups were generated by rapid growth and fairly low inequality in access to productive inputs such as land and human capital.[21]

From the 1970s' reforms to 1985, China's main strategy to reduce poverty was to focus on rural economic growth. After 1985, however, the government, recognizing that growth was necessary but insufficient to reduce poverty, adopted a development-oriented strategy, providing assistance through various programs in poor regions.[22] Nonetheless,

direct redistributive interventions have not been prominent in China's efforts to reduce poverty.[23]

India's strong growth—focused since the 1980s on moving from a state-controlled, inward-looking economy to an outward-oriented, market-led economy—has not been damped by its poorly performing targeted programs.[24] Similarly, Vietnam's remarkable gains in economic growth and poverty reduction were the product of market reforms and a loosening of state control.[25] It was only after growth was established that policy makers turned their attention to poverty reduction strategies and ethnic minority development;[26] and, even then, such programs focused on developing local economic activities rather than targeting the poor, as in Latin America.

Latin American countries with large indigenous populations also have had some success in equalizing human capital and expanding access to basic services, starting from very unequal conditions. Indigenous people often have political representation, and their rights are generally well established. All Latin American countries but one have national bilingual education programs,[27] some of which may benefit indigenous populations (box 4.4). And 17 have conditional cash transfer (CCT) programs.[28]

Despite these efforts, slow growth has hampered progress in overall poverty reduction and more equitable income distribution.[29] The Latin American countries with the largest indigenous populations experienced per capita growth rates of no more than 1 percent in the 1990s and not much more since then. High inequality, slow growth, and little participation by indigenous peoples in the economic progress that did occur meant that indigenous peoples made little progress in poverty reduction. Most distributive programs, as currently designed and implemented, have not reduced poverty among indigenous people. One significant exception is Mexico's CCT program *Oportunidades*, an important part of the country's antipoverty program that has benefited indigenous people disproportionately (box 4.5). It is characterized as well targeted (to the poor,

---

BOX 4.4   Bilingual education in Guatemala

Bilingual education is an efficient public investment. According to a crude cost–benefit exercise, a shift to bilingual schooling for indigenous people in Guatemala would result in considerable cost savings because of reduced grade repetition. The higher quality of education would probably help students complete the primary education cycle and substantially increase total education levels at lower cost.

The cost savings from bilingual education are estimated at $5 million, equal to the cost of providing primary schooling to 100,000 students a year. A reduction in the number of dropouts and the effect on personal earnings would thus be significant.[a]

a. Patrinos and Velez 2009.

MAP 4.2   For girls in some African countries, secondary education remains elusive

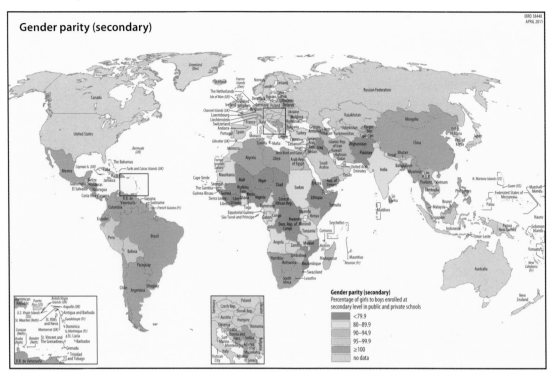

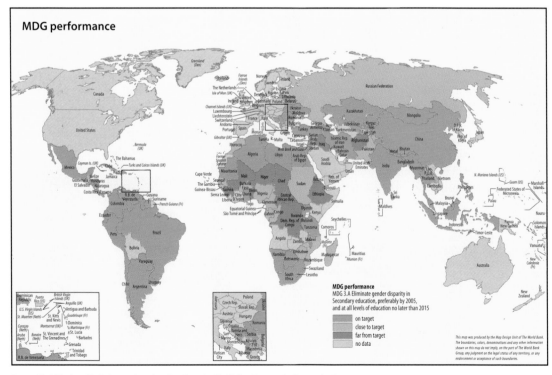

Source: World Bank staff calculations based on data from the World Development Indicators database.

BOX 4.5   Examples of successful targeted programs

CCT programs have become very popular for attacking poverty. They provide assistance conditioned on the beneficiary's actions—that is, the government provides money only to beneficiaries who fulfill certain criteria, such as enrolling children in school, ensuring that they attend regularly and complete grades, and receiving regular medical attention. CCTs have become the largest social assistance program in some countries, covering millions of households—for example, in Brazil (*Bolsa Família*) and Mexico.[a]

The program in Mexico—PROGRESA (now *Oportunidades*)—started early (1997) and evolved thoughtfully. The program produced successive waves of data to evaluate its impact and put the data in the public domain. Hundreds of studies attest to its success in confronting poverty and disadvantage. Although targeted generally to the poor, the program has improved indigenous children's schooling attainment relative to Spanish-speaking or bilingual children (see figure at right). Before the program, indigenous children had lower school attainment than did Spanish-speaking or bilingual children. After three years of implementation, school attainment among indigenous children increased, reducing the gap. Ecuador's CCT—*Bono de Desarrollo Humano*—also

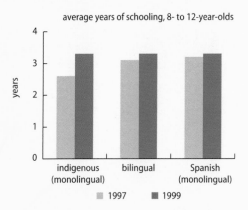

average years of schooling, 8- to 12-year-olds

Sources: Bando, Lopez-Calva, and Patrinos 2005; Godoy et al. 2005, 2006.

recorded success in reaching indigenous populations.[b] Cambodia's Education Sector Support Project has a CCT that targets ethnic minorities. Exported from the developing world to the developed, CCTs have also been used in New York City and for indigenous communities in Australia.

a. Fiszbein and Schady 2009.

b. Ibid.

among whom the indigenous in Mexico are overrepresented), transparent, and evidence based—with the results of impact evaluations used to adjust and improve it.

The differing experiences in China and Latin America underline the importance of growth for poverty reduction.[30] Considerable reductions in poverty can be achieved through rapid growth, at least at first. But given the typical widening of inequality with rapid development (as in China and India), there is a desperate need to design effective programs that target underprivileged groups. This is one area where Asia can learn from the successes of such programs in Latin America (including *Oportunidades* and a similar program in Brazil)[31] that combine careful identification of beneficiary groups, transparent program delivery, and learning from experience.

Empowering indigenous people can improve their development prospects

To properly empower vulnerable groups so that broad-based growth and targeted poverty reduction programs work in their favor, the groups need greater political representation and greater voice. Political representation in legislatures or parliaments, for instance, could significantly increase their say in the design of programs and delivery of services. It could also ensure that they are referred to in plans to achieve the MDGs and that they are consulted in the development and design of national programs.

Although beneficial, effecting change through the political process takes time, as made evident in Latin America. Empowering stakeholders directly—for example, enabling parents to influence school policies or patients to choose health providers—holds more immediate promise. In Mexico, parents are given the right to exercise voice and decision-making authority over the use of small sums of money for improving schooling in rural areas. These programs target disadvantaged and poorly performing schools, including a substantial number that provide services to indigenous groups. A randomized evalua-tion of one such program shows that parental pressure produced efficiency gains, increasing access and improving test scores.[32]

To work, such empowerment must be accompanied by real efforts to generate, use, and disseminate disaggregated data and information on vulnerable groups—some-thing that can be done well only to the extent that those groups play a role in conceptualiz-ing and implementing the data gathering, and in formulating policy.

Although much of the economic disad-vantage of indigenous and excluded groups is the result of lower human capital, there is also evidence of labor market discrimi-nation.[33] In decompositions of the earnings gap, the portion of the difference between indigenous and nonindigenous peoples that is "unexplained"—perhaps because of discrim-ination or other unidentified factors—repre-sents one quarter to more than one half of the total differential. This means that although about half the earnings differential can be influenced by improvements in human capital (education, skills, and abilities that an indig-enous person brings to the labor market), another half may result from discriminatory labor market practices or other factors over which the indigenous person has little con-trol. So efforts to empower excluded groups and increase their human capital need to look at how the labor market can be made more fair for them.

Small and largely untouched groups

Indigenous peoples across the globe have very different exposures to nonindigenous peoples and varying degrees of cooperation with gov-ernments and government programs. It is hard to design programs that would benefit

those who are least exposed to a modern national economy and allow them to main-tain their identity and choice of livelihood. The prime consideration of such programs is the need to tread lightly and be well informed by on-the-ground research.

Indigenous peoples have dealt with the expansion of western influence and market systems in at least two broad ways: some have confronted the expansion and either adapted to it or been deracinated, and oth-ers have retreated farther into the backlands to avoid exposure and deal with the modern world at arm's length.[34] We know a great deal about the vulnerability and well-being of the first group, but little about the second.[35] Nor is it clear what role, if any, the govern-ment should play in enhancing the well-being of people who eschew the modern economy. Two examples illuminate the issues.

Persistent poverty in Central Africa

Among the oldest inhabitants of Africa, the Pygmy peoples lead a nomadic or semino-madic lifestyle (depending on the country) that has persisted largely unchanged for thousands of years, with livelihoods based on hunting, fishing, and gathering wild fruits and nuts. Because of urbanization and deforesta-tion, however, many Pygmies have become sedentary, leaving them disadvantaged and vulnerable. In the Democratic Republic of Congo, for example, Pygmies have tradition-ally been closely attached to the rain forest—the source of their spirituality, livelihood, and protection. They once lived in camps of 30–40 families, maintaining regular links with each other. But today their lifestyle is in danger, as they become more sedentary, lose access to the forest, and face a deteriorating relationship with Bantu farmers. Census data for the Central African Republic and Gabon show that Pygmies lag behind the general population in wealth, education, and access to basic infrastructure.

Their poverty rates are extremely high. In the Democratic Republic of Congo, 85 per-cent of the Pygmy population is estimated to be poor, compared with 72 percent of the gen-eral population.[36] Unemployment is typically lower among Pygmies, perhaps because they are so poor that they cannot afford not to work. But the share of workers who are not paid cash for their work is much higher, suggesting low-productivity jobs.

School enrollment rates and average years of schooling among Pygmies in the Central African Republic and Gabon are dramatically lower than among other groups. The Central African Republic's gross primary enrollment is only 21 percent for Pygmies, compared with 73 percent for nonindigenous peoples; Pygmy men average 0.3 years of schooling and women average 0.1 years, compared with 2.8 years for non-Pygmy men and 1.4 years for non-Pygmy women. Gabon's gross secondary enrollment is only 4 percent for Pygmies, but 80 percent for non-Pygmies; and the average years of schooling are 3.0 for men and 2.8 for women among Pygmies, compared with 6.5 years for both non-Pygmy men and women. Lower school enrollment among Pygmies may result from high cost, distance to schools, weaker cultural emphasis, and the need for children to work.

Pygmies in the Central African Republic and Gabon are less likely to have access to safe water and electricity; more likely to live in a dwelling with walls, roof, or floor made of temporary materials; and less likely to have adequate sanitation. Even compared with other rural households, Pygmies in Gabon fare worse in all housing dimensions.

In the Central African Republic, the share of households living in a village or area with a health facility is smaller for Pygmies than for the population as a whole, although the differences in distances to health facilities are small. Access to condoms is much lower for Pygmies; and the share of households that lost a member to a long-term illness is higher among Pygmies than among the overall population (although the share of households that have lost a member to HIV/AIDS is smaller).

The Pygmies embody a valuable cultural heritage that should be protected and preserved, one of the most original forms of human adaptation to the ecology of the rain forest. They have a sophisticated knowledge

of their environment and the possibilities for humans to adapt to it sustainably. They are increasing their integration into broader society as they become more sedentary, and this process—unmanaged and with little input from the Pygmies—is linked to their impoverishment, exploitation, and poor health and education outcomes. Although these findings do not point to specific policies that the government could implement to improve Pygmies' living conditions, they do suggest the need for more qualitative and institutional analysis of measures to target this especially vulnerable group.

Lack of interaction with wider society: the case of the Tsimane' of Bolivia

The Tsimane', a native Amazonian society of foragers and farmers in Bolivia, provide an intriguing example of the benefits and costs when an indigenous group exercises significant autonomy in its exposure to the outside world. Active withdrawal into the backlands and collaboration with Protestant missionaries since the late 1940s have enabled Tsimane' to retain a great deal of their traditional culture and territory.[37] They show no change in core cultural values[38] or in ethnobotanical knowledge,[39] although a more recent unpublished study by Reyes-García et al.[40] suggests they may be losing that knowledge at the rate of 2 percent a decade.

Close to 75 percent of the population follows the traditional preferential system of cross-cousin marriage (that is, a man marries his mother's brother's daughter or father's sister's son),[41] which produces a tight endogamic group. With ample access to farmlands, Tsimane' daily personal income (adjusted for inflation and in purchasing power parity) reaches $9 a day per person, much higher than the international poverty line of $1–$2 a day.[42] And, over the period 2002–06, many indicators of individual well-being improved, including real income, real wealth, consumption, body-mass index, social capital, and happiness.[43] Little wonder that permanent outmigration is rare; but they are being encroached on by highland colonist farmers, cattle ranchers, and logging and oil firms.[44]

Tsimane' experience little damage in physical stature,[45] widespread parasitism[46] and child growth stunting, and vulnerability to adverse weather conditions (such as excessive rainfall). Such events during gestation, infancy, and early childhood suppress adult physical stature, particularly among women.[47] And when adverse shocks strike households (illness, theft, crop loss, floods), people weather them on their own, without help from kith, kin, or formal institutions. That suggests the Tsimane' remain poorly insured against mishaps that strike either the individual or the village.

Conclusions

Indigenous groups make up a sizable share of the world's people and even a greater share of the world's poor. But their isolation reduces their gains from overall growth and makes them difficult to reach through targeted poverty programs. As we come closer to 2015, reaching even more isolated people will become progressively more difficult. Addressing their needs will require widespread and sustainable economic growth and poverty reduction, along with strategies to reach those who need a special lift. Helping indigenous groups will require better understanding of their needs and of how they interact with the modern economy.

Nevertheless, some programs have improved their lot. For example, well-implemented bilingual education programs promote school completion and subsequent earnings gains, thus contributing to multiple goals; and these programs can be cost effective. CCT programs can promote schooling, health, and poverty reduction goals; and in countries with large vulnerable populations, CCTs show disproportionate gains for the minority population. Empirical research suggests that investments in early childhood development and improving school attendance and completion are the most promising means of

breaking the intergenerational transmission of social exclusion.

The international community needs a knowledge base of what specific programs and policies work best, and for which vulnerable populations. It is widely held that outright discrimination may explain some of the observed differential in poverty outcomes among minority groups,[48] and there is evidence consistent with labor market discrimination against indigenous peoples.[49] But overt tests for discrimination against indigenous peoples (such as tests in the United States comparing call-back rates for blacks and whites with otherwise similar profiles)[50] are distinctly lacking.

To properly address the needs of the world's excluded populations, more and better data are needed. That is, one needs to analyze disaggregated data that are collected regularly and consistently. This data collection and analysis effort can only be done successfully to the extent that the minority populations play a role, thus ensuring coverage and relevance.

Extending the gains from development to indigenous people will not be easy. It will be necessary to continue progress in overall poverty reduction; to overcome physical, institutional, and social obstacles to their participation in broader society; and to empower them by supporting their political and social rights.

Notes

1. In formal terms, "indigenous" is more suitable for describing socially excluded groups in the western hemisphere and other areas of mass migration than in areas where majority groups have been in place for many centuries. However, "indigenous peoples" has been used generally to refer to socially excluded groups, and we will continue that usage here.
2. Hall and Patrinos 2011.
3. Ibid 2011. This gap is expressed as the money required to raise the poor from their present income to the poverty line, as a proportion of the poverty line, and averaged over the total population.

4. Garcia-Moreno and Patrinos forthcoming.

5. Ravallion 2010.

6. Das et al. forthcoming.

7. Hoff and Pandey 2004; UNESCO 2010.

8. For example, Alesina et al. 2003.

9. Lewis and Lockheed 2006.

10. WHO 2010, p. 8.

11. Parodi, Muñoz, and Sanhueza 2010.

12. UN 2010b.

13. Lewis and Lockheed 2006, p. 8.

14. Das et al. forthcoming.

15. King and Van de Walle forthcoming.

16. Figure 1.3 and table 1.1 in chapter 1 and table A1.1 in the appendix show the countries by MDG status.

17. Borja-Vega, Lunde, and Garcia Moreno 2007.

18. Das et al. 2010.

19. MacDonald forthcoming.

20. Dang 2010.

21. Ravallion 2010.

22. World Bank 2009.

23. Ravallion 2010.

24. Ravallion 2010; Lanjouw and Ravallion 1999.

25. Dollar, Glewwe, and Litvack 1998.

26. Baulch et al. 2007.

27. Hall and Patrinos 2006.

28. Fiszbein and Schady 2009.

29. Hall and Patrinos 2011.

30. See, for example, Dollar and Kraay (2002).

31. Ravallion 2010.

32. Gertler, Patrinos, and Rodríguez-Oreggia 2010.

33. Nopo, Chong, and Moro 2010; Patrinos, Skoufias, and Lunde 2010; Hall and Patrinos 2006; Psacharopoulos and Patrinos 1994.

34. Godoy et al. 2005; Rubio et al. 2009.

35. But see Scott (2009), who provides a comprehensive overview of various Southeast Asia groups who have avoided contact with modern society.

36. Ben-Achour, Backiny-Yetna, and Wodon 2011.

37. Huanca 2008; Ringhofer 2009.

38. Rubio et al. 2009.

39. Godoy, Reyes-García, Broesch et al. 2009.

40. Reyes-García et al. 2009.

41. Godoy, Eisenberg et al. 2008.

42. Godoy et al. 2005.

43. Godoy, Reyes-García, Gravlee et al. 2009.

44. Reyes-García and others 2010.

45. Godoy et al. 2006.

46. Tanner et al. 2009.

47. Godoy, Tanner et al. 2008.

48. Becker 1971.

49. Daley and Lui 1995; Patrinos and Sakellariou 1992; Brosnan 1984; Kimmel 1997; Hall and Patrinos 2006; Ohenjo et al. 2006.

50. Bertrand and Mallainathan 2003.

References

Alesina, A., A. Devleeschauwer, W. Easterly, S. Kurlat, and R. Wacziarg. 2003. "Fractionalization." *Journal of Economic Growth* 8: 155–94.

Bando, R., L. F. Lopez-Calva, and H. A. Patrinos. 2005. "Child Labor, School Attendance, and Indigenous Households: Evidence from Mexico." Policy Research Working Paper 3487, World Bank, Washington DC.

Baulch, B., T.T.K. Chuyen, D. Haughton, and J. Haughton. 2007. "Ethnic Minority Development in Vietnam." *Journal of Development Studies* 43 (7): 1151–76.

Becker, G. S. 1971. *The Economics of Discrimination*. 2nd edition. Chicago: University of Chicago Press.

Ben-Achour, A., P. Backiny-Yetna, and Q. Wodon. 2011. "Socioeconomic Status of the Pygmies in the Democratic Republic of Congo." Unpublished manuscript, Human Development Network, World Bank, Washington, DC.

Bertrand, M., and S. Mallainathan. 2003. "Are Emily and Greg More Employable Than Lakisha and Jamal? A Field Experiment on Labor Market Discrimination." Working Paper 9873, National Bureau of Economic Research, Cambridge, MA.

Borja-Vega, C., T. Lunde, and V. Garcia-Moreno. 2007. "Economic Opportunities for Indigenous People in Mexico." Background paper for the study Economic Opportunities for Indigenous Peoples in Latin America, Conference Edition. World Bank, Washington, DC.

Brosnan, P. 1984. "Age, Education and Maori-Pakeha Income Differences." *New Zealand Economic Papers* 18: 49–61.

Daley, A. E., and J. Lui. 1995. "Estimating the Private Rate of Return to Education for Indigenous Australians." Discussion Paper 97, Centre for Aboriginal Economic Policy Research, Australian National University, Canberra.

Dang, H.-A. H. 2010. "Growth in Vietnam Is Strong But Not Shared Equitably across Ethnic Groups." *Indigenous Peoples* Country Brief (Vietnam) No. 1, World Bank, Washington, DC.

Das, M. B., G. Hall, S. Kapoor, and D. Nikitin. 2010. "India's Adivasis." *Indigenous Peoples Country Brief (India) No. 4*, World Bank, Washington, DC.

———. Forthcoming. "India: The Scheduled Tribes" In *Indigenous Peoples, Poverty and Development*, ed. G. Hall and H. A. Patrinos. Cambridge, UK: Cambridge University Press.

de Laat, J. 2010. "Economic Costs of Roma Exclusion." Europe and Central Asia Topic Brief, Human Development Department, World Bank, Washington DC.

Dollar, D., P. Glewwe, and J. Litvack, eds. 1998. *Household Welfare and Vietnam's Transition.* Washington, DC: World Bank.

Dollar, D., and A. Kraay. 2002. "Growth Is Good for the Poor." *Journal of Economic Growth* 7 (3): 195–225.

Fiszbein, A., and N. Schady. 2009. *Conditional Cash Transfers: Reducing Present and Future Poverty.* Washington DC: World Bank.

Garcia-Moreno, V., and H. A. Patrinos. Forthcoming. "Education and Poverty in Mexico: Indigenous Peoples." Teachers College, Columbia University, New York; and Human Development Department, World Bank, Washington, DC.

Gertler, P., H. A. Patrinos, and E. Rodríguez-Oreggia. 2010. "Parental Empowerment in Mexico: Randomized Experiment of the Apoyos a la Gestión Escolar (AGE) in Rural Primary Schools in Mexico: Preliminary Findings." Unpublished manuscript, Human Development Network, World Bank, Washington, DC.

Godoy, R., D.T.A. Eisenberg, V. Reyes-García, T. Huanca, W. R. Leonard, T. W. McDade, and S. Tanner. 2008. "Assortative Mating and Offspring Well-Being: Theory and Empirical Findings from a Native Amazonian Society in Bolivia." *Evolution and Human Behavior* 29: 201–10.

Godoy, R., W. R. Leonard, V. Reyes-Garcia, E. Goodman, T. McDade, T. Huanca, S. Tanner, and V. Vadez. 2006. "Physical Stature of Adult Tsimane' Amerindians, Bolivian Amazon, in the 20th Century." *Economics and Human Biology* 4: 184–205.

Godoy, R., V. Reyes-García, J. Broesch, I. C. Fitzpatrick, P. Giovannini, M. R. M. Rodríguez, T. Huanca, W. R. Leonard, T. W. McDade, and S. Tanner. 2009. "Long-Term (Secular) Change of Ethnobotanical Knowledge of Useful Plants: Separating Cohort and Age Effects." *Journal of Anthropological Research* 65 (1): 51–67.

Godoy, R., V. Reyes-García, C. C. Gravlee, T. Huanca, W. R. Leonard, T. W. McDade, and S. Tanner. 2009. "Moving Beyond a Snapshot to Understand Changes in the Well-Being of Native Amazonians." *Current Anthropology* 50 (4): 563–73.

Godoy, R., V. Reyes-García, T. Huanca, W. R. Leonard, V. Vadez, C. Valdés-Galicia, and D. Zhao. 2005. "Why Do Subsistence-Level People Join the Market Economy? Testing Hypotheses of Push and Pull Determinants in Bolivian Amazonia." *Journal of Anthropological Research* 61 (2): 157–78.

Godoy, R., S. Tanner, V. Reyes-García, W. R. Leonard, T. W. McDade, M. Vento, J. Broesch, I. C. Fitzpatrick, P. Giovannini, T. Huanca, and N. Jha. 2008. "The Effect of Rainfall during Gestation and Early Childhood on Adult Height in a Foraging and Horticultural Society of the Bolivian Amazon." *American Journal of Human Biology* 20 (1): 23–34.

Hall, G., and H. A. Patrinos, eds. 2006. *Indigenous Peoples, Poverty and Human Development in Latin America.* London: Palgrave Macmillan.

———. 2011. *Indigenous Peoples, Poverty and Development.* Cambridge, UK: Cambridge University Press.

Hartley, B. 2008. "MDG Reports and Indigenous Peoples: A Desk Review." Report prepared for the Secretariat of the United Nations Permanent Forum on Indigenous Issues, New York.

Heckman, J. J. 2006. "Skill Formation and the Economics of Investing in Disadvantaged Children." *Science* 312: 1900–02.

Hoff, K., and P. Pandey. 2004. "Belief Systems and Durable Inequalities: An Experimental Investigation of Indian Caste." Policy Research Working Papers 3351, World Bank, Washington DC.

Huanca, T. 2008. *Tsimane' Oral Tradition, Landscape, and Identity in Tropical Forest.* La Paz, Bolivia: Imprenta Wagui.

Kimmel, J. 1997. "Rural Wages and Returns to Education: Differences between Whites, blacks, and American Indians." *Economics of Education Review* 16 (1): 81–96.

King, E. M., and D Van de Walle. Forthcoming. "Laos: Ethno-Linguistic Diversity and Disadvantage." in *Indigenous Peoples, Poverty and Development*, ed. G. Hall and H. A. Patrinos. Cambridge, UK: Cambridge University Press.

Kremer, M., E. Miguel, and R. Thornton. 2009. "Incentives to Learn." *Review of Economics and Statistics* 91 (3): 437–56.

Lanjouw, P., and M. Ravallion. 1999. "Benefit Incidence, Public Spending Reforms, and the Timing of Program Capture." *World Bank Economic Review* 13 (2): 257–73.

Lewis, M. A., and M. E. Lockheed. 2006. *Inexcusable Absence: Why 60 Million Girls Still Aren't in School and What to Do about It.* Washington DC: Center for Global Development.

MacDonald, K. Forthcoming. "Indigenous Peoples and Development Goals: A Global Snapshot." in *Indigenous Peoples, Poverty and Development,* ed. G. Hall and H. A. Patrinos. Cambridge, UK: Cambridge University Press.

Nopo, H., A. Chong, and A. Moro, eds. 2010. *Discrimination in Latin America: An Economic Perspective.* Washington DC: World Bank.

Ohenjo, N., R. Willis, D. Jackson, C. Nettleton, K. Good, and B. Mugarura. 2006. "Health of Indigenous People in Africa." *Lancet* 367: 1937–46.

OSI (Open Society Foundation). 2010. *No Data—No Progress: Country Findings. Data Collection in Countries Participating in the Decade of Roma Inclusion 2005–2015.* New York.

Parodi C. T., S. Muñoz, and A. Sanhueza. 2010. "Acceso y gasto de salud para grupos étnicos/raciales en la región de las Américas." *World Health Report 2010* background paper, no. 46. http://www.who.int/healthsystems/topics/financing/healthreport/whr_background/en.

Patrinos, H. A. 2007. "Living Conditions of Children." In *Solutions for the World's Biggest Problems: Costs and Benefits,* ed. B. Lomborg, 358–75. Cambridge, UK: Cambridge University Press.

Patrinos, H. A., and C. N. Sakellariou. 1992. "North American Indians in the Canadian Labour Market: A Decomposition of Wage Differentials." *Economics of Education Review* 2 (3): 257–66.

Patrinos, H. A., E. Skoufias, and T. Lunde. 2010. "Social Networks among Indigenous Peoples in Mexico." *Latin American Research Review* 45 (2): 49–67.

Patrinos, H. A., and E. Velez. 2009. "Costs and Benefits of Bilingual Education in Guatemala: A Partial Analysis." *International Journal of Educational Development* 29 (6): 594–98.

Psacharopoulos, G., and H. A. Patrinos, eds. 1994. *Indigenous People and Poverty in Latin America: An Empirical Analysis.* Washington, DC: World Bank.

Ravallion, M. 2010. "A Comparative Perspective on Poverty Reduction in Brazil, China and India." *World Bank Research Observer* 26 (1): 71–104.

Reyes-García, V., E. Kightley, I. Ruiz-Mallén, N. Fuentes-Peláez, K. Demps, T. Huanca, and M. Martínez-Rodríguez. 2009. "Schooling and Local Environmental Knowledge: Do They Complement or Substitute Each Other?" Unpublished manuscript, Tsimane' Amazonian Panel Study, Brandeis University, Waltham, MA.

Reyes-García, V., M. Orta-Martínez, M. Gueze, A. C. Luz, J. Paneque-Gálvez, M. J. Macía, J. Pino, J. Cristobal, and TAPS Bolivian Study Team. 2010. "Does Participatory Mapping Increase Conflict? A Randomized Experimental Evaluation in the Bolivian Amazon." TAPS working paper 59. http://tsimane.org/research/pgs/workingpapers.html.

Ringhofer, L. 2009. *Fishing, Foraging and Farming in the Bolivian Amazon: On a Local Society in Transition.* New York: Springer.

Ringold, D., M. A. Orenstein, and E. Wilkens. 2005. *Roma in an Expanding Europe: Breaking the Poverty Cycle.* Washington DC: World Bank.

Rubio, K., E. Undurraga, O. Magvanjav, C. Gravlee, T. Huanca, W. R. Leonard, T. W. McDade, V. Reyes-García, S. Tanner, R. Godoy, and TAPS Team. 2009. "Modernization and Culture Loss: A Natural Experiment among Native Amazonians in Bolivia." Tsimane' Amazonian Panel Study Working Paper. http://tsimane.org/research/pgs/workingpapers.html.

Schlotter, M. 2010. "The Relationship between Human Capital Quality, Governance and Educational Institutions: First Steps towards a Panel Approach." Unpublished manuscript, Human Development Network, World Bank, Washington, DC.

Scott, J. 2009. *The Art of Not Being Governed: An Anarchist History of Upland Southeast Asia.* Yale Agrarian Studies Series. New Haven, CT: Yale University Press.

Tanner, S., W. R. Leonard, T. W. McDade, V. Reyes-García, R. Godoy, and T. Huanca. 2009. "Influence of Helminth Infections on Childhood Nutritional Status in Lowland Bolivia." *American Journal of Human Biology* 21: 651–56.

Telles, E. E. 2007. "Race and Ethnicity and Latin America's United Nations Millennium Development Goals." *Latin American and Caribbean Ethnic Studies* 2 (2): 185–200.

UN (United Nations). 1981. "Study of the Problem of Discrimination against Indigenous

Populations." Final Report submitted by the Special Rapporteur, Jose R. Martinez Cobo, United Nations Economic and Social Council, Commission on Human Rights, Sub-Commission on Prevention of Discrimination and Protection of Minorities, 34th session, E/CN.4/Sub.2/476, New York.

————. 2009. *State of the World's Indigenous Peoples*. New York.

————. 2010a. *Human Rights and the Millennium Development Goals in Practice: A Review of Country Strategies and Reporting*. New York.

————. 2010b. *The Millennium Development Goals Report*. New York.

UNESCO (United Nations Educational, Scientific, and Cultural Organization). 2010. *Education for All Global Monitoring Report 2010: Reaching the Marginalized*. Oxford, UK: Oxford University Press.

WHO (World Health Organization). 2010. *World Health Report 2010: Health Systems Financing: The Path to Universal Coverage*. Geneva, Switzerland.

World Bank. 2009. "From Poor Areas to Poor People: China's Evolving Poverty Reduction Agenda. An Assessment of Poverty and Inequality in China. Washington, DC.

————. 2010. "Roma Inclusion: An Economic Opportunity for Bulgaria, Czech Republic, Romania and Serbia." Policy Note, Human Development Sector Unit, Europe and Central Asia Region, Washington, DC.

Progress in the International Development and Trading Framework

The global economy has weathered the financial crisis, but the recovery remains fragile. Governments and international institutions cooperated in the face of recession, thus avoiding the perils of a protectionist spiral, maintaining aid levels, and boosting emergency financial resources. Because a beneficial global environment also supports progress toward the Millennium Development Goals (MDGs), this chapter reviews recent changes in the international development framework—in the context of the gradual transformation of development policies over the past decade.

Aid in 2010 rose in real terms over 2009, despite fears that the sharp rise in fiscal deficits during the crisis would severely constrain donor budgets. Even so, recent research suggests that declines in aid have tended to deepen for a period of years following past banking crises. Some major donor governments remained dedicated to maintaining aid in 2010, while others announced cuts.

New donors that are not members of the Organisation for Economic Co-operation and Development (OECD) Development Assistance Committee (DAC) may provide some $12 billion to $15 billion in aid disbursements a year. There is keen interest to engage with them at the Fourth High Level Forum on Aid Effectiveness, to be held in Busan, Republic of Korea, at the end of 2011. The objective is to forge a new consensus on development assistance coming out of Busan—one that reflects the growing role of non-OECD-DAC countries. Developing countries are also receiving more assistance from private sources. Philanthropic flows to developing countries from the private sector in advanced countries may have exceeded $60 billion in 2008, more than 10 times the amount received early in the decade.

Nonetheless, new donor flows will not compensate for any significant fall in aid from traditional donors, particularly if they pursue different development priorities and practices. The changing aid landscape could also have implications for the transparency of official flows and for the policies and programs that aid supports.

World trade, recovering at about double the 2002–08 rate of growth, remains well below the precrisis peak and even lower than it would have been if trade had continued to follow the rising 1995–2008 trend. The new protectionist measures during the crisis, which hit the exports of least-developed countries (LDCs), appear to be receding. Solidifying an

A human flood chokes the mud-slick remnants of a highway, the main vein for commerce through the Ituri, Democratic Republic of the Congo. Rough and rutted during dry weather, the roads are nearly impassable in the wet season. But rain can't stop the toleka traders, who push goods hundreds of miles by bicycle.

125

open, rules-based international trade regime can best be accomplished by (finally) concluding the Doha Round. Efforts to increase trade integration of the poorest developing countries should focus on extending duty-free, quota-free access to their exports, providing financial resources and technical assistance to improve trade facilitation, and simplifying rules of origin in preference agreements. Regional trade agreements should support open trade through low external tariffs, and technical assistance to developing-country trade negotiators would support deeper regional integration. International efforts to avoid a collapse in trade finance during the crisis were timely and successful. But further steps are required to ensure that low-income countries can obtain trade finance at reasonable cost, along with improvements in data and a review of whether banking regulations impose excessive capital requirements on trade finance transactions.

The past tumultuous decade has ushered in significant changes in the assistance policies of the international institutions. The multilateral development banks have developed a results-based, country-driven assistance framework grounded in regular reviews of country strategy and independent evaluations. A more diverse and flexible range of financing facilities has helped tailor assistance to the needs of particular countries (such as those affected by conflict) and in particular situations (such as disaster relief and crisis assistance). The international financial institutions (IFIs) also are doing more in providing knowledge in the context of loans and technical assistance to their clients, both through global projects and programs and through the free provision of information to the global community. The financing provided to crisis-affected countries jumped sharply with the onset of the crisis, leading to a general increase in IFI resources.

An unprecedented decade for aid

Economic and political events since the Millennium Declaration in 2000 have reordered the aid framework. Booming economic growth, higher capital flows, and surging trade flows were followed by the worst economic crisis since the Great Depression. Wars have led to shifts in priorities among international donors. And China and India, with some other developing countries, have emerged as economic powerhouses.

Over the last decade, donors reaffirmed their commitments to increasing aid flows and improving aid quality, as in the Monterrey Declaration at the 2002 Financing for Development conference in Mexico and the Gleneagles G-8 and Millennium +5 summits in 2005. At the September 2010 United Nations Summit on MDGs, held in New York, representatives of key stakeholders—including governments, international organizations, and private and public sectors—reaffirmed their commitment to work together to achieve the MDGs in the five years left.

Will the crisis undermine recent commitments?

This reaffirmation was all the more remarkable, given the potential impact of the crisis on donor budgets. These may be threatened as high income countries struggle to control fiscal deficits. Even so, aid flows from DAC donors rose in 2010 (to $128.7 billion in 2010 from $119.8 billion in 2009, a 6.5 percent increase in real terms). Despite various shortfalls against commitments, the impact of the financial crisis on aid, at least in 2009 and 2010, was relatively mild. Official development assistance (ODA) as a percentage of gross national income (GNI) rose from 0.26 percent in 2004 to 0.31 percent in 2009 and to 0.32 percent in 2010.

The United States remained the largest donor in 2009 ($28.8 billion), with France ($12.6 billion), Germany ($12.1 billion, the United Kingdom ($11.5 billion), and Japan ($9.5 billion) following. With a net inflow of $6.1 billion, Afghanistan was the largest recipient in 2009, followed by Ethiopia ($3.8 billion), Vietnam ($3.7 billion), West Bank and Gaza ($3.0 billion), and Tanzania ($2.9 billion) (box 5.1). The amount of aid for debt relief and technical assistance as a share of total net official development assistance declined.

BOX 5.1   Aid recipients

Aggregate aid flows often reflect geopolitical priorities and/or responses to major global events. It is therefore not a surprise that Iraq and Afghanistan were the largest aid recipients over the last decade (top table below). In per capita terms, the pattern is also mixed at the country level. The top 10 recipients in per capita net official development assistance in 2008 were West Bank and Gaza ($659), Botswana ($373), Liberia ($330), Iraq ($321), Lebanon ($257), Timor-Leste ($253), Georgia ($206), Afghanistan ($168), Serbia ($142), and the Democratic Republic of Congo ($140).

Low-income countries captured the largest share net official development assistance in 2008 and received the highest amount in per capita terms. By geographic region, Sub-Saharan Africa received the highest aggregate aid flows, but it is second to the Middle East and North Africa in per capita terms (lower table below)

Largest aid recipients by decade
billions, constant 2008 US$

1960–69		1980–89		2000–09	
India	64.7	India	42.4	Iraq	68.1
Pakistan	25.1	Egypt, Arab Rep.	31.0	Afghanistan	35.5
Algeria	20.7	Bangladesh	29.6	Nigeria	29.2
Vietnam	17.5	Israel	23.2	Ethiopia	27.4
Korea, Rep.	14.5	Indonesia	20.9	Vietnam	27.4
Brazil	13.1	Pakistan	20.5	Tanzania	25.4
Turkey	12.6	China	19.5	Congo, Dem. Rep.	24.8
Indonesia	12.4	Syrian Arab Republic	18.7	Pakistan	23.4
Congo, Dem. Rep.	8.4	Sudan	18.6	Mozambique	21.1
Israel	8.1	Tanzania	16.9	India	20.6
1970–79		**1990–99**		*Source:* DAC database.	
India	44.8	Egypt, Arab Rep.	41.1		
Egypt, Arab Rep.	44.8	China	33.6		
Indonesia	25.1	India	25.0		
Pakistan	21.2	Bangladesh	21.3		
Bangladesh	19.5	Indonesia	18.9		
Syrian Arab Republic	18.2	Mozambique	16.3		
Vietnam	15.6	Tanzania	15.2		
Israel	13.6	Israel	14.4		
Jordan	12.4	Pakistan	14.0		
Korea, Rep.	10.5	Ethiopia	13.3		

Aid flows by income groups and region, 2008

Income groups and regions	Total ($ billions)	Per capita ($)
Income		
Low	41.4	42
Lower middle	37.1	10
Higher middle	11.8	12
Regions		
East Asia and Pacific	9.1	5
Europe and Central Asia	8.2	19
Latin America and the Caribbean	9.3	16
Middle East and North Africa	23.6	73
South Asia	12.3	8
Sub-Saharan Africa	40.1	49

Source: Word Development Indicators database.

The largest increases in real terms in ODA between 2009 and 2010 were recorded by Australia, Belgium, Canada, Japan, Korea, Portugal, and the United Kingdom. Many countries (for example, the United Kingdom) have maintained their original commitments to aid flows made at the Gleneagles G-8 and Millennium +5 summits in 2005. Other donor countries, however, have announced shifts in their aid policy because aid budgets are under strain and economic growth in many high-income countries is slow in recovering to pre-crisis levels. The Dutch government plans to cut foreign aid from 0.8 percent to 0.7 percent of gross national income. Ireland and Spain have already cut their aid budgets, and France has announced a postponement of its commitments.

The year 2010 marked an important target for DAC countries that are part of the European Union. In 2005, they collectively agreed to increase aid to 0.56 percent of gross national income within five years, with a minimum country requirement of 0.51 percent. Some countries—including Belgium, Finland, Denmark, Ireland, Luxembourg, the Netherlands, Spain, Sweden, and the United Kingdom—appear to be on track to meet this goal.[1] Others—including Austria, France, Germany, Greece, Italy, and Portugal—appear unlikely to reach it. Similarly, the United States set the goal of doubling its aid to Sub-Saharan Africa between 2004 and 2010. It achieved this in 2009. Japan, by contrast, fell short of its Gleneagles promise that its aid during 2005–09 would equal $10 billion more than if it had remained at the 2004 level, owing to serious budgetary constraints.

Overall, donor countries have remained pretty much on track in meeting their aid commitments, despite the economic downturn. But we will only really know the true impact of the crisis on aid several years down the road. Reinhart and Rogoff argue that the full impact on aid flows of a recession following a banking crisis can be felt for several years after the crisis, owing to enduring effects of the crisis on the country's fiscal position and growth prospects.[2] Similarly, Dang, Knack, and Rogers find that aid flows during 1977–2007 fell by 20–25 percent, on average, from donor countries with banking crises, beyond any income-related effects (figure 5.1).[3] And the effects can last as long as 10 years after the onset of a crisis.[4] Is this pattern going to repeat itself?

New donors appear on the scene

During most of the last half of a century, DAC donors, with international organizations, accounted for most aid flows. Since 1960, the United States, Japan, Germany, France, and the United Kingdom have been the largest donors in absolute terms; and the Nordic countries have given the most, relative to gross national income.[5]

But the global balance of aid has started to shift rapidly in the past five years because some developing countries' recent strong growth gives them more resources to share in development. There is a clear lack of reliable data. Until recently, the DAC Creditor Reporting System, which captures only a partial picture of total aid flows, was the only available database. DAC donors are required to report their financial flows to the OECD, whereas non-DAC donors can voluntarily provide the information to the organization.

FIGURE 5.1   Impact of banking crises on net disbursed aid provided by crisis-affected donors, 1977–2007

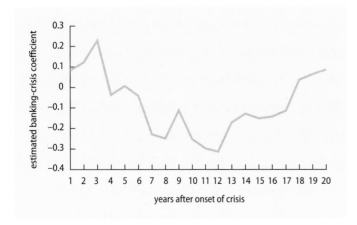

Source: Dang, Knack, and Rogers 2009.

Twenty non-DAC donors now report to the OECD. Some of them—such as Saudi Arabia, Thailand, and Turkey—provide significant amounts of aid. Overall, non-DAC donors reporting to the DAC contributed 5 percent of net aid ($6.7 billion in current dollars) in 2009. But other non-DAC donors making significant contributions to development assistance are not recorded by DAC, including Brazil, China, India, Malaysia, the Russian Federation, and República Bolivariana de Venezuela.

In total, non-DAC donors provided about $12 billion to $15 billion in aid in 2008.[6] Arab countries together would constitute the largest non-DAC donor, contributing $5.9 billion.[7] Development assistance from the BRIC countries (Brazil, Russia, India, and China) is estimated in the range of $2.3–$5.1 billion in fiscal 2006/07, with Chinese assistance at $1.4 billion to $3.0 billion. These figures may be underestimated. China's aid to Africa alone was estimated at nearly $2.5 billion in 2009.[8]

Flows from multilateral institutions grew to $28 billion in 2009, and the number of institutions has increased. There are now more than 260 multilateral aid agencies, including development banks, the United Nations, and specialized funds that have become important or have been set up in recent years.[9] These funds tend to deliver aid with a special focus, such as HIV prevention and treatment, vaccines, or disaster prevention and relief.

Other key aid flows in recent years have come from civil society organizations and private philanthropists. No reliable figures exist for total aid from this group, but one recent estimate has their total aid reaching $53 billion in 2008, more than 10 times the amount early in the decade.[10] The largest is the Gates Foundation, which has a total asset trust endowment of more than $35 billion and annual disbursements of $3 billion to $4 billion.[11] Additional work is clearly needed to systematically gather more reliable data.

Still, the emergence of new aid flows and actors has led to changes and increased the complexity of the aid architecture, requiring a new consensus on aid effectiveness. With so many actors, donor activities are less likely to be coordinated effectively in recipient countries. Aid-funded projects are also likely to follow different rules, increasing the risk of more fragmentation and higher transaction costs for donors and recipients. Moreover, differences in aid policies may undermine aid effectiveness through a lack of transparency, possible violations of international aid and governance standards, and unfair competition. Incorporating the viewpoints of new actors is likely to enrich the discussions and bring key voices of the international community into this important global dialogue.

Aid effectiveness

Aid effectiveness is a critical agenda for partner-countries, donors, and other aid providers—including the World Bank. The importance of results of development efforts, including external assistance, is the fourth pillar of new research directions at the World Bank.[12] The 2005 Paris Declaration on Aid Effectiveness and the 2008 Accra Agenda for Action have focused on the following principles, intended to improve the quality and effectiveness of aid:

1. strengthening country ownership of development,
2. building more effective and inclusive partnerships for development, and
3. delivering and accounting for development results.

Monitoring tools have been developed to improve the accountability of donors and aid recipients. The Survey on Monitoring the Paris Declaration was developed to monitor the implementation of these principles by measuring progress against the commitments made by both partner-countries and donors. To measure progress between 2005 and 2010, surveys—consisting of 12 quantitative indicators and qualitative information—were conducted in 2006 and 2008, with the third survey scheduled for 2011. An evaluation tool called the Evaluation of the Implementation of the Paris Declaration is intended to provide more comprehensive understanding of how increased aid effectiveness contributes to meeting development objectives (results forthcoming in the spring of 2011).

Several assessment tools have focused on the quality or effectiveness of donors, including by observers such as Easterly and Pfutze,[13] Roodman,[14] and the Brookings Institution's Quality of Official Development Assistance Assessment (QuODA, developed in 2010). Other attempts sponsored by bilateral donors include the Multilateral Organizational Performance Assessment Network, the United Kingdom's Multilateral Aid Review, and self-evaluations such as the Common Performance Assessment System. More recently, Knack, Rogers, and Eubank developed an index to compare donor performance and assess how well donors are delivering on their mandates.[15] Two of these assessments are described here to provide a sense of the results:

- In Knack, Rogers, and Eubank 2010, the selectivity subindex reviews policies and measures of poverty reduction, based primarily on GDP per capita and the World Bank's Country Policy and Institutional Assessment index. The index covers the four most common dimensions of aid quality in the relevant literature—selectivity, alignment, harmonization, and specialization. Alignment focuses on ways that donor countries match their aid to support country priorities and policies outlined in country development strategies. Harmonization involves coordination among donors that is designed to avoid duplication and high transaction costs in recipient countries. The specialization subindex attempts to capture the fragmentation of donor aid, including geographic concentration of aid, concentration of aid by sector, and average size of projects. In the overall ranking of the quality index (the average of the four subindexes), Denmark came first among bilateral donors, followed by Ireland, the Netherlands, Sweden, and the United Kingdom; the Asian Development Bank

(ADB) scored the highest among multilateral donors, followed by the World Bank, the International Monetary Fund (IMF), the International Fund for Agricultural Development, and the Global Alliance for Vaccines and Immunisation.

- The QuODA Index, compiled by Nancy Birdsall and Homi Kharas, takes into account four broad categories covering 30 aid-related indicators: maximizing efficiency, fostering institutions, reducing the burden on recipients, and transparency and learning.[16] Different from Knack, Rogers, and Eubank, QuODA does not aggregate across sectors because of the low correlations among the four categories. It also looks at both bilateral and multilateral agencies. The International Development Association (IDA) and Ireland scored in the top 10 for all four categories.

Transparency is emerging as a major component of aid effectiveness because it is essential to enhancing accountability. For donors, one of the most important initiatives is the International Aid Transparency Initiative, which aims at establishing common global reporting standards on aid and publishing aid information in a way that is accessible to various stakeholders for the purposes of global reporting and improving budget management by partner-countries. Progress on how donors rank on their transparency has been monitored in the 2010 report on "Aid Transparency Assessment."[17] For partner-countries, transparency in public finances is critical for accountability. Several frameworks attempt to measure fiscal transparency—frameworks such as the IMF's Good Practices on Fiscal Transparency; the OECD's Best Practices for Budget Transparency; the Public Expenditure and Financial Accountability assessments supported by the World Bank Group (WBG); and public sector accounting standards from the International Federation of Accountants, the International Organization of Supreme Audit Institutions, and the International Budget Project's Open Budget Index.

The aim of these indexes is to give donor countries and organizations a metric for comparison as well as an objective framework for ways to improve the quality of aid over time. But aid is measured; a more fundamental question remains: does aid contribute to development at all?

The impact of aid

For decades, researchers have grappled with the question of whether foreign aid inflows lead to positive changes in a recipient country—economic and otherwise—and, if so, in what form. Does aid lead to long-term improvements in the recipient country in the form of increased growth? Or does it harm the economy in some way? And if it helps, what type of aid helps best?

Resolving these questions is critical for aid policy, particularly given the huge sums. Some studies find that aid has a positive impact on a country's growth, others that a positive impact depends on certain economic and political factors, and still others that aid has no impact on growth. Indicators include macroeconomic factors, openness or trade variables, governance and political conditions, and geographic location.[18] Burnside and Dollar's seminal paper concluded that aid has a positive effect on growth in countries with good policy environments.[19] But according to Doucouliagos and Paldam, no clear conclusion emerges from the aid literature.[20]

Analyzing the effectiveness of particular forms of aid, Clemens, Radelet, and Bhavnani find a positive relationship between economic growth and "short-impact aid."[21] Mavrotas, reviewing the impact of different types of aid on Uganda's fiscal sector, finds that project and food aid reduces public investment, whereas program aid and technical assistance increase it.[22] Reddy and Minoiu, distinguishing between what they call developmental aid and geopolitical aid,[23] find that the former has a strong, positive impact on growth, and the latter has a weak but negative relationship with growth.[24] Heyman, in her sectoral analysis of the link between aid and economic improvement, finds that only humanitarian aid has a positive impact on per capita GDP.[25]

Much aid is, of course, targeted at improving health, nutrition, and education, as well as at such nondevelopmental objectives as disaster relief. Such interventions are primarily directed at welfare, particularly of the poor, although they also can have an important impact on growth. For example, the German and Irish governments' funding for the Kalomo cash transfer program in Zambia was likely intended to reduce poverty and malnourishment, rather than to raise GDP directly.

Some researchers have looked at the impact of social sector aid on country progress in achieving the MDGs. Michaelowa and Weber find aid for education (both per capita and as a share of GDP) increases primary enrollment and completion rates.[26] Dreher, Nunnenkamp, and Thiele find that increased per capita aid for education significantly increases primary school enrollment.[27] Mishra and Newhouse, using a data set of 118 countries for 1973–2004, find that doubling per capita health aid is associated with a 2 percent reduction in the infant mortality rate. Therefore, increasing per capita health aid from $1.60 to $3.20 will lead to roughly 1.5 fewer deaths per 1,000 births—a lift that is encouraging but small, relative to the MDG targets.[28]

These results show that not all aid is effective. Bourguignon and Sundberg point out the need to "open the black box" and better understand the relationship between aid and development outcomes.[29] This can be done through analyses that focus on three basic relationships: the impact of policies on outcomes (knowledge, either ex post from impact evaluation or ex ante from modeling or economic reasoning), the influence of policy makers on policy, and the influence of external donors and international financial institutions on policy makers.

Myriad factors play on whether aid achieves its desired impact—or any positive impact. Some examples include the level of recipient-country ownership and the conditions imposed by donors, the predictability of future flows of aid, the investment climate of the recipient country, whether aid is tied, and the apparatus to monitor and evaluate progress. The changing aid architecture, which has new faces, new priorities, and a new structure, will play a major role in the next years.[30] Aid quality, together with strong international coordination, will continue to be a focus to improve the delivery and effectiveness of aid and its impact on developing countries

Trade and the global economic recovery

In the aftermath of the recent financial crisis, trade has recently begun its path to recovery. Sustaining it will be critical. But many developing countries continue to face considerable challenges in reaching global markets as a result of limited or weak trade-related infrastructure and institutions, unfavorable business climates, limited access to trade finance, and protectionist restrictions. High and volatile food prices also create vulnerabilities, particularly for low-income countries with high shares of food imports and limited fiscal space.

After a brief review of the ongoing trade recovery, this section discusses the key challenges and opportunities to strengthen the international system and enhance the ability of developing countries—particularly the more vulnerable low-income countries—to

benefit from greater trade integration. To maintain the recent momentum toward recovery, concerted efforts will be required to keep protectionist tendencies in check and to recommit to building a stronger and more effective multilateral trading system that serves developing countries through the conclusion of the Doha Round. It will be important to ensure that regional trade agreements, which can enhance market access, promote open regionalism. Also needed are measures to support access to trade finance and trade facilitation to connect vulnerable low-income countries, landlocked countries, and lagging regions to regional and international markets—and an expansion of aid for trade to ensure that the developing countries can implement such reforms and reap the gains of trade integration.

Trade remains crucial after the "great" trade collapse

World merchandise trade has recovered since early 2009, but it remains below precrisis levels (see figure 5.2). The world import value increased nearly 30 percent since its low point in February 2009, recovering at twice its growth rate during 2002–08. The recovery in trade is much faster among developing countries than among high-income countries. In the first 10 months of 2010, high-income-country export volumes grew at 10.4 percent a year, compared with 15.5 percent among developing countries. But the world import value remains 18 percent lower than the precrisis peak, even lower than if the world economy had continued to grow at the 1995–2008 trend. The pace of trade recovery is now decelerating, and the prospects are unclear. Although the global GDP growth projection for 2011 has been revised upward (by a quarter of a point to 4.4 percent) in anticipation of stronger growth in the United States, persistent high food prices threaten to undermine it.

Trade bounced back in all developing regions (figure 5.3), driven by a vibrant rebound in emerging economies. By 2010, all developing regions recovered to their precrisis export volumes, with East Asia and the

FIGURE 5.2   Exports have yet to recover their precrisis trend

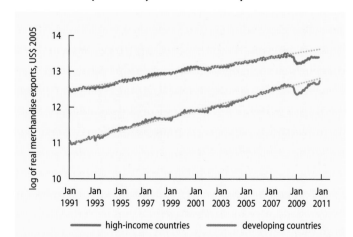

Sources: Datastream; World Bank Development Prospects Group.

FIGURE 5.3   **Merchandise export volume**

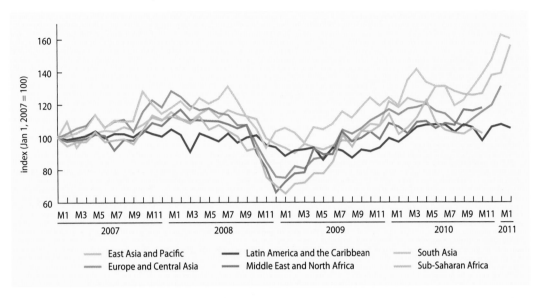

Legend:
- East Asia and Pacific
- Europe and Central Asia
- Latin America and the Caribbean
- Middle East and North Africa
- South Asia
- Sub-Saharan Africa

Source: World Bank Development Economics Prospects Group data.

Pacific and South Asia (especially China and India) leading this recovery. Export volumes in South Asia and East Asia and the Pacific peaked higher than precrisis levels. Trade volumes in the Middle East and North Africa also rebounded, but continue to be constrained by the sluggish growth in their main markets in the European Union. The downturn in exports in Europe and Central Asia turned a corner in August 2010, led by strong intraregional trade that saw the region more than recover its precrisis levels by the end of 2010. Exports in Latin America and the Caribbean remained lackluster, with sharp drops in October 2010 in Argentina and Chile as a result of strikes and disruptions in metal supply and weather-related agricultural shocks. Export growth in Africa has recovered from its trough during the crisis, but remains volatile. Globally, low-income countries have been insulated not only from the economic downturn, but also from the recovery, reflecting their lack of integration in the world economy. Their exports and imports, in both volume and value terms, remained comparatively flat during both the crisis and the postcrisis recovery.

Benefits from global trade require continuing vigilance against protectionist tendencies

Given the importance of trade and investment for the global economic recovery, the G-20 commitment to resist all forms of protectionist measures, to keep markets open, and to liberalize trade and investment to promote economic progress for all is welcome. This commitment, reiterated during the November 2010 meeting in Seoul, Republic of Korea, has been a centerpiece of the G-20 response to the global economic crisis. It may have spared the world economy from falling into a 1930s Depression-era scenario.

The World Trade Organization (WTO) reports some progress in lifting protectionist measures imposed in the wake of the financial crisis (figure 5.4). The latest WTO Trade Policy Review (November 2010) indicates that 415 measures were reported by members between November 2009 and October 2010, down from 430 in the aftermath of the crisis between October 2008 and October 2009. Whereas more than three-quarters of the measures were trade restrictive in the

FIGURE 5.4   Trade-restrictive measures have fallen since 2008

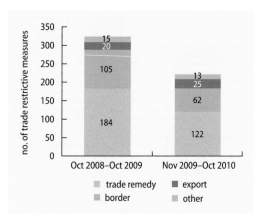

Source: WTO Trade Policy Review OV 13.

first year, newly reported restrictive measures came down to two-thirds in the second year. Retrenchment in protectionism since the start of the crisis has nonetheless been slow, as only 15 percent of the restrictive measures introduced in 2008 have been terminated so far. Moreover, newly imposed export measures increased by 25 percent over the same period—primarily export bans and quotas on agricultural products partly resulting from higher food prices. According to WTO estimates, total import-restrictive measures

introduced since the end of 2008 now account for about 1.9 percent of world imports.

G-20 countries remained the most active instigators of restrictive—and liberalizing—measures. About 60 percent of the trade-restrictive measures implemented between November 2009 and October 2010 were imposed by G-20 nations, led by BRICs (85 measures) with India at the head, followed by high-income OECD countries (35 measures). The United States had imposed the second-highest number of trade-restrictive measures in the year after the crisis but reported only four new restrictive measures in the last year. Whereas restrictions imposed in high-income OECD countries were mainly the result of trade remedy investigations—almost all antidumping initiations by the European Union—BRICs brought out both nontariff measures and trade remedy investigations. More detailed information on the number of WTO member–initiated temporary trade barrier investigations (antidumping, safeguards, and countervailing duty policies) from the World Bank's Temporary Trade Barriers database indicates that their number has gone down since the third quarter of 2009 and is back to precrisis levels (figure 5.5). But overall estimates of the impact of these border and behind-the-border measures (including

FIGURE 5.5   Newly initiated trade remedy investigations have peaked

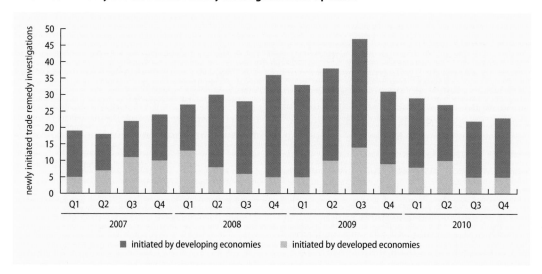

Source: World Bank Temporary Trade Barriers database.

bailouts and subsidies) implemented since the crisis indicate that they contributed to an annual aggregate distortion to global trade of at least $35 billion.[31]

The number of trade-liberalizing measures introduced in 2010 increased by 71 percent over those introduced in 2009. More than a third of the new measures were tariff reductions, introduced primarily by BRICs and lower-middle-income countries, such as Pakistan and Bolivia. Reductions in nontariff measures made up a quarter of all liberalizing measures, mainly from the BRICs. Despite global economic uncertainty, new measures to liberalize trade increased in 2010 (figure 5.6).

The LDCs are particularly harmed by G-20 protectionism. New analysis by the Global Trade Alert[32] indicates that, since November 2008, 141 trade measures imposed by countries worldwide harmed the commercial interests of LDCs. Of these, about 100 measures (70 percent of those imposed) were introduced by G-20 members. Among the G-20, developing countries initiated 70 percent of the measures, led, in order, by India, Argentina, Indonesia, and Russia. Among LDCs, Bangladesh has been affected by the largest number of measures, followed by Tanzania, the Republic of Yemen, Senegal, and Sudan. These measures may significantly restrict LDC exports, particularly for some products they specialize in, thus contravening the undertaking at the G-20 summit.

High and volatile food prices are also creating vulnerabilities, particularly for low-income countries with high shares of food imports and limited fiscal space. Whereas individual governments can insulate themselves to some degree from increases in world prices by imposing export bans or making tactical reductions in import tariffs, these measures increase the volatility of world prices. Trade policy is generally not the appropriate instrument to achieve food security and rural development. High protection hurts households that are net consumers. Long-term solutions include, among other things, higher agricultural productivity to raise farmer incomes and lower consumer prices, liberalization around the world and commitment to multilateral trade rules, public access to information on

FIGURE 5.6   Trade-restrictive and trade-liberalizing measures, November 2009–October 2010

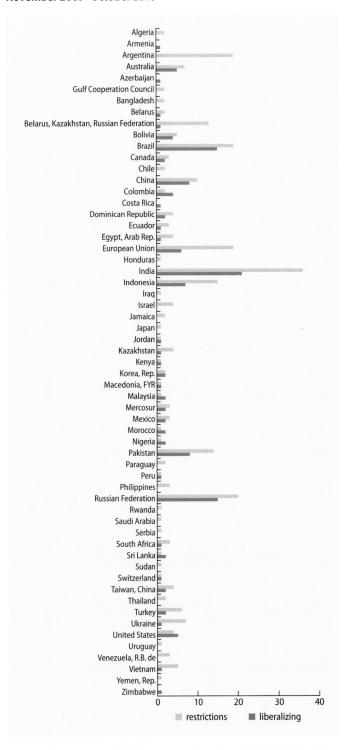

Source: World Bank International Trade Department calculations based on WTO Trade Policy Review Overview Annex 1, November 2010.
Note: Of the 486 trade-related measures listed in the annex, 19 were unclassifiable because of insufficient information regarding their trade effect.

the quality and quantity of grain stocks, and effective safety nets.[33]

Keeping markets open for LDC exports would help lift those countries out of poverty. Extending 100 percent duty-free, quota-free (DFQF) access to all exports of LDCs would promote new export opportunities for LDCs, particularly market access for products in which LDCs have a comparative advantage. Although trade preference programs provide high levels of product coverage, preferences are often underused and exclude products important to LDC exporters—for example, agricultural goods (for African exporters) and textiles, apparel, and footwear (for Asian exporters).

Extending DFQF from 97 percent to 100 percent could have a significant impact. Overall export gains for WTO-member LDCs could be on the order of $2 billion if G-20 OECD countries extended to 100 percent product coverage; this amount could be even larger if BRICs also offered full market access. For example, full DFQF access to all G-20 markets could increase Malawi's GDP by some 10 percent; for Tanzania, the benefits of full DFQF granted by non-OECD G-20 countries are double those generated through DFQF enacted by only the OECD members. Given the size of the economies of low-income countries and the apparent complementarities with the G-20 countries, the additional imports are unlikely to pose undue costs or disruptions to G-20 markets.[34] More comprehensive efforts to harmonize and coordinate trade preferences would also increase the overall effectiveness of trade preferences.

Concluding the Doha Round

The global financial crisis underlined the critical role of a multilateral, rules-based trade system. The WTO's monitoring and reporting of trade measures during the crisis helped distinguish WTO-compatible policies from discriminatory policies, crucial to ensuring a transparent and fair trading system. It also certainly contributed to restraining governments from adopting more pervasive and numerous trade-restrictive policy measures to curtail the domestic impact of the crisis.

As unemployment rates rise despite the global economic recovery, governments should continue to ensure that benefits of an open multilateral trading system are not compromised by short-run pressures to protect domestic markets. Keeping markets open will also be paramount to countering the effects of the withdrawal of expansionary fiscal and monetary policies.

An effective and strong multilateral trading system remains critical for improving market access and accommodating new dynamics of trade. The structure of global production has undergone a major transformation, with global value chains much more prevalent and elaborate, involving more developing countries (including low-income countries). Although weak domestic policies, regulations, and institutions (particularly those increasing the cost of logistics) are the main binding constraint to progress, more gains may be achieved through a concerted, internationally integrated approach to reform, given the multilateral nature of vertical production chains.

Now is the right time to reach an agreement on Doha. Commissioned by a group of developed and developing economies, Peter Sutherland and Jagdish Bhagwati made the case for a deadline to complete the talks before the end of 2011, highlighting three prevailing conditions as opportune. First, higher commodity prices can dissipate resistance by farmers benefiting from subsidies. Second, the weak recovery enhances the attraction of a potential stimulus of approximately $360 billion on global trade. And, third, the new global trade dynamics need to be addressed.[35] Consider the growth and rising complexity of global supply chains: they mean that today's protectionists are more likely to resort to targeted rules than to tariffs, making trade negotiators' traditional goal of dismantling tariffs less relevant.

The November 2010 G-20 meeting in Seoul and the Japan summit of the Asia-Pacific Economic Cooperation renewed hopes for progress in the Doha negotiations in the first half of 2011. G-20 and Asia-Pacific Economic Cooperation leaders saw a new window of opportunity to intensify negotiations in 2011,

MAP 5.1   Across the world, 884 million people lack access to safe water—around 80 percent of them in rural areas

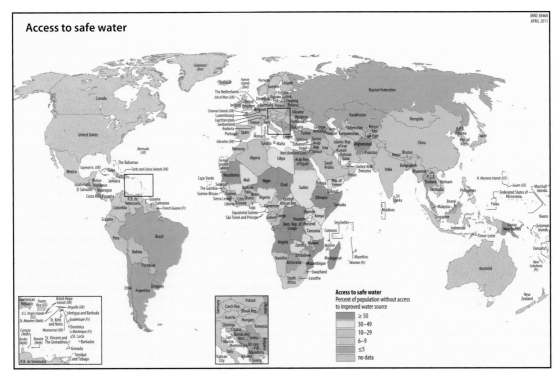

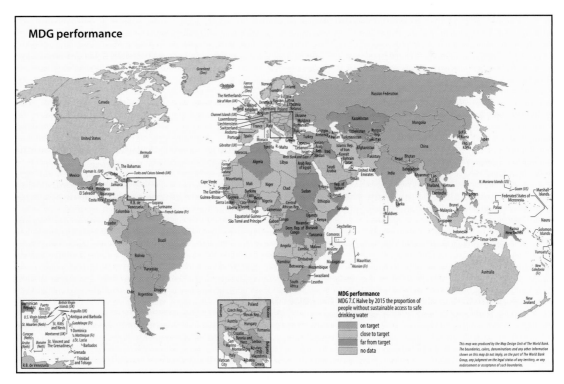

Source: World Bank staff calculations based on data from the World Development Indicators database.

calling for multilateral cooperation to pursue a comprehensive and balanced trade agreement. WTO Director-General Pascal Lamy asked WTO ambassadors to engage in informal sessions with the goal of breaking long-standing stalemates (including sessions on the sidelines of the World Economic Forum Davos meeting in January 2011). He called the chairs of the negotiating committees for revised texts by late-April 2011 and urged WTO ambassadors to also pursue bilateral and small-group discussions to resolve key differences and catch up with work among the full membership on refining texts. Negotiations and consultations are scheduled to commence on all Doha topics—agriculture, nonagricultural market access, services, dispute settlement, facilitation, trade and environment, intellectual property rights, and the development agenda.

Locking in the Doha Round is also crucial so that the international community can address emerging issues beyond those existing in the Doha agenda.[36] A fundamental shift is taking place in the world economy, but the multilateral trading system has not adapted. Mattoo and Subramanian point out that the world economy is moving broadly from conditions of relative abundance to relative scarcity, so economic security has become a paramount concern for consumers, workers, and ordinary citizens.[37] Addressing these new concerns—relating to food, energy, and economic security—requires a wider agenda of multilateral cooperation involving not just the WTO but other multilateral institutions as well. Although these issues are growing in importance and require a multilateral approach, abandoning the present Doha negotiations in favor of an entirely new round of talks with a more up-to-date agenda, as some have advocated, has even less chance to get anywhere than has the Doha effort.

Building capacity to support deeper but open regional integration

Regional integration can complement multilateral liberalization. Regional trade agreements can mitigate potential adverse effects through parallel efforts to support unilateral liberalization or open access.[38] Supporting the regional integration efforts of low-income countries through the promotion of trade facilitation and regional infrastructure could accelerate the pace of achievement for many MDGs. But regional trade agreements could be trade diverting and further complicate developing countries' global integration prospects—for example, through complex rules of origin. Developing countries should be strategic about what is included in preferential trade agreements, be selective about which trading partners to include in such agreements and treaties, and avoid signing on to one-size-fits-all trade agreements that might not be suitable for their developmental stages.

In light of the growing number of preferential trade agreements, efforts should concentrate on building the capacity of trade negotiators from developing countries. With some 474 regional trade agreements notified to the WTO as of July 2010, regional integration has become an unavoidable feature of the international trading regime. More of these agreements included "deep regional integration" measures, involving regulatory and policy issues such as investment, intellectual property rights, environmental protection, technical and sanitary standards, migration and labor policies, and an array of other behind-the-border regulations. The breadth and coverage of deep regional integration is new for many developing countries. Negotiating and implementing such policies could be complicated and, without proper guidance and sufficient information, they could be tactically and commercially destructive. Many developing-country trade negotiators and government agencies may not have the legal or policy knowledge to strategically negotiate the appropriate regulatory components of regional agreements.

To provide more information about preferential trade agreements to developing countries and the international community, the World Bank recently launched a Web-based portal, the Global Preferential Trade Agreement Database,[39] which provides real-time information on preferential trade agreements around the world (including agreements that have not been notified to the WTO). Designed to help trade policy makers, scholars, and business operators better understand and navigate the world of preferential trade agreements, the database was merged with the revamped Web-based World Integrated Trade Solutions, multiagency software providing access to trade-related data and integrated trade simulation tools.

A services "platform" could help fill in the information gap for services negotiations. Bringing together government agencies, regulators, and private sector stakeholders to discuss regulatory reforms related to services would improve policy makers' expertise.[40] Considering that services trade is paramount to the export strategies for many LDCs and that multilateral negotiations on further services liberalization and issues of labor mobility (beyond the General Agreement on Trade and Services) are inevitably tied to the eventual conclusion of the Doha Round, this would provide important information that developing countries need as they pursue services trade liberalization through unilateral reforms or regional and bilateral trade agreements.

As developing countries pursue regional integration, a better understanding of non-tariff measures (NTMs)—their prevalence, impact, and ways to streamline them—should be at the forefront of governments' export competitiveness agenda. By definition, NTMs encompass a broad range of barriers, including quotas, import licensing systems and procedures, sanitary regulations, technical requirements, product standards, and labeling requirements. As a result of this broad definition, there is a lot of discretion in the application of NTMs, whether for legitimate policy objectives (health and consumer protection) or as protectionist measures. Poorly designed NTMs can also harm the competitiveness of developing countries by constraining the ability of companies to outsource key inputs, putting them at a competitive disadvantage on global markets. Enhancing transparency on the adoption and application of NTMs is thus crucial for developing countries

as they aim to become more integrated with the global economy.

As a follow-up to the Multi-Agency Support Team's work on NTMs that revised the NTM classification and collected data in a pilot phase, the World Bank, the International Trade Centre, and the United Nations Conference on Trade and Development have initiated data collection and dissemination efforts worldwide. As of December 2010, data had been collected in about 30 countries and should soon populate the World Integrated Trade Solutions database.[41] Data collection and dissemination are accompanied by capacity-building programs at country and regional levels to improve the governance of NTMs, streamline them, and assess their impact on trade. More transparent information on NTMs should lead to more informed policy making for developing countries and facilitate the harmonization and streamlining of these measures.

To further increase the benefits of their preferential trade programs, developed countries should also consider simplifying the rules of origin pertaining to their preference programs. The estimated administrative cost for LDCs to comply with such rules is relatively high—in the range of 3–4 percent of the value of the goods traded. But because the majority of most-favored-nation tariffs in high-income countries are below this range, many LDCs choose not to use the preference margin. Harmonizing multilaterally would bring the administrative costs down. Those costs can also be reduced by adopting more trader-friendly approaches, such as allowing self-certification methods. The rules can be further eased by allowing less restrictive cumulation rules (such as diagonal or full cumulation), allowing duty drawback, and setting higher de minimis levels.[42]

Trade facilitation for LDCs, landlocked countries, and lagging regions

Exporters in many developing countries continue to face weak transport infrastructure and burdensome trade procedures. Landlocked LDCs, in particular, face unique

---

BOX 5.2   The donor community is enhancing Africa's trade facilitation

The international community has reinforced its support to LDCs, especially in Africa. In addition to the Multi-Donor Trade Facility, the World Bank multidonor Trade Facilitation Facility, launched in July 2009, helps developing countries implement trade facilitation reforms and scale up trade-related infrastructure and institutions. As of June 2010, the facility was supporting 29 projects, with $20 million approved. Most projects are in Africa (Cameroon, Democratic Republic of Congo, Lesotho, Nigeria, Rwanda, South Africa, Togo, Zimbabwe, and regional projects with the Economic Community of

West African States and the Economic Community of Central African States). The facility also has provided funding for regional transportation integration in East Asia and the Pacific, Europe and Central Asia, and Latin America. The aim is to provide initial funding to support technical advisory services and capacity building for project preparation that would later lead to concrete and measurable trade facilitation improvements. In addition, the facility supports the Doha negotiations by funding case studies to assess the implementation challenges of trade facilitation agreements for LDCs.

---

infrastructure and institutional hurdles to overseas markets. For many landlocked LDCs, connecting to global supply chains is a formidable challenge caused by long distances from seaports and the need to cross borders. Landlocked countries tend to trade, on average, 30 percent less than coastal countries. Connecting landlocked LDCs to global supply chains could expand their employment, income, and consumption opportunities. With 20 of 54 low-income countries landlocked (mostly in Sub-Saharan Africa), trade facilitation that connects landlocked regions with international markets will open considerable economic opportunities (box 5.2). It could include streamlining transit regimes, implementing border and customs reform, improving transport service quality, and coordinating multimodal nodes within the supply chain. Limited competition on domestic routes is an explanatory factor behind the high prices charged for domestic shipments.[43] So constraining monopoly power and removing barriers to entry and exit would lower costs for importers and exporters.

Logistical improvements can connect rural and remote areas within developing countries.[44] Even with the sharper focus on connecting countries to trade corridors and supply chains, there is still a gaping divide between lagging areas in developing countries

and better-connected leading areas. Moreover, logistics costs are exceptionally high because of poor logistics services and infrastructure, low economies of scale (transporting small consignments across long distances), and highly fragmented supply chains with numerous intermediaries exacting time and cost at each link. So producers and exporters in lagging areas do not reap the full benefits of trade. Policy actions should ensure better coordination and cooperation among producers within the supply chain and leverage public-private partnerships to improve transport infrastructure, to apply information technology, and to reduce the information asymmetry within supply chains (figure 5.7).

Trade facilitation through support to trade finance in low-income countries

The international community should continue to increase the availability of trade finance in developing countries—particularly low-income countries—to facilitate trade. Trade finance, which includes a range of financial instruments for trade transactions, underpins the financial infrastructure that enables countries and firms to trade with one another. The lack of trade finance can have severe implications for a pro-development global trading system. The issue of trade finance availability

MAP 5.2   With half the people in developing regions without sanitation, the 2015 target appears to be out of reach

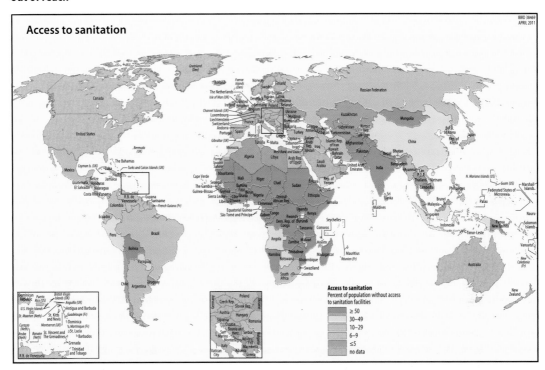

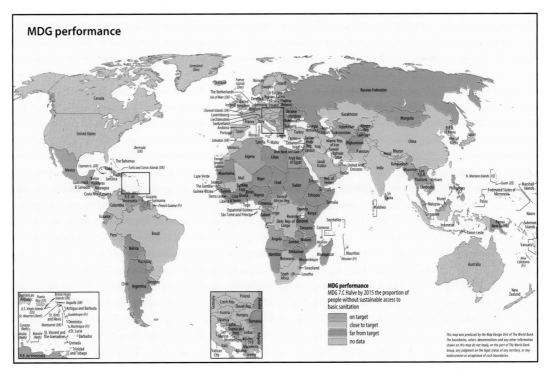

Source: World Bank staff calculations based on data from the World Development Indicators database.

FIGURE 5.7   Local-to-global connectivity

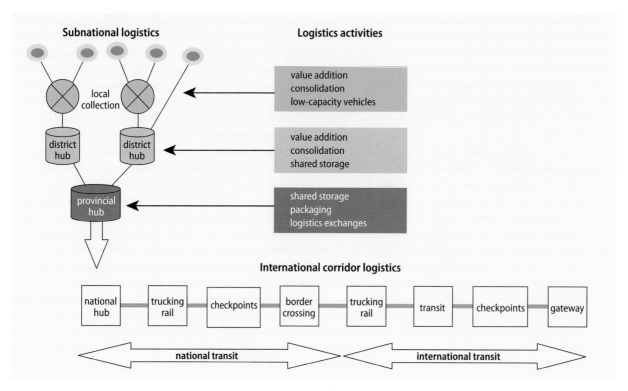

Source: Kunaka 2010.

became especially relevant during the global financial crisis in 2008–09, when higher lending costs, higher risk premiums, and liquidity pressures caused by scarcity of capital led to a sudden shortage in trade finance.

Lack of affordable trade finance has probably constrained the trade activities of small and medium enterprises (SMEs), particularly in low-income countries. Results from financial market and firm surveys (undertaken during the crisis by the IMF, the International Chamber of Commerce, and the World Bank to overcome the lack of data on trade finance) and postcrisis empirical analyses all indicate the prevalence of tighter trade finance conditions during the crisis and significant adverse effects on trade flows. The lack of data can hamper clear conclusions. Although survey results indicate that the shortfall in trade finance has contributed to the sharp drop in global trade flows during the crisis, it seems that it played a moderate role in one study.[45] In manufacturing, where volumes fell but

prices actually rose postcrisis, the evidence is consistent with a negative supply shock that might be associated with credit constraints.[46] The trade collapse was mostly a result of the spillover of the financial crisis to the real economy and lower activity and inventory destocking. Nevertheless, the lack of affordable trade finance likely constrained trading activities of SMEs, especially those based in low-income countries that have underdeveloped financial systems and banks that could not fulfill the counterparty criteria of overseas banks. Postcrisis surveys and data on trade finance indicate signs of improvement.

The institutional response in providing trade finance during the crisis was timely and substantial. In the midst of the crisis, the international community responded swiftly—spearheaded by the G-20—in committing $250 billion over the course of two years in funding for cofinancing arrangements that support trade transactions. This was implemented through a partnership between development banks, export credit agencies, foreign commercial banks, private insurance underwriters, and investment funds. Whereas the G-20 support was mainly directed at large banks and international banking institutions, the World Bank's International Finance Corporation (IFC) and the regional development banks stepped in as well to target their efforts at smaller banks and banks in developing countries. With the continued uncertainty in trade finance markets, particularly for low-income countries and small firms, governments and international organizations need to be cautious of the timing and pace of withdrawal of such trade finance programs.

Despite recent positive developments, concerns about trade finance have not completely dissipated. At the Seoul G-20 meeting in November 2010, the international community expressed particular concern about low-income countries that may still be facing severe difficulties in accessing trade finance at affordable cost. These concerns are exacerbated by the lack of available data for trade finance, which has constrained the ability to properly monitor and evaluate existing trade finance flows and to measure their impact on trade flows during and after the crisis. The building up of the Trade Registry by the International Chamber of Commerce is a significant step forward because it will create a living database of the trade finance market and may help demonstrate the resilience of the trade finance business.

Other concerns relate to the new Basel regulations, which are viewed as potentially constraining the supply of trade finance. Banks argue that the increase in the new liquidity and capital prudential requirements, and the nonrecognition of trade assets as a highly liquid and safe asset, would lead to a significant increase in banks' cost in providing trade finance—a situation that will lead to lower supply, higher prices, or both. Regulators have insisted that the Basel II and III increase in capital for trade finance exposures is not any greater than for other exposures. In light of these different views, the Basel Committee established a working group to study the impact of regulations on trade finance. At the request of the World Bank and the WTO, the G-20 will take stock of the situation at its 2011 meeting.

Renewed support for effective aid for trade

The G-20 has renewed its commitment to support LDC trade capacity building through aid for trade. At the November 2010 Seoul meeting, the G-20 pledged to maintain aid for trade commitments in 2011 and beyond, despite fiscal and budgetary constraints. Launched at the G-8 meeting in Gleneagles and the follow-on WTO Ministerial Conference in Hong Kong SAR, China, in 2005, aid for trade aims to facilitate the integration of developing countries (particularly the LDCs) into the global economy by lowering cumbersome trade barriers, reducing transaction costs, and enhancing trade competitiveness. Aid for trade remains an effective way to support LDCs to improve supply-side capacities and reap the benefits of increased market access.[47]

After a sharp increase in donor aid for trade commitments in 2007 and 2008, the latest OECD data indicate that new commitments in 2009 plateaued at $39.5 billion (2008 constant prices). In 2009, the World Bank's concessional arm, IDA, was the largest provider of aid for trade, accounting for about 21 percent of the total. Japan and the United States were the largest bilateral donors, providing 14 percent and 12 percent of total aid for trade, respectively. Africa was, for the first time, the largest recipient of aid for trade (41 percent); and the level of commitments increased over those of 2008. Aid for trade in Africa was mainly directed to Nigeria, Uganda, Kenya, and Ethiopia. Asia was the second-largest recipient of aid for trade (39 percent), with Vietnam, India, and Afghanistan the major recipients. Aid for trade mainly supported projects involving trade infrastructure and capacity building (particularly trade development programs), while technical assistance for institutional capacity building and training for trade regulations have been on the decline (figure 5.8).

FIGURE 5.8   Regional trends in aid for trade, 2002–09

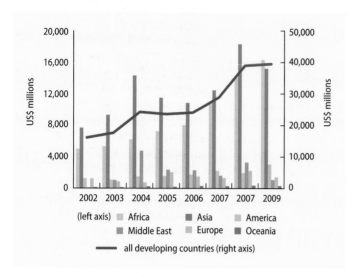

Source: OECD, Aid for Trade Statistical Queries 2010, http://www.oecd.org/document/21/0,3746,en_2649_34665_43230357_1_1_1_1,00.html.

Besides concerted efforts to channel aid for trade to developing countries, the international community is exploring the effectiveness of aid for trade. At the initiative of the WTO and the OECD, donors are currently collecting case studies that illustrate the impact of trade-related assistance and lending programs and the lessons learned from these projects. These case studies will be discussed at the July 2011 WTO/OECD Aid for Trade meeting. Moreover, with the emergence of a multipolar world with rising economic powers and multinational private sector firms, the quality of delivery of aid for trade has become more critical. This new paradigm calls for more public-private partnerships to strengthen trade capacity-building assistance delivered to LDCs. The IFIs can focus more on leveraging partnerships between government agencies and private sector firms. By combining the policy experience of the government and the ingenuity of the private sector, trade development projects may have the potential to be more far-reaching and effective. A good illustration of such programs is the deployment of modern information and communications technologies from the private sector to streamline trade facilitation and minimize at-the-border barriers.

International financial institutions' support for development

The IFIs are adapting their policies, procedures, and tools to country heterogeneous circumstances and needs.[48] They strive to provide all member-countries with development solutions appropriate to meet their development needs and capacity by using a mix of lending policies, financial facilities, and knowledge services, and by supporting the global public goods agenda. Moreover, the financial crisis, and the food and fuels crisis preceding it, have shown the crucial role of IFIs in supporting responses to crises and development emergencies, swiftly shifting toward a more countercyclical approach to mitigate social and economic impacts of the crises.

The response to recent crises provided a snapshot of the untapped potential of the IFIs to address the challenges and opportunities of the postcrisis world. It also provided a glimpse of how transformed IFIs will work on an ongoing rather than emergency basis. In recognition of the changing development landscape and country development needs, the IFIs have embarked on comprehensive modernization agendas involving actions and reforms to enhance financial capacity, transform governance, reform organization, and refresh and refine their priorities. Efforts to bolster their performance, ensuring relevance and results focus on country strategies and operations in the postcrisis world (including helping countries develop their own capacity to manage for results) are key objectives of the ongoing reform agendas and the driving force in the development of the results-based approaches that will guide IFIs' actions in the future.

The evolution of assistance policies and resources

Given developing countries' diverse needs and heterogeneous characteristics, the approach of the multilateral development banks (MDBs) has increasingly been tailored to country conditions and grounded in national strategies setting out countries' development visions, objectives, and priorities.[49] All of the major MDBs now formulate country strategy documents, generally, every two to four years, with more frequent progress reports and independent evaluations. At the World Bank, the Country Assistance Strategy has evolved over the past decade to adopt an explicit results framework that specifies the expected links between the World Bank's interventions and long-term development goals, along with measurable indicators to monitor results.[50]

Donors have stepped up financial resources to low-income countries through the MDBs' affiliates that provide grants and no- (or low-) interest credits. Disbursements by the World Bank's IDA, the African Development Fund, the Asian Development Fund, the Inter-American Development Bank (IADB)'s Fund for Special Operations, and the European Bank for Reconstruction and Development (EBRD)'s Early Transition Countries Initiative (under which the EBRD accepts higher risks in projects in low-income members) have steadily risen over the years. Strong pledges from both traditional and new donors in the last IDA replenishment recognize that restoring momentum to the MDGs leading to 2015 requires ambitious efforts to deliver on the economic growth and access agenda for basic services (health, education, and basic infrastructure). A total of 51 donors endorsed a $49.3 billion funding package for the next cycle of IDA (IDA16, which covers July 2011 to June 2014), an increase of 18 percent from the previous round. At the African Development Bank (AfDB), the level of concessional aid resources was similarly maintained as a reflection of donor commitment to the achievement of MDGs by 2015. This commitment was similarly demonstrated during the 12th General Replenishment of the African Development Fund, whereby negotiations with 27 donor countries resulted in a 10.6 percent increase from the previous replenishment cycle and a funding package of approximately $9.5 billion to support the fund's work in low-income countries in Africa between January 2011 and December 2013. MDBs' operational and financial approach to address specific challenges or vulnerabilities has evolved and

expanded over the last decade. For instance, the World Bank has enhanced its financial support to provide increased access to highly concessional resources for small IDA countries. Two measures were agreed to strengthen IDA support for small states during the IDA16 period: first, to eliminate the maximum per capita allocation ceiling, currently set at special drawing right (SDR) 19.8, which has constrained the allocations of several small states; and, second, to raise the base allocation for small states from SDR1.5 million to SDR3.0 million per year. This second measure would result in a substantial increase of IDA resources for small states with small populations.

IDA also has continued its efforts to help countries recover from natural disasters. Following the 2009 tsunami, IDA was able to provide significant additional resources to both Samoa and Tonga. Following the earthquake in Haiti, the World Bank pledged $479 million toward Haiti's reconstruction for the first 24 months after the earthquake, two-thirds of which was delivered in the first 12 months. The portfolio in Haiti was restructured toward meeting pressing post-earthquake priorities; and, by end-2010, the WBG had provided $340.0 million to Haiti, including $139.5 in new grants, $129.0 million in disbursements, debt cancellation of $39.0 million (May 2010), and investments of $32.5 million from the IFC (box 5.3). Similarly, the IMF established a Post-Catastrophe Debt Relief Trust that allows the fund to join international debt relief efforts for very poor countries hit by the most catastrophic of natural disasters. Such debt relief is intended to free up additional resources to meet exceptional balance-of-payments needs created by the disaster and the recovery, complementing fresh donor financing and the fund's concessional liquidity support. The Post-Catastrophe Debt Relief Trust Fund provided timely assistance to Haiti equivalent to around $268 million in fund-financed debt stock relief, eliminating Haiti's entire outstanding debt to the IMF. This decision adds to the $1.2 billion of debt relief delivered to Haiti by the IMF and other financial organizations in June 2009, under the Heavily Indebted Poor Countries and Multilateral Debt Relief initiatives.

BOX 5.3   Special reconstruction allocation for Haiti

The earthquake that struck Haiti on January 12, 2010, was a human tragedy. More than 230,000 people perished, 300,000 more were wounded, and well more than a million were displaced. The earthquake ravaged cities including Port-au-Prince, the capital, destroying whole neighborhoods, wiping away roads, collapsing public buildings, and damaging businesses. The disaster struck the country's political, economic, and administrative nerve center, where an estimated 65 percent of GDP and 85 percent of government revenues were generated. A year later, conditions remain difficult for the Haitian population. About 1 million people continue to live in tent camps and depend on aid organizations for water, food, sanitation, health, and education services. Furthermore, on October 21, 2010, an outbreak of cholera was confirmed. The latest United Nations data indicate that about 149,000 cases have been reported and more than 3,000 people have died.

International response. Innumerable public and private organizations were mobilized in an unprecedented outpouring of international support after the earthquake. At the International Conference on Haiti in March 2010, $9 billion was pledged ($5.3 billion of which was for 2010–11 to support the Government Action Plan for Reconstruction and National Development. At the end of 2010, the international community had delivered more than half of its pledge for the first 24 months: $1 billion in debt relief had been provided and $2.7 billion approved for projects and programs, with $1.2 billion of these funds spent.

Haiti Reconstruction Fund. At the request of the government of Haiti, in April 2010, the World Bank set up the Haiti Reconstruction Fund (HRF), a multidonor trust fund. The World Bank serves as a trustee for the HRF. In March 2010, donors pledged more than $500 million to the fund. To date, 12 donors have confirmed their pledges for a total of $267 million, all of which has been received. Since June 2010, the HRF has allocated $193 million for reconstruction.

WBG support. The World Bank Group pledged $479 million toward Haiti's reconstruction for the first 24 months after the earthquake, two thirds of which was delivered in the first 12 months. The portfolio in Haiti was restructured toward meeting pressing post-earthquake priorities; and, by end-2010 the WBG had provided $340.0 million to Haiti, including $139.5 in new grants, $129.0 million in disbursements, debt cancellation of $39.0 million (May 2010), and investments of $32.5 million from the IFC.

WBG disbursements and debt relief. The World Bank portfolio currently includes 16 active projects for a total of $337 million. The Bank has also provided $42.5 million in budget support to the government of Haiti since January 2010. IDA, the Bank's fund for the poorest countries, has disbursed more than $11 million a month, on average, since the earthquake. Following the earthquake, the Haiti portfolio was restructured to direct resources toward urgent post-earthquake priorities through the reallocation of funds and the modification of activities to adapt to institutional capacity changes. In May 2010, the Bank was able to cancel Haiti's remaining $39 million debt to IDA, thanks to contributions by IDA.

New WBG programs. In early 2011, the WBG will launch the following programs and projects from newly approved resources: $95 million for a neighborhood upgrading and housing reconstruction program financed by IDA and the HRF; $15 million for an emergency cholera project; $11 million for a line item budget support operation to cover specific expenditures in education and agriculture; and $3 million to establish a $35 million Partial Risk Guarantee Fund for private operators in Haiti, cofinanced by the Inter-American Development Bank (IADB), the U.S. Treasury, and the HRF.

Support for the private sector. Since the earthquake, the WBG's IFC has approved five projects for a total of $49.6 million. Three of these projects (worth $15.3 million) in the garments, hotels, energy, and mining industries, are already under implementation, in addition to a trade finance guarantee facility, an equity investment in a local bank to expand access to finance to SMEs, and a 30-megawatt energy project approved prior to the quake. IFC advisory services also ramped up operations to foster a better investment climate, improve access to finance, and develop management skills for more than 600 small entrepreneurs. The IFC's combined investment and advisory projects are supporting the creation of 5,000 new jobs and safeguarding 5,000 existing jobs. The IFC also completed the structuring of the international bidding process for TELECO, which is bringing the country's largest foreign direct investment since the earthquake—a $100 million investment by Vietnam's biggest mobile telephone operator, Viettel—to expand telecommunications services in Haiti.

The approach to address the specific challenges of fragile and conflict-affected countries has also increasingly evolved over the last decade. In terms of resources, eligible postconflict and reengaging countries receive exceptional allocations, and some have benefited from exceptional pre-arrears clearance grants and allocations to help clear arrears. The IDA phase-out period for exceptional allocations, for instance, was increased from 3 to 6 years, resulting in 10 years of support for postconflict countries, which otherwise would have exited the window during IDA15. For the IDA16 period, postconflict countries will also be eligible for an extension of their phase-out period on a case-by-case basis, provided that they meet a predetermined set of criteria. Fragile and conflict-affected countries have also benefited significantly from

policies on debt relief (through the joint World Bank-IMF Heavily Indebted Poor Countries and Multilateral Debt Relief initiatives) and from grants allocated through IDA's grant allocation framework to help them avoid the reemergence of debt problems.

Although all fragile states are characterized by weak policies and institutions, country context varies considerably and operational approaches must be carefully calibrated to take this into account. The World Bank will incorporate the lessons of the 2011 *World Development Report* (box 5.4)—a report focused on conflict, security, and development challenges in fragile and conflict-affected countries—into the revision of its policies. Moreover, the World Bank committed in the IDA16 replenishment to develop plans to enhance the implementation of United

---

BOX 5.4   *World Development Report 2011: Conflict, Security, and Development*

Repeated cycles of political and criminal violence have left more than 440 million people in poverty. Strengthening the institutions that provide justice, jobs, and citizen security is crucial to break these cycles. Restoring confidence and transforming security, justice, and economic institutions is possible within a generation. But that requires determined national leadership and an international system "refitted" to address 21st-century risks of violence: *refocusing* assistance on preventing criminal and political violence, *reforming* the procedures of international agencies, and *renewing* cooperative efforts between lower-, middle-, and higher-income countries.

Why do some parts of the world face repeated cycles of violence? Violence can be spurred by a range of internal and external stresses—infiltration of trafficking networks and foreign fighting forces; youth unemployment; economic shocks; and tensions between ethnic, regional, or religious groups. But other areas of the world, including some very poor countries, have managed and contained similar pressures. The common "missing factor" explaining repeated cycles of violence is that state and societal institutions are too weak to manage high internal and

external stresses. States or subnational governments do not provide protection and access to justice. Markets do not provide legal employment opportunities. And communities have lost the social cohesion to contain conflict.

What works in breaking repeated cycles of violence? The key differences between situations of violence and stable developing environments are the need to restore confidence before undertaking wider institutional reforms; the priority given to basic institutional functions of security, justice, and provision of employment; and the role of regional and international action to contain external stresses. Pragmatic, responsive, and accountable leadership at national and local levels also plays a crucial role.

What policy tools make a difference, and how can they be adapted to country circumstances? The programs listed in the table on the next page have been used successfully in different country circumstances. Few countries have combined all of them, and most have faced challenges at some point either on fast confidence-building or on longer-term institutional transformation. The toolbox presented here thus provides a mechanism to learn from both successes and failures.

continued

BOX 5.4   *World Development Report 2011: Conflict, Security, and Development* (continued)

A policy toolbox

Tools	Politics and justice	Security	Jobs and services
Restoring and building confidence Forming inclusive-enough coalitions Delivering early results	Political action to build national and international stakeholder support and manage expectations: strategic communications, appointments, decision-making processes Policy decisions and realistic timelines to political reform, decentralization, and transitional justice where relevant Extended reach and responsiveness of local justice services	Military and police doctrine and planning adapted to citizen security goals Designed to deliver benefits in ease of production, trade, workplace attendance, access to services, human rights principles, and simple mechanisms to redress citizen complaints	Multisectoral community programs, combining security operations with action on employment, local justice, infrastructure, education, and community empowerment Regulatory simplification and recovery of basic infrastructure and transit facilities to remove bottlenecks to private sector job creation Humanitarian delivery to support improvements in intercommunity and state-community relations
	All areas: transparency and willingness to consider independent monitoring by independent or multisectoral government agencies to lock in the credibility of changes		
Transforming institutions Prioritizing and sequencing institutional reform to underpin security, justice, and jobs Taking pragmatic approaches—first-best in the political context, second-best in technical terms Global and regional approaches for external stresses that national actors can initiate	Justice sector reform: focus on basic functions and use of state-community and state-traditional systems for justice Phased anticorruption measures to first show that national resources can be used for the public good; then to combat grand corruption; and then to roll back minor corruption Platforms to coordinate supply- and demand-side responses between producing and consuming countries Joint investigations and prosecutions across jurisdictions	Security sector reform: capacity increases linked to repeated realistic performance outcomes; vetting and civilian oversight Traditional low-capital systems for rural and community policing Supplementary capacity and over-the-horizon guarantees	Employment policy: mix of long-term public programs at the community level, employability programs, value chain approaches, infrastructure, informal sector support, and labor migration agreements Temporary options for second-best service delivery: high service coverage, high unit cost, under phase-out agreements; planned transitions from international humanitarian support Pooled supplementary administrative capacity Cross-border development programming

Source: World Bank 2011.

Nations–World Bank partnership agreements, evaluate IDA's work in fragile and conflict-affected countries during 2012–13, strengthen collaboration with partners on multidonor trust funds administered by the World Bank, and revise the postconflict performance indicators and publicly disclose them before the start of IDA16.

Like IDA's special assistance, the African Development Fund's postconflict enhancement factor enables countries to benefit from additional resources beyond their performance-based allocation for a limited period after they are designated postconflict countries. The AfDB has established the Post-Conflict Country Facility to help countries emerging from conflict clear these arrears on their debt. Similarly, the ADB has deployed innovative means to strengthen the effectiveness of country-led models of engagement in the complex environments of fragile and conflict-affected situations. In particular, ADB has sought to sustain its commitments for longer periods; partner closely with other funding agencies; and pursue deeper, more flexible, and longer engagements in capacity and institutional development. The IADB used special measures for its engagement in Haiti—including simplified startup requirements, broader eligible expenditure categories, and elimination of counterpart financing requirements. In 2004, the EBRD launched the Early Transition Countries Initiative to increase its impact in the region's lowest-income and least-advanced transition countries[51] by developing specific financial facilities targeted at local enterprises, including the separate facilities to fund equity investments, directly finance long-term loans, cofinance loans with local commercial banks, and lend to microfinance institutions.

Development finance

Over the years, the MDBs have expanded the range of their instruments and modernized them to make them more responsive, results oriented, and amenable to an enhanced business model and country needs. For example,

important refinements to the development policy lending (DPL) instrument were made at the World Bank immediately prior to and during the crisis. First, the World Bank adopted enhancements for DPL with a deferred drawdown option (DDO) that allows International Bank for Reconstruction and Development (IBRD) borrowers to postpone disbursement of a loan for a defined period, instead of drawing down funds immediately after approval. Second, the World Bank introduced a DPL instrument that provides liquidity immediately after a natural disaster (the CAT DDO) to support a disaster risk management program, assuming a state of emergency is declared. And, third, the Bank adopted reforms for the Special DPL, available to countries that are approaching or are in a macroeconomic crisis, contingent on a disbursing IMF program being in place. Since April 2008, the board has approved 12 DPL DDOs for a total of $5.6 billion, and $4.8 billion of that amount had been disbursed by the middle of fiscal 2011. Several CAT DDOs for countries vulnerable to natural catastrophes have since been approved, totaling $400 million. Moreover, in recognition of the vulnerabilities that low-income countries face in terms of both financial crises and natural disasters, the World Bank and the IDA deputies have recently agreed to establish a dedicated Crisis Response Window (CRW) within IDA to enhance its capacity to respond to crises. The CRW will provide IDA countries with timely access to additional resources to respond to the impact of severe economic crises or natural disasters; and it will strengthen IDA's capacity to respond rapidly to such crises in collaboration with other agencies, development banks, and donors. Resources for the CRW have been capped at 5 percent of total IDA16 resources, and an amount of SDR1,335 million has been set aside to finance expenditures under the CRW.

Finally, a major effort is also under way to reform the World Bank's investment lending model to focus on results and risks, with the goal of improving its responsiveness to borrowers' needs and to a changing global environment.[52] Guarantees are currently one of three development finance instruments (along with DPLs and investment lending) that the World Bank offers, and a number of actions are being put in place to improve the attractiveness of the guarantee product and encourage country teams and client governments to actively consider guarantee operations.

Similarly, the ADB has introduced new and innovative instruments to finance large individual projects and longer-term investment programs. The following instruments expand the options available in ADB's development finance portfolio while preserving its credit standing: Multitranche Financing Facility, which allows the ADB to finance a long-term investment program based on a sector assessment (road map) and organized in a series of funding blocks, or tranches; Nonsovereign Public Sector Financing Facility, which provides debt finance (loans and guarantees) directly to selected nonsovereign public sector entities without a central government (sovereign) guarantee; Local Currency Loan Product, which allows the ADB to offer loans denominated in a local currency to reduce the mismatch between income received in a domestic currency and debt repayments in a foreign currency; and new forms of cofinancing through active financial syndications and risk sharing with commercial financing partners that have since been mainstreamed into the ADB's operations.[53]

The global financial crisis undoubtedly also had a lasting effect on the AfDB's lending. In March 2009, the AfDB's board endorsed four initiatives aimed at better responding to the needs of its client countries: an Emergency Liquidity Facility to assist eligible AfDB regional member-countries and nonsovereign operations suffering from lack of liquidity ($1.5 billion); a Trade Finance Initiative ($1 billion) that comprises a line of credit ($500 million) and a Global Trade Liquidity Program ($500 million) to allow eligible African commercial banks to support trade finance operations; an accelerated replenishment process for the 12th General Replenishment of the African Development

Fund; and enhanced Policy Advisory Support to support countries where advisory capacity remains challenging.

The EBRD has also expanded the existing pool of financial instruments available to the private sector in its countries of operation. This includes the introduction of various facilities and frameworks aimed at different aspects of private sector development—regional energy efficiency, direct mid-size lending, and regional micro, small, and medium enterprises lending. The crisis response packages introduced in 2008 are good examples of the EBRD's reaction to the changing economic environment in its countries of operation.[54] Similarly, the IFC also undertook new initiatives to support private sector activities in the wake of the crisis by providing liquidity support, rebuilding financial infrastructure and mobilizing investment in distressed asset pools, and providing advisory services to enhance the efficiency of distressed asset markets.[55]

Knowledge services

The IFIs are also increasingly providing more flexible and ad hoc analysis, research, global public goods in the form of databases and free data, advice, and technical assistance. In low-income countries and some lower-middle-income countries, knowledge services are often bundled with lending, which is seen as a tool of public policy for designing and implementing reform/knowledge agendas. More sophisticated middle-income countries are mainly interested in obtaining stand-alone knowledge support in cutting-edge areas. Between these two extremes, there is a variety of hybrid requests that are accommodated by an increased flexibility in the delivery modalities. For instance, the EBRD's unique mandate of fostering transition toward open market–oriented economies has shaped its specific role in knowledge services. Technical cooperation provided to clients (including through donor programs) is aimed at different "transition-oriented" aspects of an operation, such as development of management skills, legal advice to promote regulatory development and improve legislation and corporate governance, and skills transfer. Another example of knowledge services is the EBRD's Turn Around Management and Business Advisory Services programs, which have been valuable instruments for the promotion of good management in the SME sector, providing consultancy advice at the enterprise level. Turn Around Management supports the introduction of international best practice SME enterprises, while the Business Advisory Services Program acts as a facilitator for the use of local, private sector consultants by micro, small, and medium enterprises to obtain a diverse array of services.

Increasingly, cutting-edge knowledge is generated in the South through the countries' own development experiences. And as policy analysis and development research are increasingly conducted by countries themselves, the IFIs can play a vital role both as generators of research and as providers of a forum for bringing together knowledge from both the North and the South—acting as a global connector of practitioner knowledge, a broker of development, and a facilitator of capacity development and client learning. The World Bank, for instance, has established partnerships with researchers and analysts in developing countries: the China Center for Economic Research, the New Economic School in Moscow, the Economic Research Forum in Cairo, the Global Development Network in collaboration with 11 regional partners and headquartered in New Delhi, and others. A South-South Experience Exchange Facility has been set up to help developing countries share expertise.[56] So far, that facility has received 88 proposals to support South-South activities in World Bank products and services in more than 40 countries.

As MDBs strengthen their role as providers of global public goods (such as data and research) and their role in linking country practitioners and policy makers to sources and centers of knowledge and innovation dispersed around the world, knowledge platforms that involve external stakeholders in coproducing knowledge have been set up to provide a framework for sustained global collaboration

around selected strategically significant issues. For instance, the World Bank knowledge platform initiative focuses resources—both within the World Bank and across the development community—on strategic, and cross-sectoral transformational issues to fill critical knowledge gaps and seek cogeneration of knowledge from diverse sources and institutions. The first three knowledge platforms are becoming operational, and they focus on urbanization, the e-Transform Initiative (information and communications technology for accountability and development); and green development. The World Bank also is taking steps to improve access to its data and research (box 5.5).

Global programs and partnerships

The MDBs are stepping up their efforts to address common social sector and environmental challenges through global programs and partnerships. World Bank support for global programs began three decades ago, with the establishment of the Consultative Group on International Agricultural Research that was recently restructured. Global programs are now reflected in World Bank corporate strategy papers and operational activities, with more than 100 programs (managed by either the World Bank or external recipients). Recent initiatives include the World Bank's role in the Climate Investment Funds, including the Clean Technology Fund and Special Climate Change Fund, which provide financing for projects to address climate change (box 5.6). The Pilot Program on Climate Resilience helps highly vulnerable countries integrate risk and resilience into core development planning; the Forest Investment Program supports efforts to reduce deforestation and forest degradation, cut emissions, and maintain carbon reservoirs; and the Scaling Up Renewable Energy Program aims to demonstrate low-carbon energy development in low-income countries.

The regional banks are also involved in global and regional programs covering financial stability, trade, environment, postconflict assistance, and knowledge; and all

BOX 5.5   Open data, open knowledge, and open solutions

User expectations for public information are changing rapidly; and clients and other stakeholders expect easy access to World Bank–generated data, knowledge, and solutions. Open access is meant to increase the development impact of the World Bank's information. Three areas are receiving top priority:

• **Open data**—In April 2010, the World Bank released its development data free of charge. The Open Data work builds on the success of this initiative. Its priorities are to expand the Web site and create a data resource center to serve as a clearinghouse for researchers, to develop new applications to enable easy access to data across platforms and devices, and to strengthen capacity-building activities in developing countries to help ensure the quality of data.

• **Open knowledge**—With a shift in the focus of research teams, there is now an emphasis on four strategic themes: economic transformations around emerging issues, such as macroeconomic growth, agriculture, and rural development, urbanization, and green development; the broadening of opportunities by trade and integration and access to finance; the understanding of risk and vulnerability across countries and sectors; and the measuring of results and aid effectiveness.

• **Open solutions**—To engage in the "wholesaling of research," the World Bank plans a greater focus on the creation of software tools, training products, and researcher communities. Significant efforts are under way to improve and to broaden the focus of such existing tools as ADePT and iSimulate. The programs are expected to be collaborative efforts within the World Bank and with technology partners (such as Google and Microsoft) and multilateral organizations (such as the United Nations and the IMF).

but the EBRD are involved in the control of infectious diseases. In many cases, the banks are focused on regional public goods (RPGs) or on regional aspects of global public goods, looking to the World Bank on the global aspects. They also are involved in helping their regional clients build country capacity to meet requirements under global agreements. For the AfDB, critical issues are postconflict assistance and health, especially in the face of the HIV/AIDS epidemic. For the ADB, key issues are the environment, health, and knowledge, with a particular focus on those issues where there are spillover effects within the region or within the ADB's subregional coverage. For the EBRD, nuclear safety is an area of special focus, where the World Bank has the international lead in supporting transition countries in decommissioning capacity and resolving other environmental liabilities from the Soviet era. Another focus area is financial stability, especially the adoption of the standards and codes underpinning market economies. The IADB has five priority

areas in the provision of regional and global public goods—financial sector assessments, regional integration, curbing of infectious diseases, promotion of environmental services, and support for research in agriculture and regional policy dialogue. It has prepared a new policy framework for its support for RPGs, including a financing facility geared to providing grant financing for what it calls "early-stage RPGs" (where dialogue among countries is needed), "later-stage RPGs" (where larger institutional resources to manage the emerging program are needed), and the initial stages of "club RPGs" (which will likely be financially self-sustaining once they are up and running).

The regional development banks are also stepping up their efforts to promote regional cooperation and integration. The AfDB supports the New Partnership for Africa's Development Secretariat, the African Union, the Global Environment Facility (especially on the development of the Environmental Action Plan for Africa), and the Africa Regional Coordination Unit for the United Nations

---

BOX 5.6   Climate change, natural disasters, and the World Bank Group

To address the threat of climate change, development needs to become "climate smart." It must deal with adaptation efficiently and mitigate the growth of greenhouse gases. This will require additional resources, beyond existing development finance. Synergies between climate-related investment and development need to be fully exploited. Adaptation programs can be pro-poor, such as converting degraded cropland into resilient agroforestry systems.

The WBG is helping countries address climate change through projects and partnerships. A key partnership is the Climate Investment Funds (established in 2008) to which contributing countries have pledged more than $6 billion for climate-resilient and low-emissions development. It is a partnership among the MDBs through which developed and developing countries come together with stakeholders. The World Bank plays a critical tripartite role—as trustee of the funds, as implementing agency, and as host of the administrative unit. More than 40 countries are currently undertaking Climate Investment Funds pilot programs. The Pilot Program on Climate Resilience helps highly vulnerable countries integrate risk and resilience into core development planning. The Forest Investment Program supports efforts to reduce deforestation and forest degradation, cut emissions, and maintain carbon reservoirs. Mitigation is addressed through the Clean Technology Fund, which supports scaled-up financing for low-carbon technologies in middle-income countries. The Scaling Up Renewable Energy Program aims to demonstrate low-carbon energy development in low-income countries.

The WBG also addresses climate change through Development Policy Operations, technical assistance, investment lending, and analytical work. Development Policy Operations provide support to governments implementing climate-related policies. In Ghana, for example, the Agriculture Development

Policy Credit supports efforts to integrate climate risk management into agriculture-led growth. In Bangladesh, 320,000 homes have been provided with solar electricity, and thus with lighting for education and for women's economic empowerment. The IFC is supporting climate-related investments that help meet the needs of the poor for modern services in an efficient manner, such as the Lighting Africa Program.

Natural disasters are another area where the WBG is increasingly focusing its attention. The Global Facility for Disaster Recovery and Reconstruction has established a Disaster Risk Financing and Insurance Program to enhance capacity building and knowledge sharing on disaster risk financing and to mainstream disaster risk financing and insurance into World Bank operations. New regional initiatives can build the Caribbean Catastrophe Risk Insurance Facility, which is in its fourth year of providing hurricane and/or earthquake insurance to 16 Caribbean countries and territories. With reinsurance, it has the capacity to handle claims arising from a series of events having a statistical probability of occurring only once in 1,000 years without drawing more than $20 million of its own assets (which now exceed $100 million). The World Bank's convening power is proving valuable to other pooling initiatives designed to reduce costs and achieve efficiencies in risk financing. In partnership with the ADB and regional partners, the Pacific Catastrophe Risk Assessment and Financing Initiative has been developing several disaster risk management applications: disaster risk financing solutions, including a regional insurance facility; disaster risk preparedness through identification of critical infrastructure; and disaster risk reduction through the identification of high-risk areas. Other similar new programs include the Catastrophe Risk Insurance Facility for Southeastern Europe and the Africa Risk Capacity, an effort to pool drought risk across the continent.

Convention to Combat Desertification. In Asia, the Greater Mekong Subregion Program has long been a prominent area of ADB support, promoting cross-country cooperation in a number of sectors through investments in infrastructure, policy initiatives, and institutional mechanisms. Other regional

programs cover the Pacific Islands, Central Asian regional economic cooperation, South Asian subregional economic cooperation, and the Association of Southeast Asian Nations. Similarly, the IADB works very closely with regional associations in Central and South America and the Caribbean.

IFIs' response to crises

The IMF has taken the lead in responding to crises by providing financial support to countries to permit orderly adjustment to payments crises. With the onset of the global financial crisis, the IMF moved quickly to establish new instruments to better assist its members—for example, a new Flexible Credit Line (FCL) to provide large and up-front financing to members with very strong fundamentals and policies. The facility can be used on a precautionary basis or for actual balance-of-payments needs. Because access to the FCL is restricted to those countries that meet strict qualification criteria, drawings under it are not tied to ex post conditionality. Countries that do not qualify for the FCL may receive financial assistance under High Access Precautionary Stand-by Arrangements, which can be frontloaded and must take account of the strength of a country's policies and the external environment. The Precautionary Credit Line (PCL) was introduced to meet the needs of countries that, despite having sound policies and fundamentals, have some remaining vulnerabilities that preclude them from using the FCL. Decisions have been made on a doubling of access levels, and conditionality has been reformed to make it more focused and tailored to country circumstances.

IMF actions were complemented by the MDBs. Much of the increase in MDB financing over the past two years took the form of budget support to quickly disburse funds to protect the most vulnerable people against the fallout of the crisis, to maintain planned infrastructure investment, and to sustain private sector–led economic growth and employment creation. The countercyclicality of the financial support provided during the crisis by the IFIs was particularly important, given that the overall aid levels stagnated in real terms.

The IFIs' response was tailored to the gravity, speed, and center of attention of the event. The IMF has made commitments of more than $250 billion since mid-2008, and the MDBs had record commitments and disbursements in the same period. For instance, since July 2008 when the full force of the financial crisis began to hit, the WBG has committed more than $152 billion and disbursed more than $96 billion in loans, grants, equity investments, and guarantees in support of its clients. In fiscal 2010, the IBRD's commitments of nonconcessional resources were $44.2 billion, up from a record high of $33 billion in 2009. Low-income countries have not had access to additional resources to the same extent as middle-income countries. IDA commitments in fiscal 2010 reached $14.5 billion, a 3.5 percent increase from 2009. Concessional funds from MDBs increased only slightly, given the fixed envelope of concessional windows. To accelerate their response to the crisis, however, the IFIs have boosted flows to the poorest countries by frontloading available resources. Finally, the support to private sector and nonsovereign has also been substantial. IFC investments increased by 21 percent in fiscal 2010, reaching $12.7 billion, with an additional $5.0 billion mobilized from other sources. Almost half went to IDA recipients—255 projects totaling $4.9 billion. Guarantees from the Multilateral Investment Guarantee Agency reached $1.5 billion, up from $1.4 billion in 2009.

The role of the IFIs, of course, extends beyond financing. Crucial roles for the IFIs in the context of the global economic crisis have been to inform policy making by analyzing the international spillovers of national policy actions and bringing out the interconnected nature of the challenges and to highlight the need to ensure that national responses are consistent with the global good. Amid rising pressures for policies to turn inward, the IFIs' role in warning against the risks of trade protectionism and financial mercantilism is indispensable. Drawing policy lessons from the current crisis, especially but not only in financial regulation, will be another key area. The IMF has a particularly important role in enhanced surveillance of risk in the globalized financial markets.

As the recovery progresses, it is clear that the crisis has dramatically altered the development challenges facing low-income and middle-income countries, and hence those facing the international community. Managing the availability and allocation of resources will remain a challenge for the IFIs as the recovery proceeds. To this end, the IFIs' shareholders increased the ability of the IFIs to cope with crises and address development needs through the increase in IMF resources and recent agreements on MDBs' capital increases.

Notes

1. OECD 2010.
2. Reinhart and Rogoff 2008.
3. Dang, Knack, and Rogers 2009. See also Mold et al. (2010).
4. They look at banking crises in 24 donor countries over 1977–2007. The data and the definition of "banking crisis" are based on Laeven and Valencia (2008).
5. Norway has spent 0.85 percent of its gross national income on official development assistance over the past half-century, followed by the Netherlands (0.79 percent), Sweden (0.77 percent), Denmark (0.77 percent), and Luxembourg (0.57 percent).
6. Davies 2010.
7. Ibid.
8. IPRCC 2010. See also Qi (2007).
9. Kharas 2009.
10. Hudson Institute 2010.
11. Bishop and Green 2008.
12. World Bank 2010.
13. Easterly and Pfutze 2008.
14. Roodman 2009.
15. Knack, Rogers, and Eubank 2010.
16. Birdsall and Kharas 2010.
17. Publish What You Fund: The Global Campaign for Aid Transparency, http://www.publishwhatyoufund.org/.
18. Statistical and technical problems include endogeneity, difficulty in determining the direction of causality or controlling for country-specific characteristics, multicollinearity, autocorrelation, and selection of instruments in the analysis (Roodman 2008).
19. Burnside and Dollar 2000.
20. Doucouliagos and Paldam 2005, 2006.
21. Clemens, Radelet, and Bhavnani 2004. Short-impact aid is defined as an aid disbursement funding an intervention that plausibly could increase growth within four years (balance-of-payments support, infrastructure finance).
22. Mavrotas 2005.

23. Developmental aid comprises multilateral aid and aid from some bilateral donors, with relatively high aid quality; geopolitical aid is aid from other bilateral donors.
24. Reddy and Minoiu 2006.
25. Heyman 2010.
26. Michaelowa and Weber 2006.
27. Dreher, Nunnenkamp, and Thiele 2006.
28. Mishra and Newhouse 2007.
29. Bourguignon and Sundberg 2007.
30. See, for example, Shafik (2007).
31. Henn and McDonald 2010.
32. The Global Trade Alert database is available at http://www.globaltradealert.com.
33. Chauffour 2008, Jeonghoi 2010, and Martin and Anderson 2010.
34. Bouët et al. 2010.
35. Sutherland and Bhagwati 2011.
36. For examples, see Martin and Mattoo (2010) and Hoekman, Martin, and Mattoo (2009).
37. Mattoo and Subramanian 2008.
38. This implies simultaneously cutting trade barriers to external members or allowing their participation within the rules envisaged under the agreement.
39. The database is available at http://data.world bank.org/news/global-preferential-trade-agreement-database.
40. See Hoekman and Mattoo (2010).
41. The World Integrated Trade Solution database is available at http://wits.worldbank.org/wits/.
42. Notes on some technical terms are as follows: "Rules of origin" determine whether an import shipment has "originated" in a preference-eligible exporting country and thus whether it qualifies for a reduced tariff rate. The rules may be specified according to the share of "value added" that originated in the preference-eligible country, or in other ways. "Cumulation" provisions allow intermediate inputs that originate in certain third countries (usually other preference-receiving countries) to count toward fulfilling the rule of origin, thus providing flexibility in sourcing inputs from low-cost providers. "De minimis" refers to rules permitting exemption from notification for state aid under certain thresholds to farmers, fishermen, and processing and marketing companies. See the WTO Web site (http://www.wto.org) for more discussion of various terms.
43. Raballand, Kunaka, and Giersing 2008.
44. See Arvis et al. 2010.
45. Chauffour and Malouche forthcoming.

46. Haddad, Harrison, and Hausman 2010.
47. See Hoekman and Wilson (2010) and OECD/ WTO (2010).
48. Our focus is on the five largest multilateral development banks—the African Development Bank (AfDB), the ADB, the European Bank for Reconstruction and Development (EBRD), the Inter-American Development Bank (IADB), and the World Bank—and the IMF.
49. For most low-income countries, the Poverty Reduction Strategy Paper (PRSP) is the vehicle used by the authorities to set out the national strategy. It serves as the foundation for the strategy. For middle-income countries, there is not an agreed format like the PRSP for setting out the national strategy, and the MDBs rely on a wide variety of country-specific vehicles as a basis for their country lending and nonlending programs.
50. Every Country Assistance Strategy since January 2005 is results based (following a successful pilot project during FY03/04).
51. The EBRD countries of operation within the Early Transition Countries Initiative are Armenia, Azerbaijan, Belarus, Georgia, Kyrgyz Republic, Moldova, Mongolia, Tajikistan, Turkmenistan, and Uzbekistan.
52. World Bank 2009.
53. The ADB's Trade Finance Program (TFP) provides guarantees and loans to partner banks in support of international trade. A substantial portion of the TFP's portfolio supports small and medium-size enterprises, and many transactions occur either intraregionally or between developing member-countries (DMCs). In March 2009, following the financial crisis and market needs, the TFP limit was increased to $1 billion and transaction tenor was extended to three years. The ADB established a $3 billion Countercyclical Support Facility in June 2009 to provide support to fiscal stimulus by middle-income countries. The facility helped these middle-income DMCs sustain critical development expenditures for fiscal stimulus to counter the adverse impacts of the global economic crisis during 2009–10. The facility is a short-term lending instrument and complements conventional program loans aimed at supporting structural reforms over an extended period. Its aim is to provide fast-disbursing crisis assistance to address short-term liquidity crunch and enhance DMCs' capacity to provide fiscal stimulus.
54. The EBRD has stepped up its support for banks adversely affected by the crisis in the transition region by providing equity and debt finance that was otherwise unavailable on the financial market. The enterprise response package aims at meeting short-term refinancing needs and sustaining existing investment programs. The launch of the Corporate Support Facility ensured the provision of quick-disbursing financing to help companies weather the impact of the crisis and of opportunities to strengthen and extend transition impact through loan conditionality. The EBRD is virtually doubling its Trade Facilitation Programme (to a maximum of €1.5 billion), which plays a crucial role in keeping trade flowing to and from the region in times of severely restricted access to finance.
55. The IFC's new initiatives focused on three main areas: (1) providing liquidity support through the expansion of the Global Trade Finance Program from $1 billion to $3 billion and creating the Global Trade Liquidity Pool, which was endorsed at the most recent G-20 summit in London to provide credits to support trade finance over the next three years; (2) launching the Infrastructure Crisis Facility to provide liquidity for infrastructure projects, creating the Microfinance Enhancement Facility in partnership with the German development bank, and rebuilding financial infrastructure by creating the Bank Capitalization Fund in which the IFC and the Japanese government have invested $1 and $2 billion, respectively, to provide additional capital for banks in developing countries; and (3) designing advisory programs in risk management and nonperforming-loans management and implementing a Distressed Asset Recovery Program that would mobilize investment into distressed asset pools and provide advisory services to enhance the efficiency of distressed asset markets.
56. It is envisaged that the initiative could help developing countries share expertise in areas such as managing commodity windfalls, developing efficient tax systems, adapting to new technologies, selecting public investment projects with high economic and social rates of return, reforming pensions, and creating social safety nets that benefit the poor.

References

Arvis, J.-F., M. A. Mustra, L. Ojala, B. Shepherd, and D. Saslavsky. 2010. "Connecting to Compete 2010: Trade Logistics in the Global Economy. The Logistics Performance Index and Its Indicators." World Bank, Washington, DC.

Arvis, J.-F., G. Raballand, and J.-F. Marteau. 2010. *The Cost of Being Landlocked: Logistics Costs and Supply Chain Reliability*. Directions in Development Series. Washington, DC: World Bank.

Bishop, M., and M. Green. 2008. *Philanthrocapitalism: How Giving Can Save the World*. London: Bloomsbury.

Birdsall, N., and H. Kharas. 2010. "Quality of Official Development Assistance Assessment." Center for Global Development, Washington, DC.

Bouët, A., D. Laborde Debucquet, E. Dienesch, and K. Elliott. 2010. "The Costs and Benefits of Duty-Free, Quota-Free Market Access for Poor Countries: Who and What Matters?" Working Paper 990, International Food Policy Research Institute, Washington, DC.

Bourguignon, F., and M. Sundberg. 2007. "Aid Effectiveness—Opening the Black Box." *American Economic Review* 97 (2): 316–21.

Burnside, C., and Dollar, D. 2000. "Aid, Policies, and Growth." *American Economic Review* 90 (4): 847–68.

Chauffour, J.-P. 2008. "Global Food Price Crisis—Trade Policy Options." *PREM Notes* 120 (June). World Bank, Washington, DC.

Chauffour, J.-P., and M. Malouche. Forthcoming. *Trade Finance during the Great Trade Collapse*. Washington, DC: World Bank.

Clemens, M., S. Radelet, and R. Bhavnani. 2004. "Counting Chickens When They Hatch: The Short-Term Effect of Aid on Growth." Working Paper 44, Center for Global Development, Washington, DC.

Dang, H.-A., S. Knack, and H. Rogers. 2009. "International Aid and Financial Crises in Donor Countries." Policy Research Working Paper 5162, World Bank, Washington, DC.

Davies, P. 2010. "A Review of the Roles and Activities of New Development Partners." Concessional Finance and Global Partnerships Working Paper Series No. 4, World Bank, Washington, DC.

Doucouliagos, H., and M. Paldam. 2005. "The Aid Effectiveness Literature: The Sad Result of 40 Years of Research." Working Paper 2005-15, University of Aarhus, Denmark.

———. 2006. "Aid Effectiveness on Accumulation: A Meta Study." *Kyklos* 59 (2): 227–54.

Dreher, A., P. Nunnenkamp, and R. Thiele. 2006. "Does Aid for Education Educate Children? Evidence from Panel Data." Working Paper, Kiel Institute for the World Economy, Kiel, Germany.

Easterly, W., and T. Pfutze. 2008. "Where Does the Money Go? Best and Worst Practices in Foreign Aid." Working Paper 21, Brookings Global Economy and Development, Washington, DC.

Haddad, M., A. Harrison, and C. Hausman. 2010. "Decomposing the Great Trade Collapse: Products, Prices, and Quantities in the 2008–2009 Crisis." Working Paper 16253, National Bureau of Economic Research, Cambridge, MA.

Henn, C., and B. McDonald. 2010. "Crisis Protectionism: The Observed Trade Impact." http://www.voxeu.org/index.php?q=node/5960.

Heyman, A. 2010. "Drilling Down Aid: Aid by Sector." PhD diss., Bocconi University, Milan, Italy.

Hoekman, B., and A. Mattoo. 2010. "Services Trade Liberalization and Regulatory Reform: Re-invigorating International Cooperation." Policy Research Working Paper 5517, World Bank, Washington, DC.

Hoekman, B., W. Martin, and A. Mattoo. 2009. "Conclude Doha: It Matters!" Policy Research Working Paper 5135, World Bank, Washington, DC.

Hoekman, B., and J. Wilson. 2010. "Aid for Trade: Building on Progress Today for Tomorrow's Future." Policy Research Working Paper 5361, World Bank, Washington, DC.

Hudson Institute. 2010. *The Index of Global Philanthropy and Remittances*. Washington, DC.

IPRCC (International Poverty Reduction Center in China). 2010. "Development Partnerships for Growth and Poverty Reduction." Working Paper 07, Beijing.

Jeonghoi, K. 2010. "Recent Trends in Export Restrictions." Trade Policy Working Paper 101, Organisation for Economic Co-operation and Development, Paris, France.

Kharas, H. 2009. "Development Assistance in the 21st Century." Paper prepared for the VIII Salamanca Forum, "The Fight Against Hunger and Poverty," Salamanca, Spain, July 2–4.

Knack, S., F. H. Rogers, and N. Eubank. 2010. "Aid Quality and Donor Rankings." Policy Research Working Paper 5290, World Bank, Washington, DC.

Kunaka, C. 2010. *Logistics in Lagging Regions: Overcoming Local Barriers to Global Connectivity.* Washington, DC: World Bank.

Laeven, L., and F. Valencia. 2008. "Systemic Banking Crises: A New Database." Working Paper 08/224, International Monetary Fund, Washington, DC.

Martin, W., and K. Anderson. 2010. "Trade Distortions and Food Price Surges." Paper prepared for the World Bank–University of California-Berkeley Conference on Agriculture for Development-Revisited, Berkeley, CA, October 1–2.

Martin, W., and A. Mattoo. 2010. "The Doha Development Agenda: What's on the Table?" *Journal of International Trade and Economic Development* 19 (1): 81–107.

Mattoo, A., and Arvind Subramanian. 2008. "Multilateralism Beyond Doha." Policy Research Working Paper 4735, World Bank, Washington, DC.

Mavrotas, G. 2005. "Aid Heterogeneity: Looking at Aid Effectiveness from a Different Angle." *Journal of International Development* 17 (8): 1019–36.

Michaelowa, K, and A. Weber. 2006. "Aid Effectiveness Reconsidered: Panel Data Evidence for the Education Sector." Discussion Paper 264, Hamburg Institute of International Economics. Hamburg, Germany.

Mishra, P., and D. Newhouse. 2007. "Health Aid and Infant Mortality." Working Paper 07/100, International Monetary Fund, Washington, DC.

Mold, A., A. Prizzon, E. Frot, and J. Santiso. 2010. "Aid Flows in Times of Crisis." Presentation to the Conference on Development Cooperation In Times of Crisis and on Achieving the MDGs, Madrid, Spain, June 9–10.

OECD (Organisation for Economic Co-operation and Development). 2010. "Development Aid Rose in 2009 and Most Donors Will Meet 2010 aid Targets." Paris, France. http://www.oecd.org/document/11/0,3343,en_2649_3444 7_44981579_1_.1_1_37413,00.html

OECD/WTO (Organisation for Economic Co-operation and Development/World Trade Organization). 2010. "Aid for Trade: Is It Working?" Policy Note. OECD, Paris, France.

Qi, G. 2007. "China's Foreign Aid: Policies, Structure, Practice and Trend." Presentation at the Oxford/Cornell University Conference, "New Directions in Development Assistance," Oxford, UK, June 11–12.

Raballand, G., C. Kunaka, and B. Giersing. 2008. "The Impact of Regional Liberalization and Harmonization in Road Transport Services: A Focus on Zambia and Lessons for Landlocked Countries." Policy Research Working Paper 4482, World Bank, Washington, DC.

Reddy, S., and C. Minoiu. 2006. "Development Aid and Economic Growth: A Positive Long-Run Relation." Department of Economic and Social Affairs, United Nations, New York.

Reinhart, C. M., and K. Rogoff. 2008. "Banking Crises: An Equal Opportunity Menace." Working Paper 14587, National Bureau of Economic Research, Cambridge, MA.

Roodman, D. 2008. "Through the Looking Glass, and What OLS Found There: On Growth, Foreign Aid, and Reverse Causality." Working Paper 137, Center for Global Development, Washington, DC.

———. 2009. "An Index of Donor Performance." Working Paper 67, Center for Global Development, Washington, DC.

Shafik, N. 2010. "The Future of Aid." Eighth Luca d'Agliano Lecture in Development Economics, Fondazione Luigi Einaudi, Turin, Italy, December 17.

Sutherland, P., and J. Bhagwati. 2011. "The Doha Round: Setting a Deadline, Defining a Final Deal." Interim report of the High Level Trade Experts Group. http://www.acp-eu-trade. org/library/files/High%20level%20trade%20 experts%20group_EN_010111_The%20 doha%20round%20setting%20a%20dead-line.pdf.

World Bank. 2009. "Moving Ahead on Investment Lending Reform: Risk Framework and Implementation Support." SecM2009-0442, September 9, Washington, DC.

———. 2010. "Research for Development—A World Bank Perspective on Future Directions for Research." Policy Research Working Paper 5437, Washington, DC.

———. 2011. *World Development Report 2011: Conflict, Security, and Development.* Washington, DC.

Technical Issues in Estimating Progress in the Millennium Development Goals

Measuring Millennium Development Goals performance

The Millennium Development Goals (MDGs) are typically defined in terms of the number or percentage of *people* (for example, halving the number of poor people or achieving 100 percent access to primary education). Whereas data are generally collected on a country basis, the influence of each country in the global average depends on the size of its population. When large countries like China and India are doing well—as on the poverty MDG—their progress will be reflected very visibly in the global average, but will also hide progress (or a lack of it) in smaller countries. To examine how poor countries are doing, the data in chapter 1 are also presented in terms of progress in individual countries—not to replace the standard approach, but to provide additional information.

MDG performance is measured by deviations from target values required to reach development goals. The reference year for measuring progress is officially set as 1990. Countries are classified as

- **on target:** the country has already achieved or will meet the 2015 development goal if

progress continues until 2015 at the same rate as progress from 1990 to the latest available year;
- **off target:** the country will not achieve the 2015 development goal if progress continues until 2015 at the same rate as progress from 1990 to the latest available year;
- **close to the target or off target and above average:** the country is off target, but performing better than the average off-target country; or
- **far from the target or off target and below average:** the country is off target and performing worse than the average off-target country.

To determine whether a country is on target, we calculate the linear annualized rate of improvement from the 1990 value of each MDG indicator needed to reach the 2015 goal. We restrict our attention to the six MDGs and nine development targets with quantifiable 2015 goals. A country is classified as on target if the observed MDG performance is equal to or above this required achievement path; a country is considered off target if MDG progress is below this path.

Within the off-target category, countries are classified in relation to the group's average

TABLE A1.1 Data availability by MDG, income, and geographic region, fiscal 2011

Income level and geographic region	Total number of countries	MDG 1.a extreme poverty	MDG 1.c hunger	MDG 2.a primary education completion	MDG 3.a gender parity in primary education	MDG 3.a gender parity in secondary education	MDG 4.a child mortality under five	MDG 5.a maternal mortality	MDG 7.c access to safe drinking water	MDG 7.c access to sanitation
Income										
Low income	**40**	22	24	29	36	31	40	40	40	40
Lower-middle income	**56**	34	20	44	50	47	56	46	51	51
Upper-middle income	**48**	29	11	39	41	42	48	38	41	39
Region										
East Asia and Pacific	**24**	8	3	15	19	17	24	15	21	21
Europe and Central Asia	**22**	20	4	18	19	18	22	21	18	16
Latin America and the Caribbean	**30**	20	12	26	26	26	30	24	29	29
Middle East and North Africa	**13**	7	7	11	11	12	13	12	13	13
South Asia	**8**	5	4	6	8	8	8	8	7	7
Sub-Saharan Africa	**47**	25	25	36	44	39	47	44	44	44

Source: World Development Indicators.

distance to be on target. (The average here is the mean of the off-target group, not the entire sample of countries.) Two subgroups are identified: countries that are off target and above average or close to the target (that is, countries for which development goals are possibly within reach); and countries that are off target and below average or far from the target (that is, countries lagging the most

on reaching the 2015 MDGs). Performance data for these two subgroups are presented in tables A1.2, A1.3, and A1.4.

Data constraints

Detailed historical data on MDG performance are required to calculate the achievement path for each country to meet each of the MDGs.[1]

TABLE A1.2 MDG performance: share of countries close to the target in the total number of countries off target, by geographic region

percent

Geographic region	MDG 1.a extreme poverty	MDG 1.c hunger	MDG 2.a primary education completion	MDG 3.a gender parity in primary education	MDG 3.a gender parity in secondary education	MDG 4.a child mortality under five	MDG 5.a maternal mortality	MDG 7.c access to safe drinking water	MDG 7.c access to sanitation
East Asia and Pacific	100	100	100	75	100	33	64	56	62
Europe and Central Asia	0	—	100	100	100	92	40	50	27
Latin America and the Caribbean	25	100	100	91	100	85	43	60	39
Middle East and North Africa	0	50	80	67	33	50	80	44	50
South Asia	100	67	67	50	50	60	80	33	80
Sub-Saharan Africa	81	53	48	47	50	25	38	69	29

Source: World Bank staff calculations based on data from the World Development Indicators database.
Note: — = not applicable. Shading indicates the share of countries close to target among all off-target countries that is below 50 percent.

TABLE A1.3   MDG performance: share of countries close to the target in the total number of countries off target, by income level

percent

Income level	MDG 1.a extreme poverty	MDG 1.c hunger	MDG 2.a primary education completion	MDG 3.a gender parity in primary education	MDG 3.a gender parity in secondary education	MDG 4.a child mortality under five	MDG 5.a maternal mortality	MDG 7.c access to safe drinking water	MDG 7.c access to sanitation
Low-income countries	88	50	41	36	35	34	51	67	31
Lower-middle-income countries	38	80	84	72	85	53	53	43	48
Upper-middle-income countries	17	50	100	89	100	63	37	67	39

Source: World Bank staff calculations based on data from the World Development Indicators database.
Note: Shading indicates the share of countries close to target among all off-target countries that is below 50 percent.

TABLE A1.4   MDG performance: share of countries close to the target in the total number of countries off target, by alternative typologies

percent

Alternative typology	MDG 1.a extreme poverty	MDG 1.c hunger	MDG 2.a primary education completion	MDG 3.a gender parity in primary education	MDG 3.a gender parity in secondary education	MDG 4.a child mortality under five	MDG 5.a maternal mortality	MDG 7.c access to safe drinking water	MDG 7.c access to sanitation
A. IDA classification									
Non-IDA countries	27	64	100	82	92	57	45	57	49
IDA countries	74	58	50	52	46	42	52	61	29
B. State fragility									
Little to low	25	50	100	100	100	53	47	63	47
Moderate	33	100	100	83	100	65	32	50	45
Serious	73	50	56	83	50	65	87	73	50
High to extreme	70	67	27	23	38	26	33	64	23
C. Export sophistication									
High	67	—	100	100	—	67	17	50	57
Medium high	43	60	67	100	33	59	68	50	65
Medium low	58	64	53	62	62	33	40	75	38
Low	60	50	69	67	70	52	63	58	25

Source: World Bank staff calculations based on data from the World Development Indicators database, Marshall and Cole 2010, and Lall 2000.
Note: — = not applicable; IDA = International Development Association. Shading indicates the share of countries close to target among all off-target countries that is below 50 percent.

Unfortunately, such data are not available in many countries for 1990, although estimates for recent years tend to be more complete. If no country data are available for 1990, we used the closest available information in the late 1980s or early 1990s as substitutes for the starting point (table A1.5), and then calculated the rate of progress required from that point to meet the MDG. This approach may be inaccurate if the data for the available starting point are significantly different from the level of MDG performance in 1990 or if the sample period does not capture the latest progress. The latter is a particularly important issue now because data generally are not available for 2009, the crisis year. In addition, for countries without at least two data points, progress cannot be measured, even if data are available for a recent year. Even so, the approach enables us to include more

TABLE A1.5   Development indicators, average levels circa 1990

MDG performance	MDG 1.a extreme poverty	MDG 1.c hunger	MDG 2.a primary education completion	MDG 3.a gender parity in primary education	MDG 3.a gender parity in secondary education	MDG 4.a child mortality under five	MDG 5.a maternal mortality	MDG 7.c access to safe drinking water	MDG 7.c access to sanitation
On target	24.14	19.47	88.61	90.76	97.26	73.37	150.73	23.75	30.43
Close to the target	55.97	25.66	68.22	91.97	79.75	87.94	525.39	38.15	51.19
Far from the target	9.70	23.04	26.09	73.65	50.92	112.47	485.98	24.52	53.03
Total	29.43	22.27	68.99	89.14	87.00	93.44	419.49	28.26	46.42

Source: World Bank staff calculations based on data from the World Development Indicators database.

countries than if we relied only on data from 1990 and 2008. Table A1.1 summarizes the number of observations by MDG, income group of countries, and region (World Bank's classification, table A1.13).

The multinomial logit estimates

Empirically analyzing the MDGs from a cross-country perspective imposes serious challenges, with frequent data gaps and measurement errors. Plausible functional forms are therefore difficult to derive. And several MDGs—such as access to safe drinking water and health targets—are likely to be significantly cross-correlated. Here we discuss some of the most significant issues affecting our methodological approach.[2]

We employ the multinomial logit estimation method because it is well suited to examine the likelihood that countries fall into one of the three country groups explained above (on target, close to the target, and far from the target), given changes in economic growth and the policy framework. This method is typically employed to model individual discrete choices, such as the occupational choice of households in microsimulations or demand for modes of transportation.

Dependent variable and estimation method. The multinomial logit model does not use the actual values of MDG performance indexes. Instead, MDG performance is defined in terms of three values: 1 for countries far from the target (off target and below average), 2 for countries close to the

target (off target and above average), and 3 for countries on target. Avoiding the use of the actual value of MDG indexes is important for two reasons. First, the index numbers that indicate progress in many MDG indicators display substantial variability for countries performing well below or above average. Taking account of this variability would require some form of data trimming, outlier identification procedure, or inclusion of control variables that would reduce the available degrees of freedom and therefore decrease the reliability of estimates, in a context of small data samples. Second and more important, our goal is to assess the likelihood of each country achieving or being on track to achieve the MDGs, conditional on current development performance, an empirical approach consistent with the use of models of categorical dependent variables. We are not trying to determine how much per capita GDP must grow or institutions and policies must improve to attain the development goals by 2015—for which observed values of development indicators and linear regression models are better suited (although these models, as well as nonlinear approaches, may suffer from endogeneity and multicollinearity problems).[3]

At first glance, an ordinal regression model seems appropriate to analyze the extent to which GDP growth and the policy framework determine the likelihood of being on track to achieve the MDGs. Our initial work therefore involved estimating this relationship using an ordered logistic regression model.

However, a fundamental assumption of such models is that the explanatory variables have the same impact across different values for the dependent variable (the proportional odds hypothesis), and this assumption is consistently rejected in most of the nine specifications under consideration. These rejections imply that the coefficients associated with per capita growth and institutions are not equal across levels of MDG performance. For this reason, alternative and less restrictive models that can integrate a differentiated impact of growth and policy on the dependent variable (MDG performance) are required. Consequently, we turn to the multinomial logit model, a nominal outcome estimation technique that reduces the risk of bias resulting from the rejection of the proportional odds hypothesis in the ordinal regression approach, but at the cost of a potential loss of efficiency, given the many parameters in the model.[4]

Functional form, model specification, and the use of the Country Policy and Institutional Assessment index. The empirical model follows a simple structure that addresses the fundamentals of the *Global Monitoring Report* framework,[5] builds on the current MDG literature, and takes into account data limitations. Progress toward the 2015 goals is expressed as a function of initial conditions and development progress over time (table A1.6). In this context, measuring the quality of policies and institutions represents a major challenge. We use the Country Policy and Institutional Assessment (CPIA) index, which provides a comprehensive assessment of social policies and public sector management that is fundamental for MDG attainment. For example, the CPIA index takes into consideration the extent to which the pattern of public expenditures and revenue collection affects the poor and is consistent with national poverty reduction priorities (criterion 8, equity of public resource use). However, an important limitation of the CPIA index is that values are not strictly comparable across years because of numerous methodological changes over time. Therefore, we focus on current index values, assuming

that the current level of the CPIA indexes partially reflects past performances, given the slowly evolving nature of institutions.

The independence of irrelevant alternatives. One assumption of our estimation procedure is that the results satisfy the independence of irrelevant alternatives (IIA) assumption. This assumption, which is often used in the context of public choice theory, is that the odds of an outcome (in this exercise, being on target, close to target, or far from target) do not depend on other alternatives that are available (alternatives are dissimilar). This means that the coefficients on independent variables (in this exercise, growth and the quality of institutions) would not change significantly if we were to suppress one of the categories of the dependent variable and reestimate the model. We performed Small-Hsiao tests[6] to determine whether results satisfy the IIA assumption, with generally satisfactory results (calculations of the Small-Hsiao test are shown in table A1.7).[7] In any event, it is generally acknowledged that IIA tests have little power in small samples and may even provide conflicting results.[8] According to McFadden, the multinomial logit model "should be limited to situations where the alternatives can plausibly be assumed to be distinct and weighted independently in the eyes of each decision-maker."[9] Therefore, the validity of our conclusions (in terms of the IIA assumption) relies more on the fact that our categories are conceptually independent than on this econometric test.

Endogeneity, reverse causality. Indicators of progress in human development (our dependent variables) can have an impact on growth and the quality of institutions (our independent variables). Thus, our estimations could be subject to reverse causality, which would mean that the coefficients on the independent variables are not correctly estimated. However, such concerns are likely to be less of a problem in our estimation than in regressions using the levels of MDGs (for example, where the level of the poverty head count is the dependent variable). This is because small changes in the dependent variable (for

TABLE A1.6 Growth has a clear, pervasive effect, but better policy also helps improve the odds of achieving the MDGs

multinomial logit estimates

Independent variables	(1) MDG 1.a Above average coef/se	(1) MDG 1.a On target coef/se	(2) MDG 1.c Above average coef/se	(2) MDG 1.c On target coef/se	(3) MDG 2.a Above average coef/se	(3) MDG 2.a On target coef/se	(4) MDG3.a (primary) Above average coef/se	(4) MDG3.a (primary) On target coef/se	(5) MDG 3.a (secondary) Above average coef/se	(5) MDG 3.a (secondary) On target coef/se	(6) MDG 4.a Above average coef/se	(6) MDG 4.a On target coef/se	(7) MDG 5.a Above average coef/se	(7) MDG 5.a On target coef/se	(8) MDG 7.a (water) Above average coef/se	(8) MDG 7.a (water) On target coef/se	(9) MDG 7.a (sanitation) Above average coef/se	(9) MDG 7.a (sanitation) On target coef/se
Annual growth in GDP per capita, average for 1990–2009 (2005 Id PPP)	0.262 / 0.217	0.359*** / 0.131	0.335*** / 0.051	0.427** / 0.177	0.766*** / 0.187	1.304*** / 0.197	0.627 / 0.440	0.470 / 0.340	0.922* / 0.513	1.411** / 0.558	0.240* / 0.132	0.518** / 0.211	0.187* / 0.101	0.546 / 0.397	0.105 / 0.120	0.253*** / 0.038	0.260 / 0.187	0.383*** / 0.129
CPIA 2009	0.609 / 0.892	0.211 / 1.525	1.071*** / 0.398	2.784*** / 0.330	–0.158 / 0.258	0.128 / 0.732	0.725 / 0.524	0.925*** / 0.351	–1.007 / 0.664	–0.745 / 1.437	1.119** / 0.553	1.670*** / 0.579	0.864*** / 0.173	1.382*** / 0.367	–2.033** / 1.005	–1.203 / 0.990	0.690 / 0.591	0.409 / 0.368
GDP per capita 1990 (2005 Id PPP)	–0.010 / 0.059	0.041* / 0.023	0.001 / 0.014	0.002 / 0.012	0.079** / 0.034	0.087** / 0.039	0.008 / 0.013	0.005 / 0.016	0.146** / 0.071	0.141** / 0.069	–0.005 / 0.005	–0.001 / 0.010	–0.025** / 0.012	0.002 / 0.008	0.051*** / 0.014	0.046*** / 0.010	–0.005 / 0.006	–0.012 / 0.016
CPIA 1996	0.906 / 1.020	0.740 / 1.404	0.585 / 0.741	0.294 / 0.341 ~	0.726 / 0.549	–0.511 / 0.958	–0.601* / 0.321	0.363** / 0.153	1.295* / 0.673	2.209*** / 0.629	–0.801** / 0.400	0.047 / 0.412	0.183 / 0.126	–0.360 / 0.231	1.652*** / 0.582	1.927** / 0.760	0.103 / 0.278	–0.355 / 0.457
Extreme poverty circa 1990	0.097*** / 0.015	0.079*** / 0.017																
Hunger circa 1990			–0.004 / 0.036	–0.040 / 0.049														
Primary education completion circa 1990					0.167*** / 0.027	0.221*** / 0.029												
Gender parity in primary education circa 1990							0.062** / 0.026	0.054* / 0.031										

Variable	Values (coef / se, in left-to-right column order)
Gender parity in secondary education circa 1990	0.089*** / 0.007 0.127*** / 0.014
Child mortality under five circa 1990	−0.006 / 0.005 −0.005 / 0.006
Maternal mortality circa 1990	−0.000 / 0.001 −0.004 / 0.003
Access to safe drinking water circa 1990	0.077*** / 0.011 0.041*** / 0.015
Access to sanitation circa 1990	0.003 / 0.017 −0.033 / 0.266 0.022 / 2.259
_cons	−7.751** / 3.479 −5.864*** / 0.897 −5.259** / 2.281 −9.741*** / 2.609 −11.842*** / 3.435 −5.422*** / 1.896 −6.887*** / 2.277 −7.736*** / 1.148 −14.483*** / 3.278 −0.988 / 2.204 −7.021** / 2.794 −3.069*** / 0.507 −4.741** / 2.101 −1.408 / 2.251 −3.540* / 2.085 −3.612 / 2.263
Number of observations	77 49 90 105 95 114 104 106 107
adjusted R^2	0.293 0.185 0.515 0.161 0.415 0.146 0.211 0.192 0.123

Source: World Bank staff calculations.
Note: Robust estimates with regional clusters. CPIA = Country Policy and Institutional Assessment; coef/se = coefficient/standard error; Id = international dollars; PPP = purchasing power parity.
*p < 0.1; **p < 0.05; ***p < 0.01.

TABLE A1.7   **Small-Hsiao tests of IIA assumption—null hypothesis: odds (outcome-j versus outcome-k) are independent of other alternatives**

Equation	Omitted outcome	Lnl(full)	Lnl(omit)	chi2	df	P>chi2
(1)	Close to the target	−9.65	−8.21	2.88	6.0	0.82
	On target	−2.20	0.00	4.40	6.0	0.62
(2)	Close to the target	−0.01	0.00	0.03	6.0	1.00
	On target	−0.14	0.00	0.27	6.0	1.00
(3)	Close to the target	−0.03	0.00	0.05	6.0	1.00
	On target	−8.05	−3.36	9.37	6.0	0.15
(4)	Close to the target	−21.13	−11.46	19.33	6.0	0.00
	On target	−10.43	−5.90	9.07	6.0	0.17
(5)	Close to the target	−0.01	0.00	0.02	6.0	1.00
	On target	−0.02	0.00	0.04	6.0	1.00
(6)	Close to the target	−13.66	−12.33	2.65	6.0	0.85
	On target	−24.72	−22.87	3.69	6.0	0.72
(7)	Close to the target	−14.32	−11.65	5.34	6.0	0.50
	On target	−22.85	−20.16	5.38	6.0	0.50
(8)	Close to the target	−12.54	−9.20	6.67	6.0	0.35
	On target	−20.60	−11.08	19.06	6.0	0.00
(9)	Close to the target	−24.05	−19.67	8.76	6.0	0.19
	On target	−19.08	−16.15	5.86	6.0	0.44

Source: World Bank staff calculations.
Note: IIA = independence of irrelevant alternatives.

example, poverty head count) in the latter case may have a direct impact on the independent variable (for example, growth). In our estimations, the dependent variable is inclusion in a group defined by deviations from an exogenously determined path (for example, the rate of change in poverty necessary to achieve the goal). The connection between inclusion in one of the three groups and growth is much more tenuous.

Predicted probabilities, marginal effects, and odds ratios. Table A1.8 summarizes the effect of marginal changes in independent variables on the probability of a country being in one of our three groups at average sample values. Results show that a one-unit marginal increase in per capita GDP growth is significantly and inversely related to the probability of a country being far from the target in all MDGs, excluding completion of primary schooling and gender parity in secondary education. Conversely, a one-unit increase in GDP per capita growth significantly raises the probability of a country being on target by at least 0.05, holding other variables at their mean, for primary completion, gender parity

in secondary education, and access to safe water and sanitation. In addition, CPIA scores appear to have significant marginal effects, at average values, on the probabilities of being on target (positive signs) and/or far from target (negative signs) for several health-related MDGs (hunger, child mortality, and maternal mortality). Note that for several development goals, the predicted probability of a country being close to target is significantly and inversely related to changes in per capita growth and the CPIA index (that is, higher growth may reduce the probability of being close to the target). This does not imply that high growth is correlated with poor performance. Rather, countries with relatively high growth may be on track to meet the goals, instead of off-track but close to the target.

The odds ratios or factor change coefficients (table A1.9) illustrate the dynamics among MDG performance outcomes. These coefficients depict the expected change in the probability of a country being on target versus far from the target and on target versus close to the target, following a one-standard-deviation increase in development drivers and

TABLE A1.8 Predicted probabilities and marginal effects

Predicted probabilities	MDG 1.a			MDG 1.c			MDG 2.a			MDG 3.a (primary)			MDG 3.a (secondary)			MDG 4.a			MDG 5.a			MDG 7.a (water)			MDG 7.a (sanitation)		
	On target	Close to target	Far from target	On target	Close to target	Far from target	On target	Close to target	Far from target	On target	Close to target	Far from target	On target	Close to target	Far from target	On target	Close to target	Far from target	On target	Close to target	Far from target	On target	Close to target	Far from target	On target	Close to target	Far from target
Predicted probabilities	0.69	0.19	0.13	0.43	0.40	0.17	0.42	0.58	0.00	0.75	0.22	0.03	0.73	0.27	0.00	0.20	0.44	0.36	0.10	0.44	0.47	0.57	0.27	0.15	0.23	0.31	0.46
Change in predicted probabilities following a one-unit increase in GDP per capita growth	0.04	−0.01	**−0.04**	0.05	**0.01**	**−0.06**	**0.13**	**−0.13**	0.00	−0.02	0.03	**−0.01**	**0.10**	**−0.10**	0.00	0.06	0.01	**−0.08**	0.04	0.02	**−0.06**	**0.05**	−0.02	**−0.03**	**0.05**	0.03	**−0.08**
Change in predicted probabilities following a one-unit increase in CPIA score	−0.03	0.07	−0.03	**0.50**	**−0.22**	**−0.28**	0.07	−0.07	0.00	0.05	−0.03	−0.02	0.05	−0.05	0.00	**0.17**	0.13	**−0.30**	0.09	**0.15**	**−0.24**	0.02	**−0.22**	0.16	0.02	0.12	−0.14

Source: World Bank staff calculations.

Note: CPIA = Country Policy and Institutional Assessment. Predicted probabilities and changes in predicted probabilities for each category are computed at average sample values. Results are not comparable across indicators. Numbers in bold type denote significant changes at 0.10 level or better.

TABLE A1.9   Effects of a one-standard-deviation increase in selected development drivers

percent

MDG	Due to increase in GDP per capita growth		Due to increase in CPIA index	
	on target vs. far from target	*on target vs. close to target*	*on target vs. far from target*	*on target vs. close to target*
MDG 1.a extreme poverty	**93**	19	12	−19
MDG 1.c hunger	**88**	15	**281**	**128**
MDG 2.a primary completion rate	**1,111**	**180**	7	16
MDG 3.a gender parity (primary)	141	−25	**67**	12
MDG 3.a gender parity (secondary)	**1,191**	**143**	−34	16
MDG 4.a child mortality under five	**163**	68	**152**	36
MDG 5.a maternal mortality	189	101	**120**	**34**
MDG 7.c access to safe water	**61**	32	−48	**58**
MDG 7.c access to sanitation	**102**	25	26	−15

Source: World Bank staff calculations.
Note: Percentage variations are not comparable across indicators. Average standard deviation increase in GDP per capita growth = 1.8. Average standard deviation increase in CPIA index = 0.5. Numbers in bold type denote significance at 0.10 level or better.

holding all other variables constant. (Results are discussed in chapter 1.)

Disaggregation of the CPIA index. Our main results use the aggregate CPIA index as the independent variable. However, we also did estimations using the four components of the CPIA index in 2009 (economic management, structural policies, policies for social inclusion and equity, and public sector management and institutions) separately. These results show that policies for social inclusion and equity (gender equality, equity of public resource use, building human resources, social protection, and labor) are significantly and positively correlated with the odds of a country being on target to achieve the MDGs for extreme poverty, primary completion, gender parity, and child mortality. Results are mixed for the three remaining indicators (secondary education, access to water and sanitation, and maternal mortality) and vary according to whether a country is or is not close to the target. However, these results have to be interpreted with caution because of the high collinearity between CPIA subcategories (pairwise correlations above 0.65) and the limited degrees of freedom, given the substantial number of parameters and the relatively small size of available data samples.

Alternative measures of policy and institutions. Given the uncertainties surrounding measurements of policy and institutional performance, we test the robustness of our results by including in the analysis other indicators of government performance: state fragility, as measured by Marshall and Cole's index[10] and governance indicators produced by Kaufmann, Kraay, and Mastruzzi.[11] The impact of these institutional variables, as well as the CPIA index, on the odds of being on target is summarized in tables A1.10 and A1.11.

Table A1.10 shows the links between fragility and governance variables and the odds of a country being on target or far from the target. Results are broadly consistent with our previous estimates using the CPIA index: perceptions of political stability and regulatory quality are positively related to the likelihood of achieving the hunger target; perceptions of government effectiveness, regulatory quality, rule of law, and control of corruption are positively related to achieving the targets for gender equality and primary education; perceptions of state fragility are inversely related to child mortality; and perceptions of regulatory quality are positively correlated with achieving the target for maternal mortality.

Table A1.11 displays the relationship between institutional indicators and the probability of being on target versus close to the target. Previous results are partly confirmed.

TABLE A1.10   Probability of being on target or far from the target average

Indicator	MDG 1.a	MDG 1.c	MDG 2.a	MDG 3.a (primary)	MDG 3.a (secondary)	MDG 4.a	MDG 5.a	MDG 7.c (water)	MDG 7.c (sanitation)
CPIA index (2009)		+		+		+	+		
State fragility (1995–2009)			–			–			–
Voice and accountability									
Political stability	+	+				–			
Government effectiveness	+		+	+	+				
Regulatory quality	+	+		+			+		
Rule of law				+				–	
Control of corruption		–		+	+				

Source: World Bank staff calculations.
Note: CPIA = Country Policy and Institutional Assessment. Significant at 0.1 level or better. Empty cells = no significant correlation. State fragility (1995–2009) is the difference between index values in 2009 and 1996. Governance indicators correspond to 2009 rankings.

TABLE A1.11   Probability of being on target or close to the target average

Indicator	MDG 1.a	MDG 1.c	MDG 2.a	MDG 3.a (primary)	MDG 3.a (secondary)	MDG 4.a	MDG 5.a	MDG 7.c (water)	MDG 7.c (sanitation)
CPIA index (2009)		+					+	+	
State fragility (1995–2009)						–			
Voice and accountability	–								
Political stability		+				–	–	+	
Government effectiveness		+						–	–
Regulatory quality	+							+	–
Rule of law									
Control of corruption								+	

Source: World Bank staff calculations.
Note: CPIA = Country Policy and Institutional Assessment. Significant at 0.1 level or better. Empty cells = no significant correlation. State fragility (1995–2009) is the difference between index values in 2009 and 1996. Governance indicators correspond to 2009 rankings.

Political stability and government effectiveness are positively linked to the hunger target. And political stability, regulatory quality, and control of corruption exhibit positive correlations with access to safe drinking water.

These estimations provide additional and interesting links between indicators of institutional quality and progress toward the MDGs. For instance, political stability, regulatory quality, and government effectiveness are positively correlated with poverty reduction for countries on target versus those off target and below average (table A1.10); however, per capita GDP growth loses its significance in the case of political stability and regulatory quality (results not shown). Conversely, voice and accountability—that is, civil and political rights—are not significantly related to most MDGs (tables A1.10 and A1.11); and when a significant correlation is found (table A1.11, extreme poverty), the observed sign is negative (the result is counterintuitive). In addition, a negative relationship is found between some other governance variables (particularly, political stability and government effectiveness) and the attainment of several MDGs (child and maternal mortality and access to water and sanitation [tables A1.10 and A1.11]). A complete analysis of the role of governance in achieving the MDGs is beyond the scope of this appendix. However, these apparently counterintuitive outcomes are consistent with the fact that many of the poorest countries are making important progress toward achieving the MDGs, thanks to sustained growth and despite significant institutional weaknesses— a finding that highlights the necessity of a better understanding of the mechanisms through which policies and institutions promote development.

Education outcomes versus outputs. Our results show that policies and institutions are significantly and positively correlated with several health-related MDGs, whereas correlations with education attainment are not as strong. One possibility is that these differences arise from the fact that the health targets are defined in terms of outcomes (for example, child and maternal mortality), whereas the education goals are defined in terms of access (for example, primary education coverage). In part, the selection of MDG indicators reflected the availability of data. In what follows, we try to assess how important institutions are to achieving higher levels of literacy—a broadly available outcome-based measure of educational attainment.

An explicit target for literacy was not included in the MDGs, so defining outcomes in terms of our three categories (on track, off track but above average, and off track and below average) would be difficult. Instead, we calculate the growth rate of the literacy rate between 1990 and 2009 (or the closest available year) and divide the countries into three categories:

- countries below percentile (33), thus exhibiting the slowest progress;
- countries above percentile (33) and below percentile (66), thus close to the median; and
- countries above percentile (66), the best performers.

To provide a rough comparison with access-based indicators, we perform a similar procedure on the primary completion rate. Several multinomial logit models, reproducing our core specification, are then estimated linking education outcomes and access to various proxies of institutional quality, using as the reference category the group of countries below percentile (33).

The results are mixed and, to some extent, counterintuitive (see table A1.12) so it is impossible to draw strong conclusions. However, it is interesting that the CPIA is not significantly related to the outcome indicator (literacy) but in this specification (unlike our earlier results) is significantly related to the access indicator (primary completion rate). Although these results are difficult to interpret, it does not appear that the differing results for the impact of growth and institutions on progress toward achieving the health and education MDGs can be ascribed simply to the use of outcome versus access indicators.

TABLE A1.12   Probability of being in percentile (66) or above or in percentile (33) or below

Indicator	Primary completion rate, total (% of relevant age group)	Literacy rate, adult total (% of people aged 15 and above)
CPIA index (2009)	+	
State fragility (1995–2009)		
Voice and accountability		
Political stability		+
Government effectiveness		–
Regulatory quality	–	+
Rule of law		+
Control of corruption	+	+

Source: World Bank staff calculations.
Note: CPIA = Country Policy and Institutional Assessment. Significant at 0.1 level or better. Empty cells = no significant correlation. State fragility (1995–2009) is the difference between index values in 2009 and 1996. Governance indicators correspond to 2009 rankings.

FIGURE A1.1   **Odds of achieving the MDGs improve with growth and better policy**

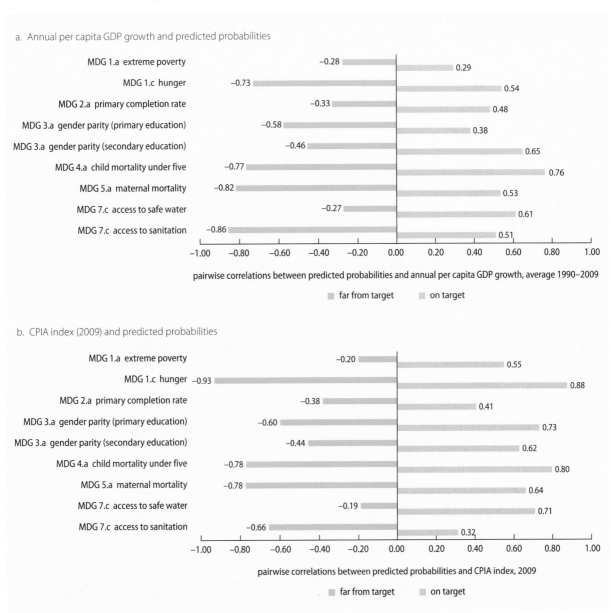

a. Annual per capita GDP growth and predicted probabilities

pairwise correlations between predicted probabilities and annual per capita GDP growth, average 1990–2009

far from target   on target

b. CPIA index (2009) and predicted probabilities

pairwise correlations between predicted probabilities and CPIA index, 2009

far from target   on target

Source: World Bank staff calculations.
Note: CPIA = Country Policy and Institutional Assessment. Pairwise correlations are significant at the 0.10 level or better.

TABLE A1.13   Classification of economies by region and income, fiscal 2011

East Asia and Pacific		Latin America and the Caribbean		Sub-Saharan Africa		High-income OECD economies
American Samoa	UMC	Antigua and Barbuda	UMC	Angola	LMC	Australia
Cambodia	LIC	Argentina	UMC	Benin	LIC	Austria
China	LMC	Belize	LMC	Botswana	UMC	Belgium
Fiji	UMC	Bolivia	LMC	Burkina Faso	LIC	Canada
Indonesia	LMC	Brazil	UMC	Burundi	LIC	Czech Republic
Kiribati	LMC	Chile	UMC	Cameroon	LMC	Denmark
Korea, Dem. Rep.	LIC	Colombia	UMC	Cape Verde	LMC	Estonia
Lao PDR	LIC	Costa Rica	UMC	Central African Republic	LIC	Finland
Malaysia	UMC	Cuba	UMC	Chad	LIC	France
Marshall Islands	LMC	Dominica	UMC	Comoros	LIC	Germany
Micronesia, Fed. Sts.	LMC	Dominican Republic	UMC	Congo, Dem. Rep.	LIC	Greece
Mongolia	LMC	Ecuador	LMC	Congo, Rep.	LMC	Hungary
Myanmar	LIC	El Salvador	LMC	Côte d'Ivoire	LMC	Iceland
Palau	UMC	Grenada	UMC	Eritrea	LIC	Ireland
Papua New Guinea	LMC	Guatemala	LMC	Ethiopia	LIC	Israel
Philippines	LMC	Guyana	LMC	Gabon	UMC	Italy
Samoa	LMC	Haiti	LIC	Gambia, The	LIC	Japan
Solomon Islands	LIC	Honduras	LMC	Ghana	LIC	Korea, Rep.
Thailand	LMC	Jamaica	UMC	Guinea	LIC	Luxembourg
Timor-Leste	LMC	Mexico	UMC	Guinea-Bissau	LIC	Netherlands
Tonga	LMC	Nicaragua	LMC	Kenya	LIC	New Zealand
Tuvalu	LMC	Panama	UMC	Lesotho	LMC	Norway
Vanuatu	LMC	Paraguay	LMC	Liberia	LIC	Poland
Vietnam	LMC	Peru	UMC	Madagascar	LIC	Portugal
		St. Kitts and Nevis	UMC	Malawi	LIC	Slovak Republic
Europe and Central Asia		St. Lucia	UMC	Mali	LIC	Slovenia
		St. Vincent and		Mauritania	LIC	Spain
Albania	UMC	the Grenadines	UMC	Mauritius	UMC	Sweden
Armenia	LMC	Suriname	UMC	Mayotte	UMC	Switzerland
Azerbaijan	UMC	Uruguay	UMC	Mozambique	LIC	United Kingdom
Belarus	UMC	Venezuela, R.B. de	UMC	Namibia	UMC	United States
Bosnia and Herzegovina	UMC			Niger	LIC	
Bulgaria	UMC	**Middle East and North Africa**		Nigeria	LMC	**Other high-income economies**
Georgia	LMC			Rwanda	LIC	
Kazakhstan	UMC	Algeria	UMC	São Tomé and Principe	LMC	Andorra
Kosovo	LMC	Djibouti	LMC	Senegal	LMC	Aruba
Kyrgyz Republic	LIC	Egypt, Arab Rep.	LMC	Seychelles	UMC	Bahamas, The
Lithuania	UMC	Iran, Islamic Rep.	UMC	Sierra Leone	LIC	Bahrain
Macedonia, FYR	UMC	Iraq	LMC	Somalia	LIC	Barbados
Moldova	LMC	Jordan	LMC	South Africa	UMC	Bermuda
Montenegro	UMC	Lebanon	UMC	Sudan	LMC	Brunei Darussalam
Romania	UMC	Libya	UMC	Swaziland	LMC	Cayman Islands
Russian Federation	UMC	Morocco	LMC	Tanzania	LIC	Channel Islands
Serbia	UMC	Syrian Arab Republic	LMC	Togo	LIC	Croatia
Tajikistan	LIC	Tunisia	LMC	Uganda	LIC	Cyprus
Turkey	UMC	West Bank and Gaza	LMC	Zambia	LIC	Equatorial Guinea
Turkmenistan	LMC	Yemen, Rep.	LMC	Zimbabwe	LIC	Faeroe Islands
Ukraine	LMC					French Polynesia
Uzbekistan	LMC	**South Asia**				Gibraltar
						Greenland
		Afghanistan	LIC			Guam
		Bangladesh	LIC			Hong Kong SAR, China
		Bhutan	LMC			Isle of Man
		India	LMC			Kuwait
		Maldives	LMC			Latvia
		Nepal	LIC			Liechtenstein
		Pakistan	LMC			Macao SAR, China
		Sri Lanka	LMC			Malta
						Monaco
						Netherlands Antilles
						New Caledonia
						Northern Mariana Islands
						Oman
						Puerto Rico
						Qatar
						San Marino
						Saudi Arabia
						Singapore
						Trinidad and Tobago
						Turks and Caicos Islands
						United Arab Emirates
						Virgin Islands (U.S.)

Source: World Bank data.
Note: OECD = Organisation for Economic Co-operation and Development. This table classifies all World Bank member-economies and all other economies with populations of more than 30,000. Economies are divided among income groups according to 2009 gross national income per capita, calculated using the World Bank Atlas method. The groups are low income (LIC), $995 or less; lower-middle income (LMC), $996–$3,945; upper-middle income (UMC), $3,946–$12,195; and high income, $12,196 or more.

Notes

1. Statistical analysis is based on available data as of January 2011. The maps in the report were created with updated data, as of end-March 2011.
2. Go and Quijada forthcoming.
3. Lofgren and Rodarte forthcoming.
4. Long and Freese 2006. An alternative to the multinomial logit model would be the generalized ordered logit model, specifically proportional and partial proportional odds models.
5. World Bank 2004.
6. Small and Hsiao 1985.
7. The null hypothesis is rejected in only two cases, when testing the independence of outcome 2 (off target and above average) in equation 4 (primary education) and outcome 3 (on target) in equation 8 (access to clean water). Our test results do not reject the assumption of independence in the seven remaining specifications.
8. Long and Freese 2006.
9. McFadden 1973, p. 113.
10. Marshall and Cole 2010.
11. Kaufmann, Kraay, and Mastruzzi 2010.

References

Go, D., and A. Quijada. Forthcoming. "Assessing the Odds of Achieving the MDGs." Background paper for *Global Monitoring Report 2011*, World Bank, Washington, DC.

Kaufmann D, A. Kraay, and M. Mastruzzi. 2010. "The Worldwide Governance Indicators: Methodology and Analytical Issues." Policy Research Working Paper 5430, World Bank, Washington, DC.

Lall, S. 2000. "The Technological Structure and Performance of Developing Country Manufactured Exports, 1985–1998." Working Paper 44, Queen Elizabeth House, University of Oxford, Oxford, UK.

Lofgren, H., and I. Rodarte. Forthcoming. "Macro Analysis of Health and Education MDGs: Brief Review and Country–Level Diagnosis." Background note for *Global Monitoring Report 2011*, World Bank, Washington, DC.

Long, J. S., and J. Freese. 2006. *Regression Models for Categorical Dependent Variables Using Stata*. 2nd edition. College Station, TX: Stata Press.

Marshall, M., and B. Cole. 2010. "Global Report 2009: Conflict, Governance, and State Fragility." Center for Global Policy, Washington, DC.

McFadden, D. 1973. "Conditional Logit Analysis of Qualitative Choice Behavior." In *Frontiers of Econometrics*, ed. P. Zarembka, 105–42. New York: Academic Press.

Small, K., and C. Hsiao. 1985. "Multinomial Logit Specification Tests." *International Economic Review* 26 (3): 619–27.

World Bank. 2004. *Global Monitoring Report: Policies and Actions for Achieving the Millennium Development Goals and Related Outcomes*. Washington, DC.

Policies to Reduce Biodiversity Loss and Enhance Human Development Require a Concerted Approach

Both poverty and economic development affect global biodiversity and the provision of ecosystem goods and services. More food, water, and firewood are needed to sustain population growth, especially in the poorer parts of the world. At the same time, expected rising levels of affluence in emerging economies will add to the demand for products like meat, construction timber, and paper. When current technologies and consumption patterns prevail, increased global consumption by a larger and richer population will drive:

- expansion of agriculture, forestry, and bio-energy production;
- intensification of production, leading to overexploitation and pollution from excess nutrients and contaminants; and
- higher exploitation of remaining natural ecosystems.

In the context of rising demand for food, water, and firewood, growing populations that lack the capabilities to minimize environmental impacts of production will be more susceptible to overexploiting and degrading their livelihoods. As a consequence of land

use expansion and more intense use, global biodiversity loss will continue unabated or accelerate without additional policies.[1] Largest losses are expected in Central and South America, South Asia, and Sub-Saharan Africa (map A2.1).

The importance of biodiversity for development is recognized by Millennium Development Goal 7, which includes targets to "reverse the loss of environmental resources" and "reduce biodiversity loss." However, there is scant quantitative evidence on ways in which especially poorer people depend on biodiversity, although patterns can be distinguished. In general, it seems that poor people depend more on renewable natural resources than on biodiversity. However, the value of biodiversity aspects in terms of risk insurance, ecosystem resilience, and larger area ecosystem services (such as temperature regulation) still represents a large knowledge gap.[2]

Traditionally, policies to reduce biodiversity loss focus on area protection measures. However, these measures have no effect on the unprotected surrounding areas. Furthermore, expanding protected areas and reducing deforestation would impose limits on

MAP A2.1 **Average change in species populations, relative to the intact situation (mean species abundance or MSA), 2000 and 2050**

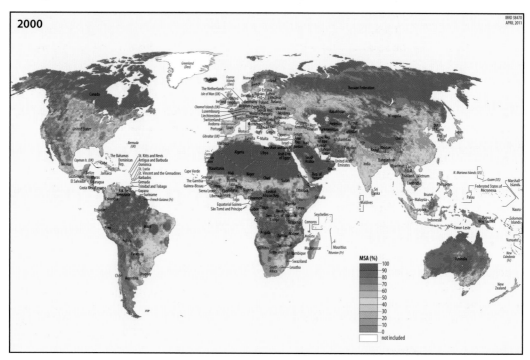

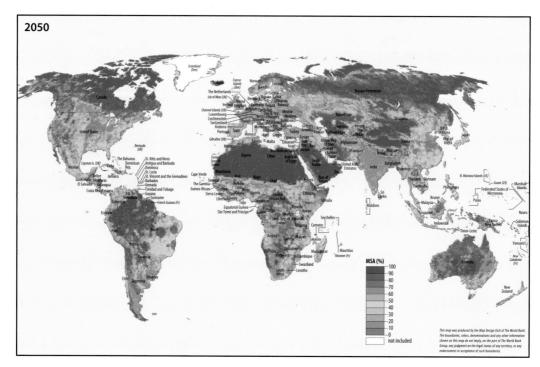

Source: PBL 2010, http://www.pbl.nl/en/publications/2010/Rethinking_Global_Biodiversity_Strategies.

agricultural land expansion, pushing land and food prices upward. This would especially affect urban people who depend on the market for their food. Therefore, additional measures should include smarter and better-managed land use, alternative consumption patterns, and the development and application of technologies to increase production efficiency per hectare. Measured by food prices, these routes would provide relief for urban poor, increasing food security and affordability. However, rural poor people are oftentimes particularly vulnerable to changes in land values and uses. Potential increases in natural rents could affect rural poor for whom land entitlements are not adequately arranged, making them vulnerable for displacement by larger landholders with access to technology and markets.

In conclusion, policies to reduce biodiversity loss and enhance human development require a concerted approach. Some of these options are already being discussed at the international level; others appear to be more contentious (changing consumption patterns), requiring careful consideration at the national level, and will be dependent on voluntary approaches. This requires broadening the scope of biodiversity policies on all levels of decision making. Although most management decisions affecting biodiversity and ecosystem goods and services are made at a local level, these local decisions are conditioned by national and international policies beyond nature conservation. International policy domains, including agricultural and forestry sector policies, development assistance (including the role of international financial institutions) and international trade provide clear opportunities to integrate biodiversity and ecosystem goods and services in their policies in ways that can support poverty reduction as well as sustainable use and conservation of natural resources.[3]

Notes

1. PBL 2010.
2. CBD 2010.
3. Kok et al. 2010.

References

CBD (Convention on Biological Diversity). 2010. "Linking Biodiversity Conservation and Poverty Alleviation: A State of Knowledge Review." Technical Series No. 55, Montreal, Canada.

Kok, M. T. J., S. Tyler, A. G. Prins, L. Pintér, H. Baumüller, J. Bernstein, E. Tsioumani, H. David Venema, and R. Grosshans. 2010. "Prospects for Mainstreaming Ecosystem Goods and Services in International Policies." *Biodiversity* 1 (1–2): 45–51.

PBL (Netherlands Environmental Assessment Agency). 2010. *Rethinking Global Biodiversity Strategies: Exploring Structural Changes in Production and Consumption to Reduce Biodiversity Loss.* Bilthoven, Netherlands.